JAVA WORKSHOP
PROGRAMMING

Java WorkShop Programming

Steven Holzner

M&T BOOKS

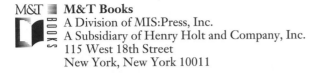 **M&T Books**
A Division of MIS:Press, Inc.
A Subsidiary of Henry Holt and Company, Inc.
115 West 18th Street
New York, New York 10011

ISBN: 1-55851-491-0

Associate Publisher: Paul Farrell
Executive Editor: Cary Sullivan
Editor: Michael Sprague
Copy Edit Manager: Shari Chappell
Copy Editor: Sara Black
Production Editor: Joe McPartland

To Betty Richardson,
      friend of so many years and so many lunches (torta...de...pescado!)

ACKNOWLEDGMENTS

Writing a book is very much a solitary act. However, after the book is written there are people too numerous to mention involved in getting the book into your hands. Thanks to everyone involved at M&T Books who worked to put this book out so quickly. Also, thanks to Erika Putre and Beth McArthur for making sure the whole world knew that it had arrived.

CONTENTS

Chapter Two:
Java: Buttons and TextFields 47

Chapter Three:
Check Boxes, Radio Buttons, and Managing Multiple Controls 71

Chapter Four:
Scrollbars, Choice Controls, and Scrolling Lists 133

Chapter Five: Windows, Menus, and Dialog Boxes 177

Chapter Six: Drawing Lines, Circles, Rectangles, and More 221

Chapter Seven: Graphics: Fonts, Canvases, Images, and Imagemaps 265

Chapter Eight: Graphics Animation 307

Chapter Nine:
Java Multithreading 353

Chapter Ten:
Handling Java
Exceptions 401

INTRODUCTION

WELCOME TO JAVA WORKSHOP

Welcome to the world of Java and the Java WorkShop. Java has been making a tremendous splash in the programming world, and we'll see why in this book. People are very excited about the power of this package and what it can do—both for Web pages and for creating stand-alone applications. In this book we'll embark on a guided tour of the world of Java, and the Java WorkShop will be our guide.

Until now, if you wanted to work with Java, you had to use the command-line version of the Java compiler, javac. However, it struck the people of Sun Microsystems, the creators of Java, as odd that you had to use a command-line program to create Java programs, which are targeted to purely graphics environments. That discrepancy was fixed with the release of the Java WorkShop, which allows us not only to edit our Java programs in a windowing environment but also to develop, compile, build, test, and debug them there. With the arrival of the Java WorkShop, Java can reach out to a tremendous new audience.

In this book, we'll see how far Java can take us, and that is very far. Have you ever thought that Web pages could pop their own windows on the screen (and even move those new windows around)? Or that such windows could support menus and dialog boxes? Or that Web pages could become multitasking things filled with utilities like calculators and spreadsheets? All this, plus the more usual Web page techniques of animation and clickable imagemaps, are part of this book, and we'll see them and more in our guided tour.

What's in This Book

There is a great deal of programming power in Java, and we are going to put it to work for us. Some of the topics we'll see in our tour include:

Using the Java WorkShop

Creating Java WorkShop projects

Java classes and objects

Textfields

Buttons, radio buttons, check boxes

Select controls

Canvas controls

Opening new windows

Menus

Dialog boxes

Exception handling

Multitasking

Synchronized functions

Graphics animation

Interactive animation

Image handling

And more

Java is an exceptionally strong and simple programming language, and we're going to see it at work for us. That's the emphasis of this book, seeing it work. We won't start with programming theory; instead, we'll start with ideas of what we want to do and let the abstract concepts come in only when they are needed and their introduction makes sense. That's why you won't see chapters entitled "Program Flow Control" or "Calling Frame Structure" in this book. Instead, you'll see chapters like "Graphics Animation" or "Textfields and Buttons" or "Drawing Lines, Circles, Rectangles, and More," topics organized around what Java programmers want to create in their Web pages. Our guided tour is studded with dozens of bite-sized examples that are clear and to the point. That's our approach: seeing Java at work and then putting it to work for us with the Java WorkShop.

What You'll Need

You'll really need only the Java WorkShop to use this book profitably. Although the code developed here is mostly targeted at the Internet, it can be run on your machine at home (because the Java WorkShop is based on a Web browser itself, allowing you to preview your Web pages). However, most people will also want to have an Internet Service Provider (ISP), which will host their Web pages and Java applets so that other people may download and use them. That's all you need, however, so let's get started without further delay.

Because Java is primarily used in Web pages, our first chapter will be a review of creating Web pages, the normal environment of Java applets. In this chapter, we'll review the language of web pages: Hypertext Markup Language (HTML), giving us a place to install the Java applets we create. If you feel confident of your HTML abilities, you might want to skip this chapter.

CHAPTER ONE

OUR REVIEW OF HTML

Welcome to our book on Java and the Java WorkShop. In this book, we'll see how to create some super Web pages—pages that display more than static information; pages that can interact with the user, ask questions, change their appearance, display animation, and support many unique interactions with the user.

When the World Wide Web first came into existence, Web browsing was a pretty passive affair. Users downloaded a page of text and graphics and looked at it, clicking links to go to other pages. That's not to downplay the magic of this relatively new medium; people were enchanted, and the Web grew quickly. Added to this attraction was the fact that the language of Web pages— Hypertext Markup Language (HTML)—was easy to learn, so people started creating their own pages, that is, their own Web publishing. This got people even more enthusiastic (there is no greater convert to the World Wide Web than someone who has their own, newly and proudly published Web page). Even corporations got into the act relatively early, producing their own Web sites. All this development made the Web a more sophisticated place, and people naturally began to ask for more.

And they got more. Pages began to hold more than just graphics, text, and hyperlinks. For example, we heard sounds (in **.WAV** or **.MID** format) that were downloaded with Web page, and began to see embedded motion pictures (in **.AVI** or **.MPG** format) that could also be downloaded with Web pages.

It wasn't long before HTML started to support new things, like *forms* in which Web page users were startled to see buttons and text boxes that they could use. For example, some clever page designers used scripts in languages like Perl to add a guestbook to their Web page. Now you not only could visit someone's page, but you also could record your appraisal of it right there and then so your words could appear in the guestbook.

In addition, Web searching became extremely popular as the Web grew; you just typed in the word or words you wanted to search for, clicked a button, and a million or so pages were searched for you automatically. This was far better than simply seeing static graphics, but there was a catch. You had to be able to create Perl scripts, your Internet Service Provider (ISP) had to support them, and you had to set them up on your ISP's computer, usually in a special area. This limited the number of people who used such scripts.

Then came Java, a language based on C++ from Sun Microsystems. You could write your Java code, compile it with a Java compiler, and upload it in a binary file to your ISP. The compiled Java—called a Java *applet*—would be downloaded with your Web page and run, if the user's Web browser supported Java. In this way, you could support animated graphics and other interesting things in your Web pages, not to mention the fact that Java is a powerful language. Understandably, it generated immense excitement.

However, even though Java applets were designed for graphics environments like Windows 95, the actual way you developed those applets depended heavily on using command-line utilities like **javac.exe**, the Java compiler. That is, you had to use the Java compiler at a command-line prompt like `javac myfile.java` to compile a Java source file named **myfile.java**. But as Java caught on (and is still catching on), people at Sun thought it odd that Java programmers had to rely on command-line utilities to create applets and applications designed for a graphics environment. So finally they brought out the Java WorkShop—an integrated design environment in which you can both design and test your Java code. And with the Java WorkShop, Java has finally arrived.

Welcome to the Java WorkShop

The Java WorkShop offers us the best of two worlds—Web page programming that is both powerful and simple to use in a graphics environment. Here, we'll design Web page applets in their own environment, a windowed environment. In this book, we'll explore what Java has to offer to us thoroughly, and we'll see it in action. We'll see a great deal in this book—from the basics to advanced techniques, from graphical methods to working with controls (the term *control* includes text boxes, buttons, list boxes, and more, that we can embed in our Web pages using Java), from graphics and image programming to animation, from Java panels to multithreaded, multitasking applets.

Java could not exist by itself, however. A Java applet must be downloaded with your Web page, and it relies on the HTML in the Web page to call it and set things up appropriately. For that reason, our first order of business in developing Java-enabled Web pages will be to review HTML, the language of Web pages. If you are confident of your HTML abilities, you can skip this chapter and start with the next chapter, where we dive right into Java. However, if you need to brush up on Web page writing in general, keep reading. The information we see here will be useful in later chapters.

Our First Web Page

Our first task will be to see what goes into a Web page. It's important to remember that a Web page at its most basic is really just text that can be interpreted by a Web browser. Although you can open many different types of files such as **.AVI** movie files or **.ZIP** compressed files with Web browsers (especially if you have a number of helper applications), Web *pages* themselves are written in straight text. With all the different possible formats, how does a Web browser know what kind of file it is working on? That's based on the file's extension. If that extension is **.html**, such as **review.html**, the Web browser expects a file written in HTML. Note that because of MS-DOS's three-letter file extension limit, many Web browsers assume that files with the extension **.htm** are also written in HTML.

The Shortest Web Page

Because the text in a Web page is interpreted based on the file's **.html** extension, we can write a Web page that is extraordinarily short, something that might contain only

```
Hello, world!
```

as long as we give the Web page's file the extension **.html**. In this case, we might put this text into a file named **hello.html**, and Web browsers would treat it as a Web page:

```
        hello.html file
        --------------
        |              |
        |Hello, world! |
        |              |
        |              |
        --------------
```

In fact, we could have a Web page as short as a single character, as long as we gave the file containing it the extension **.html**. (This also assumes that you install the Web page in your Internet Service Provider as will be detailed later.) That's all it takes to write a Web page, although we should note that the text in a Web page's **.html** file is just straight text, and on PCs that means ASCII text. If you are using a word processor like Microsoft Word for Windows, you must save your files in plain text format (i.e., as can be displayed on the screen with the **TYPE** command). We'll see in the next chapter that the Java WorkShop provides us with a suitable editor for this purpose.

In addition, we'll assume that you are familiar with the basic steps of installing a Web page on the Web. That usually means having an ISP with a computer that can run all day and night so that your Web page is always accessible and uploading your Web page properly. The actual uploading details vary from machine to machine. Uploading can mean using special uploading software that will upload Web pages at the click of a mouse button or using an FTP (File Transfer Protocol) program to transfer the Web page and any graphics files you want to include to a specially designated area of your ISP and then using UNIX commands to set the page's protections so that no one but you can modify them. The default name for a Web page is **index.html**, which is what a Web browser will look for at a given Web site if you do not specify the name of a file to open.

Our "Hello, world!" Web page isn't really all that exciting (unless you want to prove to your friends how easy it is to create a Web page), so let's start designing a more typical Web page. We'll build it up part by part during the rest of this chapter until we get a functional Web page at the end. We'll start our example Web page with the <HTML> tag.

```
                      A Web Page in Outline
        -----------------------------------------------------
  -->   |<HTML>                                             |
        |                                                   |
        |   ---------------------------------------------   |
        |  |<HEAD>                                       |  |
        |  |                                             |  |
        |  |                Head Section                 |  |
        |  |                                             |  |
        |  |</HEAD>                                      |  |
        |   ---------------------------------------------   |
        |   ---------------------------------------------   |
        |  |<BODY>                                       |  |
        |  |                                             |  |
        |  |                                             |  |
        |  |                                             |  |
        |  |                                             |  |
        |  |                                             |  |
        |  |                   Body                      |  |
        |  |                                             |  |
        |  |                                             |  |
        |  |                                             |  |
        |  |                                             |  |
        |  |</BODY>                                      |  |
        |   ---------------------------------------------   |
        |                                                   |
        |</HTML>                                            |
        -----------------------------------------------------
```

The <HTML> Tag

Usually, Web pages include both text that you want to display and HTML commands to Web browsers. Those commands are enclosed in *tags*, which are surrounded by the < and > characters. For example, the usual first line in a Web page indicates that the Web page is written in HTML with an HTML tag this way:

```
<HTML>
    .
    .
    .
```

Now a Web browser can tell that what is to follow is written in HTML, although, as mentioned, that information is usually gotten from the Web page file's extension **.html**.

The <!> Comment Tag

Because we want to explain what's going on in our first Web page, we will add comments to it with comment tags. Such a tag simply begins with a !, and Web browsers will ignore the comments that follow. (You must be careful here because early versions of some browsers had problems when they encountered a tag, such as <HTML>, inside a comment, which is why we enclose the tags we are talking about in quotes in our comments here).

```
<HTML>
<!--START THE PAGE with an HTML tag (a tag is an HTML command, and
    HTML tags appear between angle brackets) We use "HTML" to indicate
    this document is in HTML, which is the language of Web pages.>
    .
    .
    .
```

In our comment we indicated what the <HTML> tag was all about. Adding comments this way can help you recall what's going on in your own Web pages and help you understand what's going on in other people's Web pages. Keep in mind, however, that your whole Web page has to be downloaded into someone's

Web browser before they can see it. That means the comments will be down-loaded as well. For that reason, comments (which most people surfing the Web will never see) should probably be kept to a minimum. Some professional Web page writers keep a commented version of Web pages and then run software to strip the comments out of the copy they actually install. In this case, however, we'll comment our first page heavily.

The <HEAD> Tag

Web pages consist of both a head and a body.

```
                       A Web Page in Outline
        ---------------------------------------------------------
        |<HTML>                                                 |
        |                                                       |
        |   ------------------------------------------------    |
  -->   |  |<HEAD>                                         |  |
        |  |                                               |  |
        |  |               Head Section                    |  |
        |  |                                               |  |
        |  |</HEAD>                                        |  |
        |   ------------------------------------------------    |
        |   ------------------------------------------------    |
  -->   |  |<BODY>                                         |  |
        |  |                                               |  |
        |  |                                               |  |
        |  |                                               |  |
        |  |                                               |  |
        |  |                                               |  |
        |  |                   Body                        |  |
        |  |                                               |  |
        |  |                                               |  |
        |  |                                               |  |
        |  |                                               |  |
        |  |</BODY>                                        |  |
        |   ------------------------------------------------    |
        |                                                       |
        |</HTML>                                                |
        ---------------------------------------------------------
```

A Web page's head section is defined with the <HEAD> tag, and in this section we can add text that explains more about the Web page. In the past, the head section was used more often. Now Web pages usually have only a title for the Web page in the head section (see the <TITLE> tag, coming up next). It is worth noting, however, that certain advanced tags, like <BASE> and <RANGE>, can function only in the head section of a Web page. (<BASE> is an interesting and unusual tag, because it allows you to specify a page's "base location," and all other references to subdirectories and so on will be taken from that base, which allows you to move a page to another directory entirely to work on it, while the images and so on embedded in it will still be found properly.) We start our page's head section with the <HEAD> tag.

```
<HTML>

<!--The HEAD section of the Web page includes text about the page,
    although usually this section only includes the title.>

<HEAD>            <--
    .
    .
    .
```

Next is the <TITLE> tag.

The <TITLE> Tag

Although Web page programmers often skip the <HEAD> tag, they rarely skip <TITLE>. That's because a Web page's title counts; it's the text that most Web browsers will enter into the list of favorites or bookmarks when someone likes your page and wants to remember it for later. Also, it's the text that often appears in the title bar of the Web browser when it's displaying your page. In this case, we'll give our new Web page the title "Welcome to the Java WorkShop," using the <TITLE> tag. In addition, tags come in pairs in HTML, and we indicate that we are finished with the title with the tag </TITLE> and also finished with our Web page's head section with the tag </HEAD> this way:

```
<HTML>

<!--A PAGE'S TITLE is how a browser will refer to it if someone saves
    it in their Favorites or Bookmarks menu. Note that we also indicate
    we are done defining the title with "/TITLE". This second tag
    matches the first tag, "TITLE", and as mentioned, HTML tags
    always come in pairs, like the following one, which indicates that
    we are done with the page's header.>

<HEAD>                                          <--
<TITLE>Welcome to the Java WorkShop</TITLE>     <--
</HEAD>                                          <--
    .
    .
    .
```

Usually, for each tag <TAG>, there is a corresponding closing tag </TAG> (although that is not true for some tags, such as the line break <BR> tag). Although making sure that you have as many </TAG>s as <TAG>s may sometimes not be necessary in HTML (Web browsers are very forgiving), it is good form to make sure that you do. In fact, this is one of the first things that Web page *validators* (programs on the Web that check your page for errors) check for.

We've completed the head section of our Web page and are ready to turn to the body itself.

```
                    A Web Page in Outline
         ------------------------------------------------
        |<HTML>                                          |
        |                                                |
        |    -----------------------------------------   |
        |   |<HEAD>                                   |  |
        |   |                                         |  |
        |   |             Head Section                |  |
        |   |                                         |  |
        |   |</HEAD>                                  |  |
        |    -----------------------------------------   |
        |    -----------------------------------------   |
 -->    |   |<BODY>                                   |  |
        |   |                                         |  |
        |   |                                         |  |
        |   |                                         |  |
        |   |                                         |  |
        |   |                                         |  |
        |   |                                         |  |
        |   |                Body                     |  |
        |   |                                         |  |
        |   |                                         |  |
        |   |                                         |  |
        |   |                                         |  |
        |   |                                         |  |
        |   |</BODY>                                  |  |
        |    -----------------------------------------   |
        |                                                |
        |</HTML>                                         |
         ------------------------------------------------
```

The <BODY> Tag

The body follows a Web page's head section and makes up the remainder of the document (i.e., this is where the action is). We can declare the body simply with the <BODY> tag:

```
<HTML>

<HEAD>
<TITLE>Welcome to the Java WorkShop</TITLE>
</HEAD>
```

```
<BODY>   <--
   .
   .
   .
```

However, there's much more that we can do with the <BODY> tag. Here, for example, is where we set up some options. These options will indicate how we want our entire Web page to appear—what color text we want, what color hyperlinks should appear as, what color hyperlinks that the person viewing our page (the user) has already been to should look like, and so on.

In this example, let's make the text yellow, hyperlinks red, and hyperlinks that the person viewing our page has already visited yellow (to blend in with the rest of the text, although they will still appear underlined, hyperlinks that have already been visited will no longer stand out in red). This, of course, brings up the question: how do we define colors in HTML?

Setting Web Page and Text Colors

Web browsers recently defined a set of colors that you can use; the names of these colors are Aqua, Black, Blue, Fuchsia, Gray, Green, Lime, Maroon, Navy, Olive, Purple, Red, Silver, Teal, Yellow, and White. However, older Web browsers have no idea what these words are supposed to mean and ignore them, so we will not use them either because there are many people out there with older Web browsers. Instead, we will specify color using color values, which is a six-digit number in hexadecimal.

Color values work like this: rrggbb, where *rr* is the red color value, *gg* the green color value, and *bb* the blue color value. Each of these color values is a two-digit hexadecimal value from 0 to ff, that is, from 0 to 255 in decimal (i.e., hexadecimal digits go from 0 to f). In this way, we could specify pure red as #ff0000, pure blue as #0000ff, bright yellow (a combination of red and green) as #ffff00, and bright white as #ffffff, while black is simply #000000. Of course, there are intermediate values such as a more muted green, which might look like #00aa00; gray is #888888; as well as combinations of colors like a powder blue, which is set up as #aaaaff.

If you want to experiment with color values, a good shareware program is **lviewp1b.exe** (copyrighted by its author Leonardo H. Loureiro), which is available on the Web, just search for it by name. Although we will use this program occasionally, having it is not essential. There are many graphics programs with similar capabilities.

We'll add some color values to our <BODY> tag now. In this example, we intend to make the text yellow (using the TEXT keyword), hyperlinks red (using the LINK keyword), and hyperlinks that the person viewing our page has already visited yellow (using the VLINK keyword). In addition, we can specify that as the user clicks a link, it should be displayed momentarily in white (using the ALINK keyword), to indicate that we are jumping to that location.

```
<HTML>

<HEAD>
<TITLE>Welcome to the Java WorkShop</TITLE>
</HEAD>

<!--BODY OF PAGE starts with the following "BODY" tag. COLOR VALUES
    are "#rrggbb" (red, green, and blue) in hexadecimal (0-255 = 0-ff);
    for example, pure red is "#ff0000", pure green is #00ff00", and yellow
    is "#ffff00". Here we start the Web page's body, indicating we want
    yellow text, hyperlinks to be red, hyperlinks to turn white when
    pushed, and links that the user has already clicked to be
    yellow.>
<BODY TEXT  = "#ffff00" LINK  = "#ff0000" ALINK = "#ffffff" VLINK =
"#ffff00">
    .
    .
    .
```

In addition, we can specify the background color of the Web page with the BGCOLOR keyword. For example, we could make the background color white this way: <BODY BGCOLOR = "#ffffff">. For this example, however, let's use a graphics file for the background; the Web browser taking a look at our Web page will use this graphics file to "tile" the background of our Web page, which can produce some pleasing effects (you may have seen Web pages whose background mimics various cloth or paper textures or even looks like marble). We can use a graphics file named, say, **back.gif** to show how this works, and that file appears in Figure 1.1 (simply a white dot on a black background).

Figure 1.1 Our first Web page's graphics background.

We can install **back.gif** as our Web page's background with a new <BODY> tag and the BACKGROUND keyword like this:

```
<HTML>

<HEAD>
<TITLE>Welcome to the Java WorkShop</TITLE>
</HEAD>

<BODY TEXT  = "#ffff00" LINK  = "#ff0000" ALINK = "#ffffff" VLINK =
"#ffff00">

<!--BACKGROUND PICTURE (which is optional) is tiled on the page's
   background. Here, we indicate we want the Web browser to use the
   graphics file back.gif, which is in our www/gif directory (see
   explanation, below).>
<BODY BACKGROUND = "gif/back.gif">      <--
   .
   .
   .
```

Because **back.gif** is a small file, Web browsers will use it repeatedly to tile the background of our Web page, so that the background will appear as a series of white dots.

This, however, brings up the subject of graphics. How did we produce **back.gif**? Where do we store it? We'll look at that topic next, because graphics is a large part of Web page programming.

A Little About Graphics

There are a few things to review about graphics before we proceed. For example, the usual graphics file formats used in Web pages are **.gif** format and **.jpg** (or **.jpeg**) format. But how do you know which is better? That turns out to depend on your needs; **.jpg** format files can indeed be smaller, which means faster download times, but compared to **.gif** format, there is some loss of data; consequently, images can look less sharp. The best thing to do, of course, is to give it a try both ways: shareware programs like **lpview1b.exe** (mentioned previously) can easily convert from **.gif** to **.jpg** format. In fact, such programs can also convert into either format from the common Windows **.bmp** format, so you can even use the Windows Paintbrush program to design your graphics (although, of course, there are far more powerful graphics programs out there), save your work in **.bmp** format, and use a conversion program to resave the file in **.gif** or **.jpg** format.

Besides the graphics you draw, there are other sources of graphics files—scans of photos, for example. If you don't have your own scanner, you can often get this done commercially at a copy center. Ask for the standard 72 dots per inch (dpi) resolution, which is as good as screens get and make your graphics file a reasonable size (of course, if you expect people to download your file and print it on very high resolution laser printers, you can ask for better scan resolution). Another possible source of graphics are the Web pages already out there, and that can be very tempting. However, before simply copying what somebody else has done, you should be aware that such work may be copyrighted. Ask first!

Often when we insert graphics into a Web page such as the one we're designing, we'll need to know the width and height of the image in pixels (the background **.gif** or **.jpg** file is an exception) so that the Web browser can fit the page together while leaving space for our graphics. If you have a scan done, ask the people who scan the photo to tell you what the image size is in pixels; otherwise, you can use a program like **lviewp1b.exe**, which will tell you your image's dimensions. This program is also very good, incidentally, in adjusting the color and contrast of images. Given the quality of many of the commercial scanners out there, that is very useful (for example, you can brighten a dark scan easily). Adjusting contrast is also very useful for dimming images so that they can be used as background in your page.

Where do we store our images? It is customary to set up a separate directory for image files in your ISP. That is, if you store your HTML files in a directory named **www**, you might want to create and store your images in a subdirectory named, for example, **www/gif**; such a directory can be created with the **mkdir** command on UNIX machines. We will store **back.gif** in a subdirectory named **gif**. When we want to reference a file in that directory, such as **back.gif**, we do it by indicating the correct path to that file, **gif/back.gif** (note that here we use the UNIX convention of many ISPs, which is to use forward slashes to separate directories, not backward slashes as is the IBM PC convention, because the files reside in the ISP's computer).

```
<HTML>

<HEAD>
<TITLE>Welcome to the Java WorkShop</TITLE>
</HEAD>

<BODY TEXT  = "#ffff00" LINK  = "#ff0000" ALINK = "#ffffff" VLINK =
"#ffff00">

<!--BACKGROUND PICTURE (which is optional) is tiled on the page's
   background. Here, we indicate we want the Web browser to use the
   graphics file back.gif, which is in our www/gif directory (see
   explanation, below).>
<BODY BACKGROUND = "gif/back.gif">      <--
   .
   .
   .
```

Note, however, that it is not necessary to use a separate directory for your image files; many Web sites do not.

At this point, we've installed our background image from **back.gif**. The next step is to add some text to our Web page, because nothing appears there yet except the background dots. For example, we might add a heading that says: Welcome to the Java WorkShop like this.

```
-----------------------------------------------
|                                             |
|         Welcome to the Java WorkShop        |
|                                             |
|                                             |
|                                             |
|                                             |
|                                             |
|                                             |
|                                             |
|                                             |
|                                             |
-----------------------------------------------
```

This is the first time we see what our new Web page will look like.

The <Center> and Header Tags

To add a header to our Web page, we can use the header tags <H1> to <H6>.
<H1> creates the largest-font header, and we can use that here.

```
<HTML>

<HEAD>
<TITLE>Welcome to the Java WorkShop</TITLE>
</HEAD>

<BODY TEXT  = "#ffff00" LINK  = "#ff0000" ALINK = "#ffffff" VLINK =
"#ffff00">

<BODY BACKGROUND = "gif/back.gif">

<!--HEADERS. Now we are going to place a header of the largest size in
   our page, so we use the "H1" tag, as well as the "CENTER" tag.
   "CENTER" simply makes sure the following text or image is centered.
   Note that all HTML tags come in pairs -- to turn off centering, we
   use "/CENTER" at the end of our header's specification.>
<H1>Welcome to the Java WorkShop</H1>         <--
   .
   .
   .
```

Now our header will appear yellow, in the largest header style. In addition, we center our header in our page with the <CENTER> and </CENTER> tags as follows:

```
<HTML>

<HEAD>
<TITLE>Welcome to the Java WorkShop</TITLE>
</HEAD>

<BODY TEXT  = "#ffff00" LINK  = "#ff0000" ALINK = "#ffffff" VLINK =
"#ffff00">

<BODY BACKGROUND = "gif/back.gif">

<!--HEADERS. Now we are going to place a header of the largest size in
    our page, so we use the "H1" tag, as well as the "CENTER" tag.
    "CENTER" simply makes sure the following text or image is centered.
    Note that all HTML tags come in pairs -- to turn off centering, we
    use "/CENTER" at the end of our header's specification.>
<CENTER>                                  <--
<H1>Welcome to the Java WorkShop</H1>
</CENTER>                                 <--
     .
     .
     .
```

In this case, our header will appear in large yellow letters, centered in our Web page when displayed in a Web browser like the Microsoft Internet Explorer, as shown in Figure 1.2. Note that we did not have to use the <CENTER> tag; instead, we could have specified an alignment for our header in the <H1> tag as <H1 ALIGN = alignment>, where *alignment* can be LEFT, RIGHT, or CENTER.

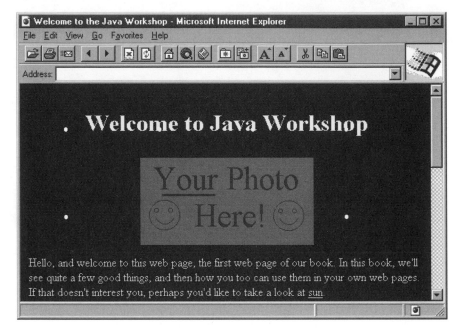

Figure 1.2 Our first Web page.

At this stage, our Web page has just started appearing. We've set up the background image and the header text. Next, we will review how to space things appropriately.

The
 Tag

The next step is to leave some space after the header and before adding any images. We do that with the line break tag <BR>. That looks like this:

```
<HTML>

<HEAD>
<TITLE>Welcome to the Java WorkShop</TITLE>
</HEAD>

<BODY TEXT  = "#ffff00" LINK  = "#ff0000" ALINK = "#ffffff" VLINK =
"#ffff00">
<BODY BACKGROUND = "gif/back.gif">
```

```
<CENTER>
<H1>Welcome to the Java WorkShop</H1>
</CENTER>

<!--LINE BREAKS. To space things vertically, we use "BR" and "/BR"
    to
    skip a line.>
<BR>                          <--
    .
    .
    .
```

Let's add some graphics next. For example, this might be a photo of yourself, **yourgif.gif**:

We insert graphics images with the <IMG> tag, which we'll review next.

The <IMG> Tag

At this point in our Web page, we will insert the image file **yourgif.gif**. We can center that image with the <CENTER> tag and actually perform the insertion with the <IMG> tag. To do this, we indicate the dimensions of the image we are inserting with the WIDTH and HEIGHT keywords. We also have to indicate

where the image file is to be found by indicating its path as well as its name with
the SRC (for Source) keyword, making our <IMG> tag look like this:

```
<HTML>

<HEAD>
<TITLE>Welcome to the Java WorkShop</TITLE>
</HEAD>

<BODY TEXT  = "#ffff00" LINK  = "#ff0000" ALINK = "#ffffff" VLINK =
"#ffff00">
<BODY BACKGROUND = "gif/back.gif">

<CENTER>
<H1>Welcome to the Java WorkShop</H1>
</CENTER>

<BR>

<!--IMAGES. We display an image, which will appear centered because of
    the "CENTER" tag, with the "IMG" tag, adding the width and height
    in pixels. Here, we display our GIF file yourgif.gif from the GIF
    directory, but this is where a photo of you could go.>
<CENTER>                                                    <--
<IMG WIDTH=236 HEIGHT=118 SRC="gif/yourgif.gif"></IMG>      <--
</CENTER>                                                    <--
    .
    .
    .
```

If you want to fill the space the image will take up on the Web page with text
while that image is being loaded, you can add that with the ALT keyword to
the IMG tag like this (and this text is all that will appear in text-only Web
browsers):

```
<IMG WIDTH = 236 HEIGHT = 118 ALT = "A photo of the Web page
    author as a young man." SRC="gif/yourgif.gif">
```

Now **yourgif.gif** appears in the Web page, as shown in Figure 1.2. It's easy to
add images to our Web page; we just have to use the <IMG> tag.

Now that we've added our first picture, let's add some text to our developing Web page.

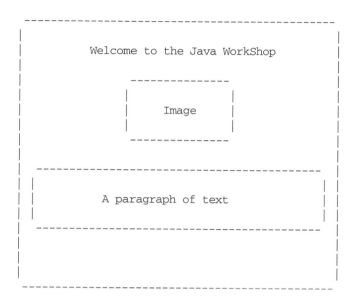

The <P> Tag

To start off our text, which will introduce the Web page to the user, we can use the <P> paragraph tag. This tag moves us to the next line and starts a paragraph of text (note that it is not necessary to use the <P> tag when inserting text). We might place this text in our Web page at this point, simply by typing it to follow the <P> tag; note that we will set up a hyperlink to **sun.com** at the very end of the paragraph.

```
Hello, and welcome to this Web page, the first Web page of our
book. In this book, we'll see quite a few good things and how
you can use them in your own Web pages. If that doesn't
interest you, perhaps you'd like to take a look at [sun.com].
```

In our Web page, we simply place the text directly into the **.html** file, like this:

```
<HTML>

<HEAD>
<TITLE>Welcome to the Java WorkShop</TITLE>
</HEAD>

<BODY TEXT  = "#ffff00" LINK  = "#ff0000" ALINK = "#ffffff" VLINK =
"#ffff00">
<BODY BACKGROUND = "gif/back.gif">

<CENTER>
<H1>Welcome to the Java WorkShop</H1>
</CENTER>

<BR>

<CENTER>
<IMG WIDTH=236 HEIGHT=118 SRC="gif/yourgif.gif"></IMG>
</CENTER>

<!--PARAGRAPHS of text start with "P".>
<P>
--> Hello, and welcome to this Web page, the first Web page of our
--> book. In this book, we'll see quite a few good things and how
--> you can use them in your own Web pages. If that doesn't
--> interest you, perhaps you'd like to take a look at
                      .
                      .
                      .
```

Now our paragraph of text appears, as shown in Figure 1.2.

The <P> tag has one keyword: ALIGN. You can align text using these key-words: ALIGN = LEFT, ALIGN = RIGHT, and ALIGN = CENTER. In this way, we have some modest control over the formatting of our text paragraph. In addition, we can use the <B> tag to make displayed text bold and the <I> tag to make it appear italicized.

However, we still have not made our hyperlink to **sun.com** at the end of the paragraph active. Let's do that next, introducing a link into our **.html** file with the <A> tag.

The <A> Tag

We add hyperlinks using the <A> (for Anchor) tag, used together with the HREF keyword. In particular, we will add a link to **sun.com**'s Web page at the end of our paragraph of text. For that, we need the page's World Wide Web address, or URL (Universal Resource Location), and that is **http://www.sun.com**. We don't want to give that as the name of the link, however; we'll just display this link as sun in the color for hyperlinks we've chosen (which is red). That looks like this with the <A> tag in our Web page:

```
<HTML>

<HEAD>
<TITLE>Welcome to the Java WorkShop</TITLE>
</HEAD>

<BODY TEXT  = "#ffff00" LINK  = "#ff0000" ALINK = "#ffffff" VLINK =
"#ffff00">
<BODY BACKGROUND = "gif/back.gif">

<CENTER>
<H1>Welcome to the Java WorkShop</H1>
</CENTER>

<BR>

<CENTER>
<IMG WIDTH=236 HEIGHT=118 SRC="gif/yourgit.git"></IMG>
</CENTER>

<!--PARAGRAPHS of text start with "P".>
<!--LINKS. We add a hypertext link with the "A" tag, using the HREF
    keyword. In particular, we add a link to sun.com's Web page at
    http://www.sun.com below. This means that the text "sun" will
    appear underlined and in the standard link color (which we've set
    to red); when the user of your page clicks that text, they will
    jump to sun's home page.>
<P>
    Hello, and welcome to this Web page, the first Web page of our
    book. In this book, we'll see quite a few good things and how
    you can use them in your own Web pages. If that doesn't
    interest you, perhaps you'd like to take a look at
```

```
    <A HREF="http://www.sun.com">sun</A>.    <--
<BR>
<BR>
</P>
    .
    .
    .
```

When someone takes a look at our Web page, this paragraph of text will appear yellow, while the word *sun* at the end will appear in red and underlined, indicating that it is a hyperlink. When clicked, this hyperlink will take us to **sun.com**. If we had wanted to use an image as a hyperlink, we would have simply used an <IMG> tag instead of *sun*.

Next we'll look at getting the format of things right. All we've done so far is to place text or images into our page and, at most, centered them. There is much more that we can do, of course. First, we'll examine the process of setting up text and images to be right next to each other. In our Web page, that might look like this:

```
 -----------------------------------------------
|                                               |
|        Welcome to the Java WorkShop           |
|                                               |
|            ---------------                    |
|           |               |                   |
|           |     Image     |                   |
|           |               |                   |
|            ---------------                    |
|                                               |
|    ----------------------------------------   |
|   | |                                  | |  | |
|   | |             Text                 | |  | |
|   | |                                  | |  | |
|   |  ----------------------------------    | |
|                                               |
|    -------    --------------------------      |
|   | |     |  | |                        | |  | |
|   | |Image|  | |          Text          | |  | |
|   | |     |  | |                        | |  | |
|    -------    --------------------------      |
|                                               |
 -----------------------------------------------
```

Aligning Images and Text

We've already reviewed how to put images and text into our Web page separately; now we will combine them, placing an image on the left and text on the right. This is actually accomplished very easily; all we have to do is to use the ALIGN keyword in the <IMG> tag. For example, if we want to add a new image named, say, **sidebar.gif**—which appears in Figure 1.3—on the left of our page, we would just specify that its alignment be LEFT (as opposed to CENTER or RIGHT):

```
<HTML>

<HEAD>
<TITLE>Welcome to the Java WorkShop</TITLE>
</HEAD>

<BODY TEXT  = "#ffff00" LINK  = "#ff0000" ALINK = "#ffffff" VLINK =
"#ffff00">
<BODY BACKGROUND = "gif/back.gif">

<CENTER>
<H1>Welcome to the Java WorkShop</H1>
</CENTER>

<BR>

<CENTER>
<IMG WIDTH=236 HEIGHT=118 SRC="gif/yourgif.gif"></IMG>
</CENTER>

<P>
   Hello, and welcome to this Web page, the first Web page of our
   book. In this book, we'll see quite a few good things and how
   you can use them in your own Web pages. If that doesn't
   interest you, perhaps you'd like to take a look at
   <A HREF="http://www.sun.com">sun</A>.
<BR>
<BR>
</P>
```

```
<!--ALIGNING PICTURES AND TEXT is done with the ALIGN keyword used in
    the IMG tag. In this case we just have to indicate that we want the
    graphics to appear on the left with ALIGN = LEFT. We also change
    the text color to green temporarily with a "FONT" tag ("FONT" only
    works in recent browsers).>
<IMG WIDTH=141 HEIGHT=126 SRC="gif/sidebar.gif" ALIGN=LEFT>      <--
    .
    .
    .
```

Figure 1.3 The image **sidebar.gif** appears next to text in our Web page.

To add our text on the right, we just type it in (i.e., we don't need to align the text RIGHT or anything). Because the image is on the left, the text will automatically fill the space on the right. To make it a little more interesting, let's switch the color of our text from our default of yellow to, say, green. We do that with the <FONT> tag.

The <FONT> Tag

The <FONT> tag is not supported in early versions of Web browsers like Netscape (i.e., in the 1.n versions), so you have to be a little careful when relying on <FONT> tags. Nonetheless, most Web browsers support it now, so we'll put it to work here. To switch the color of our text to green, we just use the <FONT> tag with the COLOR keyword:

```
<IMG WIDTH=141 HEIGHT=126 SRC="gif/sidebar.gif" ALIGN=LEFT>
<FONT COLOR = "00ff00">                <--
    We can even do green text next to graphics. This text appears next
    to the graphics on the left, allowing you to intersperse your words
    with pictures. When you take a look at the HTML for this Web page,
    you'll see how this and more is done. Although this is just a
    review, we are going to add Java to our skills soon...
</FONT>                               <--
</IMG>
    .
    .
    .
```

Note that to restore the text's default color, we also used a </FONT> tag. Now our text appears next to the sidebar image we used, as shown in Figure 1.4.

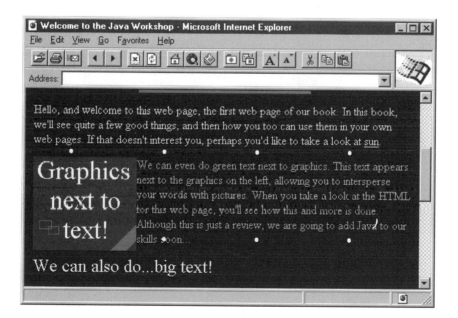

Figure 1.4 Setting up text next to images.

Besides changing the text's color, we can also change its size with the <FONT> tag and the SIZE keyword. For example, let's increase the size of our text temporarily so that it appears larger, as also shown in Figure 1.4. We might do that with this line in our **.html** file:

```
<IMG WIDTH=141 HEIGHT=126 SRC="gif/sidebar.gif" ALIGN=LEFT>
<FONT COLOR = "00ff00">
   We can even do green text next to graphics. This text appears next
   to the graphics on the left, allowing you to intersperse your words
   with pictures. When you take a look at the HTML for this Web page,
   you'll see how this and more is done. Although this is just a
   review, we are going to add Java to our skills soon...
</FONT>
</IMG>

<!--FONT SIZE is also done with the "FONT" tag; here, we set the
   size of our text temporarily to 5, a large size.>
<FONT SIZE = 5>                   <--
We can also do...big text!        <--
</FONT>                           <--
<BR>
<BR>
   .
   .
   .
```

The result appears in Figure 1.4. In addition, using the <FONT> tag with the FACE keyword, you can set the typeface used for your text, like Courier or Arial, assuming that the font you select is installed on the machine running the Web browser. (If you list a number of typefaces, the first one that is available will be used.)

Let's continue to review how to format our Web page. Here's how to put up a table in our page.

```
----------------------------------------------
|                                            |
|         Welcome to the Java WorkShop       |
|                                            |
|            ----------------                |
|            |              |                |
|            |    Image     |                |
|            |              |                |
|            ----------------                |
|                                            |
|   ------------------------------------   | |
| |                                      |  | |
| |              Text                    |  | |
| |                                      |  | |
|   ------------------------------------   | |
|                                            |
|   -------      ------------------------   | |
| |        |  | |                        |  | |
| | Image  |  | |         Text           |  | |
| |        |  | |                        |  | |
|   -------      ------------------------   | |
|                                            |
|            ----------------------          |
-->         |      TABLES TOO!      |        |
|           |----------------------|         |
|           | These | are | items |          |
|           |-------|-----|-------|          |
|           |  in   | this| table |          |
|            ----------------------          |
|                                            |
|                                            |
----------------------------------------------
```

Making Tables

Setting up a table is not very difficult, even though the resulting HTML is not very readable. To continue our review, we might aim for this table, in which we have three rows (one of which is the table's header), three columns, text centered in each table cell, and a header reading TABLES TOO! that spans all three columns:

```
-----------------------
|      TABLES TOO!      |
|-----------------------|
| These |  are | items  |
|-------|------|--------|
|  in   | this | table  |
-----------------------
```

We start our table with the TABLE tag. Here, we can indicate that our table should have a border with the BORDER keyword. In addition, we'll use the CELLPADDING keyword to add some padding around our text to improve its appearance and readability, say 4 pixels.

```
<TABLE BORDER CELLPADDING = 4>
      .
      .
      .
```

In setting up a table, we work row by row. To set up a row, we use the <TR> tag. Here, we can align the text in our table's rows with the ALIGN keyword:

```
<TABLE BORDER CELLPADDING = 4>
<TR ALIGN = CENTER>                <--
      .
      .
      .
```

We want our table's header, which we set up with the <TH> tag, to span all three columns and to read TABLES TOO!, so we set that up like this, using the COLSPAN keyword:

```
<TABLE BORDER CELLPADDING = 4>
<TR ALIGN = CENTER>
<TH COLSPAN = 3>TABLES TOO!     <--
</TH>                           <--
    .
    .
    .
```

That finishes off this row, so we use the </TR> tag.

```
<TABLE BORDER CELLPADDING = 4>
<TR ALIGN = CENTER>
<TH COLSPAN = 3>TABLES TOO!
</TH>
</TR>    <--
    .
    .
    .
```

The next step is to start the next row. We'll use the <TR> tag, aligning text in the center again, like this: <TR ALIGN = CENTER>. Now we have to set up the data for the three columns in this row. We do that with the <TD> tag. In this case, we want to set up the columns like this:

```
          -----------------------
         |      TABLES TOO!      |
         |----------------------|
   -->   | These |  are | items |
         |-------|------|-------|
         |  in   | this | table |
          -----------------------
```

To do that, we use <TD> and </TD> pairs, one for each column:

```
<TABLE BORDER CELLPADDING - 4>
<TR ALIGN = CENTER>
<TH COLSPAN = 3>TABLES TOO!
</TH>
</TR>
<TR ALIGN = CENTER>
<TD>These</TD>          <--
<TD>are</TD>            <--
<TD>items</TD>          <--
</TR>                   <--
    .
    .
    .
```

Note that at the end, we use </TR> to finish the table row. The last step is to set up the third and final row:

```
    ------------------------
    |       TABLES TOO!     |
    |----------------------|
    | These | are | items  |
    |-------|-------|-------|
-->  |  in  | this | table |
    ------------------------
```

We do that much as we did with the previous row.

```
<TABLE BORDER CELLPADDING = 4>
<TR ALIGN = CENTER>
<TH COLSPAN = 3>TABLES TOO!
</TH>
</TR>
<TR ALIGN = CENTER>
<TD>These</TD>
<TD>are</TD>
<TD>items</TD>
</TR>
<TR ALIGN = CENTER>        <--
<TD>in</TD>                <--
<TD>this</TD>              <--
<TD>table!</TD>            <--
</TR>                      <--
```

At the end of the table specification, we just include the </TABLE> tag to indicate that we are done.

```
<HTML>

<HEAD>
<TITLE>Welcome to the Java WorkShop</TITLE>
</HEAD>
    .
    .
    .
```

```
<!--TABLES. Tables are not so hard; just use the "TABLE" tag; here
    we indicate we want our table to have a border and to add space
    ("padding") around the text in each cell. You don't have to worry
    about cell widths or heights -- that's done automatically by Web
    browsers. The "TH" tag sets up a table's header (and here we
    indicate we want that header to span all three columns of our
    table), the "TR" tag sets up a table row, and we just include
    entries for each column with the "TD" tag -- if you want more
    columns, just add more "TD" tags in each table row.>
<CENTER>
<TABLE BORDER CELLPADDING = 4>
<TR ALIGN = CENTER>
<TH COLSPAN = 3>TABLES TOO!
</TH>
</TR>
<TR ALIGN = CENTER>
<TD>These</TD>
<TD>are</TD>
<TD>items</TD>
</TR>
<TR ALIGN = CENTER>
<TD>in</TD>
<TD>this</TD>
<TD>table!</TD>
</TR>
</TABLE>            <--
</CENTER>
     .
     .
     .
```

Our table is complete; the result appears in Figure 1.5. Tables enable us to organize our data in one way, but there are other ways. For example, we can set up a list that displays items vertically:

```
-----------------------------------------------------------
|                                                         |
|                Welcome to the Java WorkShop            |
|                                                         |
|                    ---------------                      |
|                    |             |                      |
|                    |    Image    |                      |
|                    |             |                      |
|                    ---------------                      |
|                                                         |
|     ---------------------------------------------     | |
|     |                                             |   | |
|     |                    Text              .      |   | |
|     |                                             |   | |
|     ---------------------------------------------     | |
|                                                         |
|     ---------     ---------------------------------     |
|     |       |     |                             |     | |
|     | Image |     |           Text              |     | |
|     |       |     |                             |     | |
|     ---------     ---------------------------------     |
|                                                         |
|              -----------------------                    |
|              |     TABLES TOO!      |                   |
|              |----------------------|                   |
|              | These | are | items |                   |
|              |-------|-----|-------|                    |
|              |  in   | this| table |                   |
|              -----------------------                    |
|                                                         |
|     *  And                                              |
|     *  here's                                           |
|     *  a                                                |
|     *  list!                                            |
|                                                         |
-----------------------------------------------------------
```

Let's review the process of setting up a list next.

Making Lists

The list we want might just have four items in it as follows:

```
*  And
*  here's
*  a
*  list!
```

There are four kinds of lists: unordered (bulleted) lists, ordered (numbered) lists, directory lists (can be arranged into columns), and menu lists (plain lists without bullets or numbers). Here we'll set up a bulleted list with the <UL> tag. To make it a little more interesting visually, we can first change the color of our list to, for example, light blue with a <FONT> tag. Next, we start the list with <UL>:

```
<FONT COLOR = "#aaaaff">
<UL>
   .
   .
   .
```

Now we simply indicate what items we want in our list with the list item <LI> tag.

```
<FONT COLOR = "#aaaaff">
<UL>
<LI> And                    <--
<LI> here's                 <--
<LI> a                      <--
<LI> list!                  <--
   .
   .
   .
```

Finally, we finish our list with </UL>:

```
<FONT COLOR = "#aaaaff">
<UL>
<LI> And
<LI> here's
<LI> a
<LI> list!
</UL>
</FONT>
   .
   .
   .
```

The list appears on our Web page as in Figure 1.5.

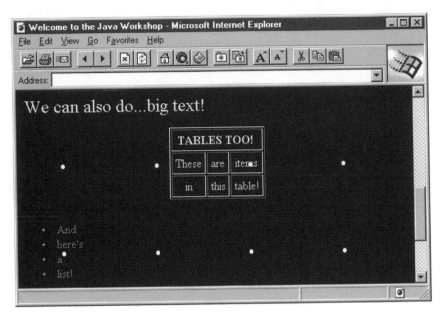

Figure 1.5 Our Web page with a table and list.

Another very popular item in Web pages is to allow people who look at your Web page to email you, and that will be the last item in our HTML review.

Enabling Email

To enable email, we simply use an anchor tag with the HREF keyword, but instead of referencing a URL, we use the MAILTO keyword. For example, to let the person viewing your Web page email the address **username@server.com**, you would do this:

```
<!--EMAIL. We let the user of our Web page email us by using an HREF
   tag with the MAILTO keyword. When the user of your page clicks on
   the underlined MAILTO address, their email program will open and
   they can write email directly to you.>
Email username: <A HREF="MAILTO:username@server.com">  <--
   username@server.com</A>                              <--
```

It's simple to enable email, as shown in Figure 1.6.

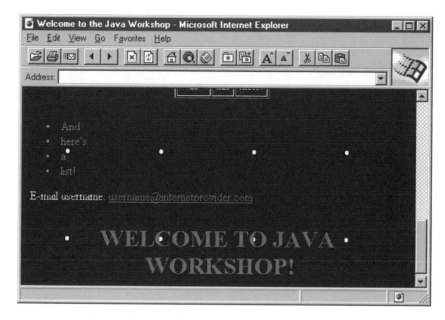

Figure 1.6 Our first Web page, with email capability.

And That's It

That's it for our review and for our first Web page. We finish it with the message WELCOME TO JAVA WORKSHOP! in large type like this:

```
<!--EMAIL. We let the user of our Web page email us by using an HREF
   tag with the MAILTO keyword. When the user of your page clicks on
   the underlined MAILTO address, their email program will open and
   they can write email directly to you.>
Email username: <A HREF="MAILTO:username@server.com">
   username@server.com</A>
<BR>
<BR>

<BR>
<FONT COLOR = "#ff0000">
```

```
<CENTER>
<H1>WELCOME TO JAVA WORKSHOP!</H1>              <--
</CENTER>
</FONT>
   .
   .
   .
```

The very last step is to finish the body of our Web page with the </BODY> tag and finish the HTML file itself with the </HTML> tag.

```
<!--EMAIL. We let the user of our Web page email us by using an HREF
    tag with the MAILTO keyword. When the user of your page clicks on
    the underlined MAILTO address, their email program will open and
    they can write email directly to you.>
Email username: <A HREF="MAILTO:username@server.com">
    username@server.com</A>
<BR>
<BR>

<BR>
<FONT COLOR = "#ff0000">
<CENTER>
<H1>WELCOME TO JAVA WORKSHOP!</H1>
</CENTER>
</FONT>

</BODY>                                         <--
</HTML>                                         <--
```

Now our Web page is ready to be installed in our ISP. The result appears in Figure 1.6; our first Web page is a success, and we included many popular HTML items. The HTML for our review Web page, **Review.html**, appears in Listing 1.1.

Listing 1.1 Review.html

```
<!--START THE PAGE with an HTML tag (a tag is an HTML command, and
    HTML tags appear between angle brackets) "HTML" to indicate this
    document is in HTML, which is the language of Web pages.>
<HTML>
```

```
<!--A PAGE'S TITLE is how a browser will refer to it if someone saves
    it in their Favorites or Bookmarks menu. Note that we also indicate
    we are done defining the title with "/TITLE". This second tag
    matches the first tag, "TITLE", and as mentioned, HTML tags
    always come in pairs, like the following one, which indicates that
    we are done with the page's header.>
<HEAD>
<TITLE>Welcome to the Java WorkShop</TITLE>
</HEAD>
```

```
<!--BODY OF PAGE starts with the following "BODY" tag. COLOR VALUES
    are "#rrggbb" (red, green, and blue) in hexadecimal (0-255 = 0-ff);
    for example, pure red is "#ff0000", pure green is "#00ff00", and
yellow
    is "#ffff00". Here we start the Web page's body, indicating we want
    green text, hyperlinks to be red, hyperlinks to turn white when
    pushed, and links that the viewer has already clicked to be
    yellow.>
<BODY TEXT  = "#ffff00" LINK  = "#ff0000" ALINK = "#ffffff" VLINK =
"#ffff00">
```

```
<!--BACKGROUND PICTURE (which is optional) is tiled on the page's
    background. Here, we indicate we want the Web browser to use the
    graphics file back.gif, which is in our www/gif directory (see
    explanation, below).>
<BODY BACKGROUND = "gif/back.gif">
```

```
<!--HEADERS. Now we are going to place a header of the largest size in
    our page, so we use the "H1" tag, as well as the "CENTER" tag.
    "CENTER" simply makes sure the following text or image is centered.
    Note that all HTML tags come in pairs -- to turn off centering, we
    use "/CENTER" at the end of our header's specification.>
<CENTER>
<H1>Welcome to Java WorkShop</H1>
</CENTER>
```

```
<!--LINE BREAKS. To space things vertically, we use "BR" and "/BR"
    to
    skip a line.>
<BR>
```

```
<!--IMAGES. We display an image, which will appear centered because of
    the "CENTER" tag, with the "IMG" tag, adding the width and height
    in pixels. Here, we display our GIF file yourgif.gif from the GIF
    directory, but this is where a photo of you could go.>
```

```
<CENTER>
<IMG WIDTH=236 HEIGHT=118 SRC="gif/yourgif.gif"></IMG>
</CENTER>

<!--PARAGRAPHS of text start with "P".>
<!--LINKS. We add a hypertext link with the "A" tag, using the HREF
    keyword. In particular, we add a link to sun.com's Web page at
    http://www.sun.com below. This means that the text "sun" will
    appear underlined and in the standard link color (which we've set
    to red); when the viewer of your page clicks that text, they will
    jump to sun's home page.>
<P>
    Hello, and welcome to this Web page, the first Web page of our
    book. In this book, we'll see quite a few good things and how
    you can use them in your own Web pages. If that doesn't
    interest you, perhaps you'd like to take a look at
    <A HREF="http://www.sun.com">sun</A>.
<BR>
<BR>
</P>


<!--ALIGNING PICTURES AND TEXT is done with the ALIGN keyword used in
    the IMG tag. In this case we just have to indicate that we want the
    graphics to appear on the left with ALIGN = LEFT. We also change
    the text color to green temporarily with a "FONT" tag ("FONT" only
    works in recent browsers).>
<IMG WIDTH=141 HEIGHT=126 SRC="gif/sidebar.gif" ALIGN=LEFT>
<FONT COLOR = "00ff00">
    We can even do green text next to graphics. This text appears next
    to the graphics on the left, allowing you to intersperse your words
    with pictures. When you take a look at the HTML for this Web page,
    you'll see how this and more is done. Although this is just a
    review, we are going to add Java to our skills soon...
</FONT>
</IMG>
<BR>
<BR>


<!--FONT SIZE is also done with the "FONT" tag; here, we set the
    size of our text temporarily to 5, a large size.>
<FONT SIZE = 5>
We can also do...big text!
</FONT>
<BR>
<BR>
```

```
<!--TABLES. Tables are not so hard; just use the "TABLE" tag; here
    we indicate we want our table to have a border and to add space
    ("padding") around the text in each cell. You don't have to worry
    about cell widths or heights -- that's done automatically by Web
    browsers. The "TH" tag sets up a table's header (and here we
    indicate we want that header to span all three columns of our
    table), the "TR" tag sets up a table row, and we just include
    entries for each column with the "TD" tag -- if you want more
    columns, just add more "TD" tags in each table row.>
<CENTER>
<TABLE BORDER CELLPADDING = 4>
<TR ALIGN = CENTER>
<TH COLSPAN = 3>TABLES TOO!
</TH>
</TR>
<TR ALIGN = CENTER>
<TD>These</TD>
<TD>are</TD>
<TD>items</TD>
</TR>
<TR ALIGN = CENTER>
<TD>in</TD>
<TD>this</TD>
<TD>table!</TD>
</TR>
</TABLE>
</CENTER>


<!--LISTS. Bulleted lists are also easy, using the "UL" tag. Just
    use the "LI" tag for each list item as follows.>
<FONT COLOR = "#aaaaff">
<UL>
<LI> And
<LI> here's
<LI> a
<LI> list!
</UL>
</FONT>


<!--EMAIL. We let the viewer of our Web page email us by using an HREF
    tag with the MAILTO keyword. When the viewer of your page clicks on
    the underlined MAILTO address, their email program will open and
    they can write email directly to you.>
Email username: <A HREF="MAILTO:username@internetprovider.com">
    username@internetprovider.com</A>
```

```
<BR>
<BR>

<BR>
<FONT COLOR = "#ff0000">
<CENTER>
<H1>WELCOME TO JAVA WORKSHOP!</H1>
</CENTER>
</FONT>

</BODY>
</HTML>
```

That completes our first Web page and our review of HTML. If you don't feel comfortable with what we've done so far, consult a book on writing Web pages before proceeding. On the other hand, if all this is old hat to you, then it's time to dig into Java and its development environment—the Java WorkShop.

CHAPTER TWO

JAVA: BUTTONS AND TEXTFIELDS

In this chapter, we'll start seeing some Java and creating Java applets. Instead of working through a lot of theory, we're going to put Java to work for us as fast as we can. We'll see how to use two very important controls: buttons and textfields. And, in the course of using those controls, we'll begin exploring how to use Java WorkShop and how to put together Java applets. Let's start with our first applet.

What is an Applet?

An *applet* is a Java-created binary file that usually has the extension **.class** and that we can embed in our Web pages with the <APPLET> tag. When run in a Web page, Java applets are downloaded automatically and run by the Web browser. They can do anything—from working with graphics to displaying animation to handling controls like the ones we'll work on in this chapter: textfields and buttons. Using applets makes your Web pages *active*, not passive, and that, of course, is their main attraction.

The process goes like this. First, you create a new applet project in Java WorkShop. Next, you design and write your new applet's Java code, placing it in a file named, for example, **myApplet.java**. You then use the tools in Java WorkShop to compile **myApplet.java** into **myApplet.class**, which is a file of *bytecodes*—binary bytes that Web browsers that understand Java interpret to run your applet. When you have your **myApplet.class** file, you upload it to your Internet Service Provider (ISP) and (usually) store it in the same directory as your HTML files. You give the applet the same protection you would give a Web page, making sure anyone can read the applet **.class** file (e.g., in UNIX, that might look like this: CHMOD 644 myApplet.class). You can embed the new applet in a Web page with the <APPLET> tag, indicating the name of the **.class** file for the applet—**myApplet.class**—and telling the Web browser how much space (in pixels) to leave for the applet, something like this:

```
<HTML>

<BODY>

<CENTER>
<APPLET CODE = "myApplet.class" WIDTH = 300 HEIGHT = 200>          <--
</APPLET>
</CENTER>

</BODY>
</HTML>
```

In this case, we set up a centered 300 x 200 pixel space in our Web page in which to display our applet, and we told the Web browser to load the **myApplet.class** file from your ISP and run it. The <APPLET> tag includes these keywords, where the optional keywords are in brackets:

```
<APPLET
    [ALIGN = LEFT or RIGHT or TOP or TEXTTOP or MIDDLE or
             ABSMIDDLE  or BASELINE or BOTTOM or ABSBOTTOM]
    [ALT = AlternateText]
    CODE = AppletName.class
    [CODEBASE = URL of .class file]
    HEIGHT = AppletPixelsHeight
    [HSPACE = PixelSpaceToLeftOfApplet]
```

```
        [NAME = AppletInstanceName]
        [VSPACE = PixelSpaceAboveApplet]
        WIDTH = AppletPixelsWidth
    >
    [<PARAM NAME = Parameter1 VALUE = VALUE1]
    [<PARAM NAME = Parameter2 VALUE = VALUE2]
                    .
                    .
                    .
    </APPLET>
```

Note, in particular, the <PARAM> tag, which we can use to pass parameters to our applet for initialization, indicating the name of the parameter and the value it should have:

```
<HTML>

<BODY>

<CENTER>
<APPLET CODE = "myApplet.class" WIDTH = 300 HEIGHT = 200>
    <PARAM NAME = MonthsInYear VALUE = 12>          <--
    <PARAM NAME = DaysInWeek VALUE = 7>             <--
</APPLET>
</CENTER>

</BODY>
</HTML>
```

What does the Java language itself look like? It's a language very close to C++, as we'll soon see. Our goal in this book is to use the Java WorkShop to write our Java language programs and then compile them to create the corresponding **.class** file, which you can embed into your Web pages with the <APPLET> tag. Let's start that process now, as we create our first working applet.

Our First Applet

In our first applet, we will use the two controls that this chapter is about, textfields and buttons. *Textfields* (also called *textboxes*) are used to display text, and everyone is familiar with buttons. Our first applet might look like this when run in a Web page, where we've set up a textfield and a button labeled **Click Me**:

When the user clicks the **Click Me** button, we can have the applet display the text "Hello World!" in the textfield this way:

Next, we can embed our applet, which we might call **First.class**, in our Web page this way:

```
<HTML>

<BODY>

<CENTER>
<APPLET CODE = "First.class" WIDTH = 300 HEIGHT = 300>  <--
</APPLET>
</CENTER>

</BODY>
</HTML>
```

Then you upload the Web page and **First.class** to your ISP so that people can see the result, as in Figure 2.1, where we view our new applet in Netscape after downloading it from the Internet. Our goal, then, is to create this first applet as it appears in Figure 2.1.

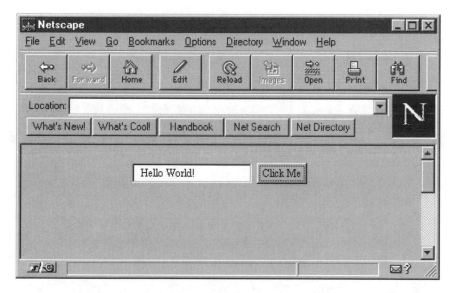

Figure 2.1 Our first applet, downloaded from the Internet.

The Java WorkShop

Now let's create our first applet with Java WorkShop. Start Java WorkShop, as shown in Figure 2.2. Java WorkShop itself is really a Web browser, and you can use it to view pages on the Web. Each tool in Java WorkShop is actually a Java applet that runs in the Web browser (that is, the whole package—Java WorkShop and all the tools—were written in Java). Here are the various tools we'll be working with in Java WorkShop:

Project Manager	Manages and edits Java projects
Build Manager	Builds applets and applications
Portfolio Manager	Manages "folders" of projects
Applet Viewer	Runs applets
Source Editor	Edits **.java** file source
Source Browser	Gives an overview of your project
Debugger	Debugs your project
On-line help system	Browses help files from disk

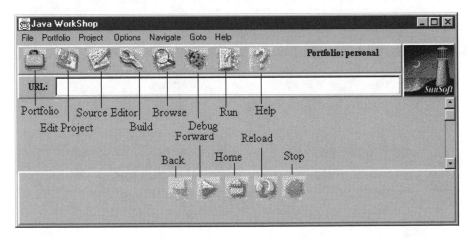

Figure 2.2 Java WorkShop.

The Java WorkShop will set up a *project* for each applet we create. Using the project file, Java WorkShop can keep track of which **.java** files are in our project, and creating that project file is the first step in creating our applet.

Creating a Java WorkShop Project

We'll start our applet by creating a project for it in Java WorkShop. Do that now by selecting the **Create** item in the Project menu, and select **Applet...** in the pop-up menu that appears. This opens the Project Manager in the Java WorkShop; the Project Manager appears in Figure 2.3.

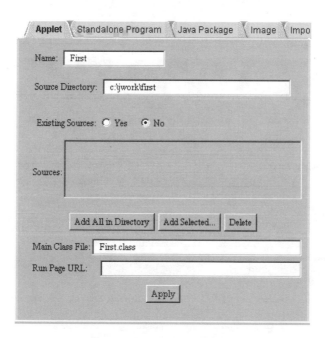

Figure 2.3 The Java WorkShop Project Manager.

This is where we set up our first Java WorkShop project, which will ultimately result in our first applet. Enter **First** in the Project Manager's Name box and enter the directory you want to use for the code and **.class** file in the Source Directory box; here, we will use **c:\jwork\first**. Finally, type **First.class** in the Main Class File box, as shown in Figure 2.3, and click the button marked

Apply to create our first Java WorkShop project, which the Java WorkShop stores for us in the file **First.prj**.

Entering the Java Code

Because we did not indicate that the project had any **.java** files already (which we would do by clicking the **Yes** button next to the Existing Sources label in Figure 2.3 and then using the **Add Selected...** button to add the **.java** files we wanted to our project), Java WorkShop opens its Source Editor for us, ready to create the file **First.java**, as shown in Figure 2.4 (one thing to note here is that case is important in the filenames Java WorkShop uses; as far as it is concerned, *First.java* is not the same thing as *first.java*).

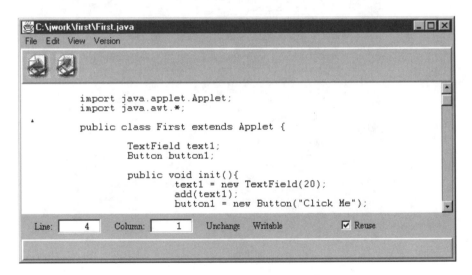

Figure 2.4 The Java WorkShop Source Editor.

Now we're ready to type in the actual Java text for our new applet. At this point, we can just type in this text, noting that case counts in Java (or get this text off the disk that accompanies this book). After we see how to get the new applet working, we will dissect the following Java code (you might be able to figure out quite a lot about Java just by looking through the code, if you are so inclined):

```
import Java.applet.Applet;
import Java.awt.*;

public class First extends Applet {

        TextField text1;
        Button button1;

        public void init(){
                text1 = new TextField(20);
                add(text1);
                button1 = new Button("Click Me");
                add(button1);
        }

        public boolean action (Event e, Object o){
                String caption = (String)o;
                String msg = "Hello World!";
                if(e.target instanceof Button){
                        if(caption -- "Click Me"){
                                text1.setText(msg);
                        }
                }
                return true;
        }
    }
}
```

After entering the Java code for our new applet, as shown in Figure 2.4, save the new file **First.java** using the Source Editor's **Save** item in the File menu. Now we are ready to build our new applet; we do that with the Build Manager and the Portfolio Manager.

Building the Java Applet

After closing the **First.java** file, our next step is to build the applet itself, **First.class**. We do that by first making sure that the First project is the *current* project in the Java WorkShop. The Java WorkShop can manage a number of projects, and you can separate them into *portfolios,* or folders of projects. The default portfolio is the personal portfolio; you can see which projects are in that portfolio by clicking the **Portfolio Manager** tool in the toolbar (it looks like a suitcase) or by choosing the Portfolio menu's **Choose** item in the Java

WorkShop and selecting the **personal** portfolio from the pop-up menu that appears. Make sure that the **First** project is selected in the portfolio, as shown in Figure 2.5. (The **First** project should be selected by default because we just created it, and it will certainly be selected if you have not set up any other projects.)

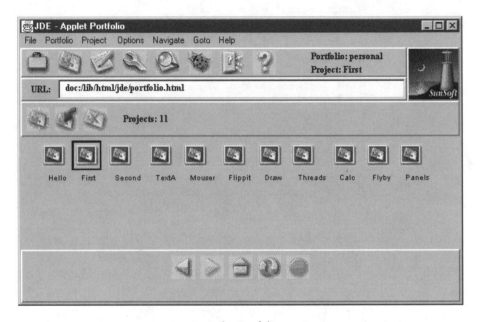

Figure 2.5 The Portfolio Manager.

The current portfolio and project are shown at the extreme right in the Java WorkShop's toolbar, as shown in Figure 2.5.

Now that we've made sure that the First project is the current project, we are ready to build our applet. Select the **Build** tool in the toolbar (it looks like a wrench) to open the Build Manager, as shown in Figure 2.6.

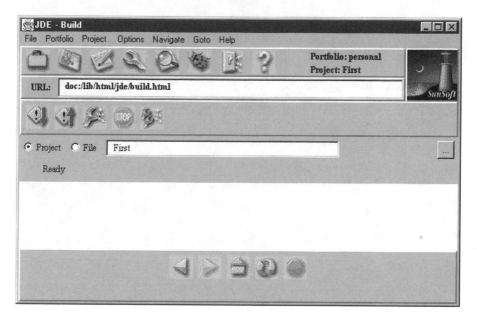

Figure 2.6 The Java WorkShop Build Manager.

To build our applet, we just need to click the **Build** tool in the Build Manager's toolbar, which appears as the single wrench with lightning coming out of it in Figure 2.6 (the double-wrench tool means that all **.java** files, including those the Build Manager thinks are up-to-date, should be rebuilt). Click the **Build** tool now to start the Java compiler and create the **First.class** file (which should happen without problems if you typed in the preceding Java code correctly). That's it; we've created our first applet, **First.class**. The next step is to test it.

Testing the New Applet

To run the new applet, we use the Applet Viewer by selecting **Run** in the Java WorkShop's Project menu and then selecting the **First** item in the pop-up menu that appears. Our new applet appears, as shown in Figure 2.7.

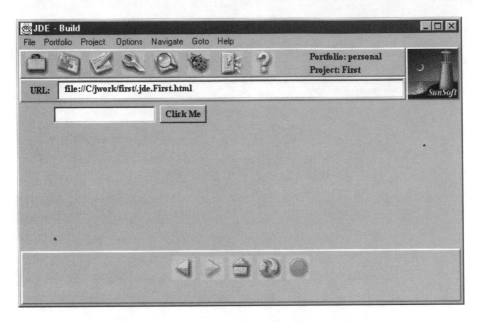

Figure 2.7 Our First applet appears in the Applet Viewer.

You can click the **Click Me** button, and the applet will display our "Hello World!" message in the textfield, as shown in Figure 2.8. Our First applet is working; if you wanted to, you could upload **First.class** to your ISP along with this HTML file:

```
<HTML>

<BODY>

<CENTER>
<APPLET CODE = "First.class" WIDTH = 300 HEIGHT = 300>
</APPLET>
</CENTER>

</BODY>
</HTML>
```

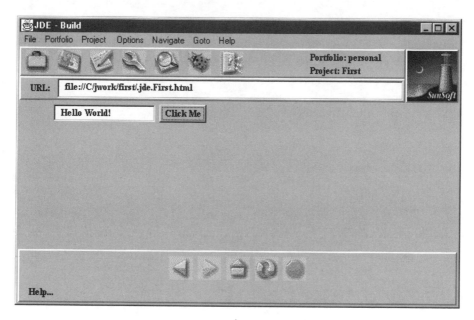

Figure 2.8 Our First applet at work.

Then you could download it into a Web browser, as was shown in Figure 2.1.

Our first applet, **First.class**, is a success; now we can dissect the actual Java code that created it.

Writing a Java Applet

We're ready to see exactly how to write the Java code for our applet by dissecting our **First.java** file. Let's see what's going on behind the scenes in our first applet. If you don't know how object-oriented programming works, hold onto your hat for the next few pages—there will be many new concepts and ideas introduced. But don't worry; everything will become clear when we start creating our own examples.

Java Classes

The very first line in **First.java** (and in most applet **.java** files) is this line:

```
import Java.applet.Applet;
        .
        .
        .
```

Here, we are *importing*, or including, a collection of prewritten Java *classes*. Java uses classes because it is *object-oriented*. Already we're buried in new terms: classes, objects, object-oriented programming. Understanding these concepts will help us understand our first Java applet, and most of what we do in this book will be based on prewritten Java classes. Let's look at objects first.

What is a Java Object?

An *object* is really just a programming construct that wraps code and data together to form a single self-sufficient programming entity. What does that mean? It means that when using objects, you don't have to worry about all the internal details of, for example, screen handling; you could just use, for example, a graphics object like this: `GraphicsObject.drawLine (x1, y1, x2, y2)` to draw a line on the screen from (x1, y1) to (x2, y2). In this case, all the details of raster scanning, memory buffers, internal data, and I/O addresses are taken care of for us by the functions internal to the graphics object. To see why this is useful, consider a refrigerator—you don't want to be responsible for regulating refrigerant flow, handling the thermostats, and working the compressor; you just want a refrigerator. There is a lot going on inside the refrigerator—internal functions interacting with internal data—that we never see. And because we never see those details, the refrigerator is a much more useful object to us.

That's what an object is: a programming construct that contains both internal data and functions, some of which are purely internal. That is, there might be dozens of internal functions in a refrigerator, but we never see them because they are internal to the refrigerator. In a programming language, that means that the object can have internal data and functions that are never seen by the rest of the program, and that divides the program up into discrete and more easily managed units.

What Is a Java Class?

A *class* is to an object as a cookie mold is to a cookie. That is, the class defines the type of object we want, and when we declare an item of that type, that's the *object*. If we were to declare an integer variable like this:

```
int myInt;
```

then the type of our variable is *int*, and the variable itself is *myInt*. In the same way, if we set up a class named *myClass*, then we could declare an object of that class named *myObject* this way:

```
myClass myObject;
```

That's the idea behind classes and objects—a *class* is like a variable type, except that it can contain functions and data, and an *object* is like a variable of that type. It turns out that Sun has already created many predefined classes for us in Java, and most of what we do will be based on these classes. For example, this first line in **First.java**:

```
import Java.applet.Applet;
        .
        .
        .
```

indicates that we want to get the Applet class from the Java libraries. This class allows us to create applet objects with all kinds of functionality built in, such as drawing the applet's background in the Web page—with the paint() function—and handling starting and stopping of applets with the start() and stop() functions. In fact, functions built into a class (like paint(), start(), and stop()) are given a special name: *methods*. Another prewritten Java class is the Graphics class, which has many built-in methods, such as drawLine() and drawRect(). When we want to work with graphics in a Java applet, we'll create an object of the Graphics class and then call the methods in it to draw lines or rectangles in our applet. Yet another prewritten Java class is the Math class, which contains math methods such as min() to find the minimum of two integers and max() to find the maximum of two integers.

Putting Classes and Objects to Work for Us

Now let's bring all this abstraction together: we are going to take the Applet class that Java provides us with and add our own additions to it to create our own applet. That's why we import **Java.applet.Applet**; we will let it handle the low-level things, such as interacting with the Web browser, to set aside space for our applet in the Web page. Because all that is already taken care of for us, we only need to add the code we want (for example, we can write the code to display a clock and base everything on the Applet class; that way, all the window handling and Web browser interaction is handled by the Java Applet class and we only have to worry about drawing our clock in the space the Applet class provides for us).

In addition to the basic Applet class, which handles low-level functions, we want to include the Java library of control classes that include prewritten buttons and textfields. These classes are referred to as *Java.awt.xxx*, where *xxx* is the class of control we want to use, such as Button, and *awt* stands for Abstract Window Toolkit. To include all the controls, we import all the awt classes:

```
        import Java.applet.Applet;
 -->    import Java.awt.*;
            .
            .
            .
```

If you're having trouble with the idea of classes and objects, keep reading; it will become very clear as we put together our examples.

Deriving a New Class

The next step is to extend the Applet class beyond the simple basics (by itself, the Applet class just places an empty region in the Web page). We do that by *deriving* a new class from the Applet class; that is, the Applet class will be our

new class's *base class*. To derive a new class from Applet, we add this line to
First.java:

```
        import Java.applet.Applet;
        import Java.awt.*;

-->     public class First extends Applet {
            .
            .
            .
```

The public keyword indicates that this new class is *public*; that is, it is available
for general use in the Java program. If a class in a file is *private* (which is the
default if you omit the public keyword), then it's only used internally by the
code in the same file.

We use the keyword *class* to show we are defining a new class, and we give
that new class the name First. It is important that the name of the public class
match (including case) the name of the **.java** file, which in this case is
First.java. When the Java compiler compiles **First.java**, it will produce
First.class, our new class derived from the Applet class. Our new class will
include all the built-in power of the Applet class to manage our applet's starting, stopping, and running. This process—where a derived class includes the
methods and data of the base class—is called *inheritance*.

To show that we are basing our new class on the Applet class, we use the
extends keyword:

```
        import Java.applet.Applet;
        import Java.awt.*;

-->     public class First extends Applet {
            .
            .
            .
```

Now we're ready to start setting up our new class for real (things will become
clearer as we start working with our actual program).

Declaring a TextField Object

The first thing we'll do in our new class is embed an object of class TextField. Recall that our applet displays a textfield and a button like this:

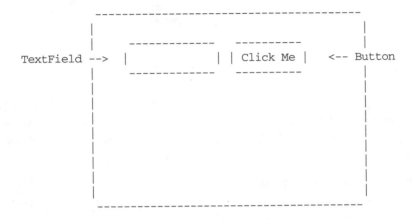

To set up a textfield called text1, we just declare an object of the awt class TextField in our Java file:

```
import Java.applet.Applet;
import Java.awt.*;

public class First extends Applet {

-->        TextField text1;
              .
              .
              .
```

Simply declaring the new textfield object is not enough, however; we still have to create this new textfield object when the applet first runs.

The init() Function

How can we create a new TextField object when the applet starts? We do that by placing our Java code in a special function named init(), which is automatically run when the applet starts. We can place initialization code in init(), and we add that function to our applet now:

```
        import Java.applet.Applet;
        import Java.awt.*;

        public class First extends Applet {

                TextField text1;

-->             public void init(){
                        .
                        .
                        .
```

The new Operator

To create a new object of class TextField, we will use the operator named *new*. The new operator sets aside memory for us in Java (i.e., it replaces the malloc() C operator in C++). To create a new TextField object, we use new and store the returned object in text1 like this:

```
        import Java.applet.Applet;
        import Java.awt.*;

        public class First extends Applet {

                TextField text1;

                public void init(){
-->                     text1 = new TextField;
                        .
                        .
                        .
```

This works, but it would actually place a textfield only one character wide in our applet. If we want a different-size textfield, we have to specify what size we want. We do that with the TextField class's *constructor*.

Java Constructors

In Java and C++, classes come with *constructors*, or special functions that we call when we make objects from those classes. In a constructor, we can specify initialization information for the new object, such as, in the case of a TextField object, how many characters wide it should be.

A class's constructor is a function that has the same name as the class itself, so the constructor for the TextField class is called TextField(). In the case of the TextField class, we can pass the number of characters we want to display in the new textfield directly to the class's constructor this way, where we ask for a textfield 20 characters wide:

```
import Java.applet.Applet;
import Java.awt.*;

public class First extends Applet {

        TextField text1;

        public void init(){
-->             text1 = new TextField(20);
                .
                .
                .
```

The possible constructors of the TextField class, as well as the TextField methods (or built-in functions), appear in Table 2.1.

Table 2.1 TextField Constructors and Methods

```
Java.lang.Object
    |
    +----Java.awt.Component
             |
             +----Java.awt.TextComponent
                      |
                      +----Java.awt.TextField
```

TextField()	Constructs a TextField
TextField(int)	Constructs a TextField with specified number of columns
TextField(String)	Constructs a TextField with specified text
TextField(String, int)	Constructs a TextField with specified text and columns
addNotify	Creates TextField's peer; the peer allows us to change the appearance of the TextField without changing its function
echoCharIsSet()	Returns true if TextField has a character set for echoing
getColumns()	Returns number of columns in TextField
getEchoChar()	Returns character used for echoing
getSelectionStart()	Returns an int with the start location of the selection
getSelectionEnd()	Returns an int with the end location of the selection
getText()	Gets the textfield's text
minimumSize(int)	Returns minimum size needed for TextField with the specified number of columns
minimumSize()	Returns minimum size needed for TextField
paramString()	Returns string of parameters for TextField
preferredSize(int)	Returns the preferred size for TextField with specified number of columns
preferredSize()	Returns preferred size needed for TextField
select(int, int)	Sets the selection
setEchoCharacter(char)	Sets echo character for TextField
setEditable(boolean)	Makes textfields read-only
setText(String)	Sets the textfield's text

You may wonder how we can call the same function, TextField(), with a different number of parameters (i.e., none, one or two), as shown in Table 2.1. This is possible because of *function overloading*, which is possible in both C++ and

Java. To overload a function, you simply define it a number of times with a different parameter list each time:

```
int function CalculateDaysFromToday(int Day){
    .
    .
    .
}
int function CalculateDaysFromToday(int Day, int Month){
    .
    .
    .
}
int function CalculateDaysFromToday(int Day, int Month, int Year){
    .
    .
    .
}
```

How will the compiler know which of these to use? It will determine that by the way you call the function; in the preceding case, for example, the compiler will use the first function definition if you call the function like this: `CalculateDaysFromToday(25);` and the third function definition if you call it this way: `CalculateDaysFromToday(25, 12, 1997);`.

Now that we've created our new textfield object, we add it to the applet's display with the add() method (we'll see more about what is happening here and how Java decides where to place our textfield in the applet in the next chapter):

```
      import Java.applet.Applet;
      import Java.awt.*;

      public class First extends Applet {

          TextField text1;

          public void init(){
                  text1 = new TextField(20);
-->               add(text1);
                  .
                  .
                  .
```

That's it—we've set up our textfield. The next step is to add the button with the caption **Click Me**.

Declaring a Button Object

As you might expect, the awt library includes a Java class named Button, and we'll use that class to create our **Click Me** button:

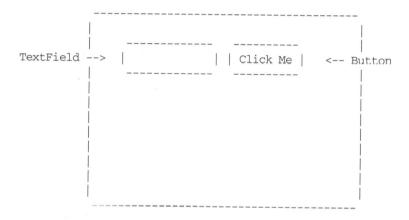

The Button class's methods and constructors appear in Table 2.2.

Table 2.2 Java Button Methods and Constructors

```
Java.lang.Object
   |
   +----Java.awt.Component
              |
              +----Java.awt.Button
```

Button()	Constructs Button with no label
Button(String)	Constructs Button with a string label
addNotify()	Creates a peer of the button; the peer allows us to change the appearance of the button without changing its function.
getLabel()	Gets the button's caption

| paramString() | Returns the parameter string of Button |
| setLabel(String) | Sets the button's caption |

In our **First.java** file, we declare the new button this way:

```
import Java.applet.Applet;
import Java.awt.*;

public class First extends Applet {

        TextField text1;
-->     Button button1;

        public void init(){
                text1 = new TextField(20);
                add(text1);
                  .
                  .
                  .
```

Next, we create a new Button object and place the pointer to it in button1. We'll use the Button(String) form of the Button class's constructor to give our button a caption of **Click Me**:

```
import Java.applet.Applet;
import Java.awt.*;

public class First extends Applet {

        TextField text1;
        Button button1;

        public void init(){
                text1 = new TextField(20);
                add(text1);
-->             button1 = new Button("Click Me");
                  .
                  .
                  .
```

Finally, we add the new button to our applet's display with add(), just as we did for the textfield, and we finish our init() function:

```
import Java.applet.Applet;
import Java.awt.*;

public class First extends Applet {

        TextField text1;
        Button button1;

        public void init(){
                text1 = new TextField(20);
                add(text1);
                button1 = new Button("Click Me");
-->             add(button1);
-->        }              .
                          .
                          .
                          .
```

At this point, our two controls—the textfield and the button—appear in our applet like this:

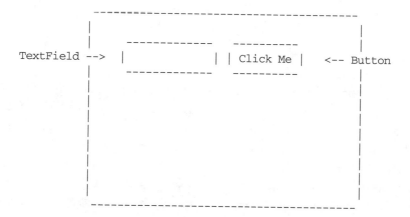

However, when you click the button, nothing happens. We have not yet connected any code to the button click. Let's do that now.

Handling Java Events

When the user clicks the button (or presses a key, moves the mouse, and so on), that creates an *event*.

We can catch these events with the action() method, which is called (if we add it to our code) for control events such as button clicks. We add it to our applet like this:

```
import Java.applet.Applet;
import Java.awt.*;

public class First extends Applet {

        TextField text1;
        Button button1;

        public void init(){
                text1 = new TextField(20);
                add(text1);
                button1 = new Button("Click Me");
                add(button1);
        }

-->     public boolean action (Event e, Object o){
                .
                .
                .
```

Here, we are passed two arguments: an Event object and an object of an unspecified type (i.e., simply of the generic type Object). The Event object tells us a great deal about the type of event that occurred—for example, the ID variable in the Event object tells us what kind of event occurred. The possible values are listed in Table 2.3. As we'll see, a variable that is part of an object is called a *member* or a *data member* of the object. To get the value in an Event object's ID member, we would refer to it this way: `mYEventObject.ID`.

Table 2.3 ID Values for Events

ID Value	Means
ACTION_EVENT	Action event
GOT_FOCUS	Component has the focus
KEY_ACTION	Key action keyboard event
KEY_ACTION_RELEASE	Key action keyboard event
KEY_PRESS	Keypress keyboard event
KEY_RELEASE	Key release keyboard event
LOST_FOCUS	Component lost the focus
MOUSE_DOWN	Mouse down event
MOUSE_DRAG	Mouse drag event
MOUSE_ENTER	Mouse enter event
MOUSE_EXIT	Mouse exit event
MOUSE_MOVE	Mouse move event
MOUSE_UP	Mouse up event
SAVE_FILE	File saving event
SCROLL_ABSOLUTE	Absolute scroll event
SCROLL_LINE_DOWN	Line down scroll event
SCROLL_LINE_UP	Line up scroll event
SCROLL_PAGE_DOWN	Page down scroll event
SCROLL_PAGE_UP	Page up scroll event
WINDOW_DEICONIFY	De-iconify window event
WINDOW_DESTROY	Destroy window event
WINDOW_EXPOSE	Expose window event
WINDOW_ICONIFY	Iconify window event
WINDOW_MOVED	Window moved event

One of the members of Event objects (like the Event object passed to us in the action() method) is the *target* member. This is the actual control for which the event was targeted. In our First class, we can check to make sure the current event was "targeted" to a button control by checking the Event object's target member like this, where we check to see if the target control was an *instance* of the Button class (objects are "instances" of their corresponding classes):

```
import Java.applet.Applet;
import Java.awt.*;

public class First extends Applet {

        TextField text1;
        Button button1;

        public void init(){
                text1 = new TextField(20);
                add(text1);
                button1 = new Button("Click Me");
                add(button1);
        }

        public boolean action (Event e, Object o){
-->             if(e.target instanceof Button){
                            .
                            .
                            .
```

Now we know a button was clicked; to make sure that it was our **Click Me** button, we can actually get the caption of the button that was clicked. In the case of button clicks, the second object o passed to us in action() holds the caption of the button. We can set up a Java text string to hold the button's caption using the Java String type this way:

```
import Java.applet.Applet;
import Java.awt.*;

public class First extends Applet {

        TextField text1;
```

```
        Button button1;

        public void init(){
                text1 = new TextField(20);
                add(text1);
                button1 = new Button("Click Me");
                add(button1);
        }

        public boolean action (Event e, Object o){
-->             String caption = (String)o;
                if(e.target instanceof Button){
                        .
                        .
                        .
```

Now we have the caption of the button that was clicked, and we can make sure it was our **Click Me** button:

```
import Java.applet.Applet;
import Java.awt.*;

public class First extends Applet {

        TextField text1;
        Button button1;

        public void init(){
                text1 = new TextField(20);
                add(text1);
                button1 = new Button("Click Me");
                add(button1);
        }

        public boolean action (Event e, Object o){
                String caption = (String)o;
                if(e.target instanceof Button){
-->                     if(caption == "Click Me"){
                                .
                                .
                                .
```

At this point, we know that the user clicked our button, so we should place the "Hello World!" string into the textfield. To do that, we first set up a string holding that text:

```
import Java.applet.Applet;
import Java.awt.*;

public class First extends Applet {

        TextField text1;
        Button button1;

        public void init(){
                text1 = new TextField(20);
                add(text1);
                button1 = new Button("Click Me");
                add(button1);
        }

        public boolean action (Event e, Object o){
                String caption = (String)o;
 -->            String msg = "Hello World!";
                if(e.target instanceof Button){
                        if(caption == "Click Me"){
                                .
                                .
                                .
```

Now we want to place that text into the textfield we have named text1:

By checking Table 2.1, we see that textfields have a setText() method, so we use that to set the text of our textfield text1:

```
import Java.applet.Applet;
import Java.awt.*;

public class First extends Applet {

        TextField text1;
        Button button1;

        public void init(){
                text1 = new TextField(20);
                add(text1);
                button1 = new Button("Click Me");
                add(button1);
        }

        public boolean action (Event e, Object o){
                String caption = (String)o;
                String msg = "Hello World!";
                if(e.target instanceof Button){
                        if(caption == "Click Me"){
        -->                     text1.setText(msg);
                                .
                                .
                                .
```

That's it—all that's left is to return a Boolean value of true to indicate that we've handled the event:

```
import Java.applet.Applet;
import Java.awt.*;

public class First extends Applet {

        TextField text1;
        Button button1;

        public void init(){
                text1 = new TextField(20);
                add(text1);
```

```
                            button1 = new Button("Click Me");
                            add(button1);
                  }

                  public boolean action (Event e, Object o){
                            String caption = (String)o;
                            String msg = "Hello World!";
                            if(e.target instanceof Button){
                                    if(caption == "Click Me"){
                                            text1.setText(msg);
                                    }
                            }
            -->               return true;
                  }
         }
```

That's all there is to our applet. We've created our first applet from start to finish, all in our first chapter on Java programming. You now have all the knowledge you need to get this applet created and installed in a Web page. Congratulations; you're a Java programmer.

It's worth noting one thing here, though: checking the button's caption is not really a good way of seeing which button was clicked:

```
                  public boolean action (Event e, Object o){
                            String caption = (String)o;
                            String msg = "Hello World!";
                            if(e.target instanceof Button){
            -->                       if(caption == "Click Me"){
                                            text1.setText(msg);
                                    }
                            }
                            return true;
                  }
```

This is because button captions can change (in fact, we'll do that in the next chapter). A better way is to use the equals() method, where we can compare the target button that was clicked with the actual button object in our program. Let's look into that technique now.

Our Second Applet

In our second applet, we might add a second button like this:

Now when the user clicks the **Hello** button, the "Hello" part of our "Hello World!" message appears in the textfield:

```
 --------------------------------------------------------
|                                                        |
|    -------------    ----------    ----------           |
|   | Hello       |  |  Hello   |  |  World!  |          |
|    -------------    ----------    ----------           |
|                                                        |
|                                                        |
|                                                        |
|                                                        |
|                                                        |
|                                                        |
 --------------------------------------------------------
```

If the user was to click the button marked **World!**, that text would appear in the textfield. In this example, we will also see a new technique that we can use to identify which of the two buttons was clicked; in applets with multiple buttons or other similar controls, accurate identification of the control that caused the event is important.

We start just as we did in our First applet—by creating a new Java WorkShop project using the Project Manager. Start the Project Manager now and enter **Second** in the Project Manager's Name box and enter the directory you want to use for the code and **.class** file in the Source Directory box; here, we will use **c:\jwork\second**. Finally, type **Second.class** in the Main Class File box, and click the button marked **Apply** to create our second Java WorkShop project, which the Java WorkShop stores for us in the file **Second.prj**.

Doing this also opens the Source Editor, allowing us to create the file **Second.java**. We start off much as we did in our First project, except of course this time the public class derived from Applet will be named Second, not First:

```
        import Java.applet.Applet;
        import Java.awt.*;

  -->   public class Second extends Applet {
                        .
                        .
                        .
```

In addition, we set up one textfield and two buttons this time, going through the creation and adding process for our new controls in the init() method:

```
        import Java.applet.Applet;
        import Java.awt.*;

        public class Second extends Applet {

  -->           TextField text1;
  -->           Button button1, button2;

  -->           public void init(){
  -->                   text1 = new TextField(20);
  -->                   add(text1);
  -->                   button1 = new Button("Hello");
  -->                   add(button1);
  -->                   button1 = new Button("World!");
```

```
  -->                     add(button1);
              }                        .
                                       .
                                       .
```

In the applet, this means that our controls will be arranged this way:

How is this determined? That is, who decides the layout of our controls in our applet? That turns out to be the job of the Layout Manager, and we'll see more about that and take more control of the process in the next chapter.

As we did in the **First.java** file, we add an action() method to our applet:

```
import Java.applet.Applet;
import Java.awt.*;

public class Second extends Applet {

        TextField text1;
        Button button1, button2;

        public void init(){
                text1 = new TextField(20);
                add(text1);
                button1 = new Button("Hello");
                add(button1);
                button1 = new Button("World!");
                add(button1);
```

```
           }

 -->           public boolean action (Event e, Object o){
                       .
                       .
                       .
```

In First, however, we examined the caption of the button to see which button had been clicked. Here, we will take a look at the actual target object of the action itself. We can compare that target to button1 (the **Hello** button) using the equals() method this way:

```
        import Java.applet.Applet;
        import Java.awt.*;

        public class Second extends Applet {

                TextField text1;
                Button button1, button2;

                public void init(){
                        text1 = new TextField(20);
                        add(text1);
                        button1 = new Button("Hello");
                        add(button1);
                        button1 = new Button("World!");
                        add(button1);
                }

                public boolean action (Event e, Object o){
 -->                    if(e.target.equals(button1)){
                                .
                                .
                                .
```

In this way, we compare the actual button clicked to our button1 object. If they are the same, we want to put the text "Hello" into the textfield named text1:

```
        import Java.applet.Applet;
        import Java.awt.*;

        public class Second extends Applet {
```

```
        TextField text1;
        Button button1, button2;

        public void init(){
                text1 = new TextField(20);
                add(text1);
                button1 = new Button("Hello");
                add(button1);
                button1 = new Button("World!");
                add(button1);
        }


        public boolean action (Event e, Object o){
                if(e.target.equals(button1)){
-->                     text1.setText("Hello");
                }               .
                                .
                                .
```

On the other hand, if button2 was clicked, we want to display the string "World!":

```
import Java.applet.Applet;
import Java.awt.*;

public class Second extends Applet {

        TextField text1;
        Button button1, button2;

        public void init(){
                text1 = new TextField(20);
                add(text1);
                button1 = new Button("Hello");
                add(button1);
                button1 = new Button("World!");
                add(button1);
        }

        public boolean action (Event e, Object o){
                if(e.target.equals(button1)){
                        text1.setText("Hello");
                }
```

```
-->                    if(e.target.equals(button2)){
-->                            text1.setText("World!");
-->                    }
                       return true;
                }
        }
```

That's it; we've added a second button to our applet, as shown in Figure 2.9.

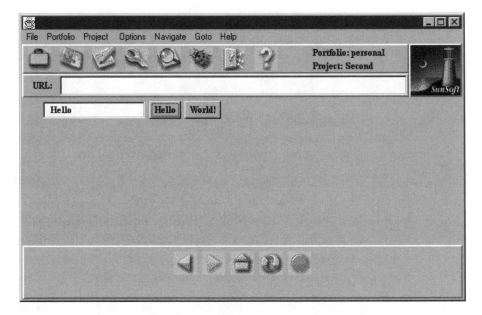

Figure 2.9 Our Second applet at work.

There's one more topic we'll cover before leaving textfields and buttons: textareas. Let's look into that now.

Textareas

Textareas are much like textfields, except that they can support multiple lines of text, as well as scrollbars, which textfields cannot. Now let's put together a textarea example in which we just replace the textfield in our previous examples with a textarea:

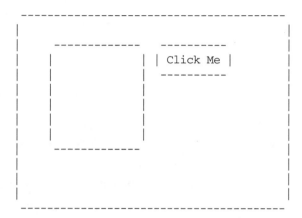

When the user clicks the **Click Me** button, we can display our message in the textarea:

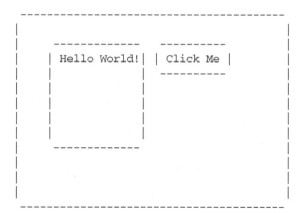

Let's see how this works; the constructors and methods of the TextArea class appear in Table 2.4.

Table 2.4 TextArea Constructors and Methods

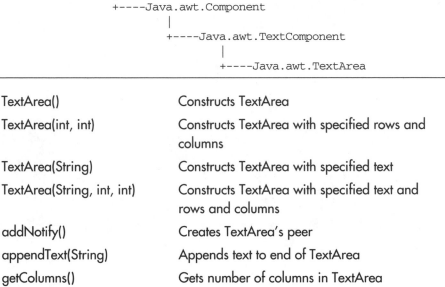

```
Java.lang.Object
        |
        +----Java.awt.Component
                |
                +----Java.awt.TextComponent
                        |
                        +----Java.awt.TextArea
```

TextArea()	Constructs TextArea
TextArea(int, int)	Constructs TextArea with specified rows and columns
TextArea(String)	Constructs TextArea with specified text
TextArea(String, int, int)	Constructs TextArea with specified text and rows and columns
addNotify()	Creates TextArea's peer
appendText(String)	Appends text to end of TextArea
getColumns()	Gets number of columns in TextArea
getRows()	Gets number of rows in TextArea
insertText(String, int)	Inserts text at specified position
minimumSize(int, int)	Gets minimum size of TextArea
minimumSize()	Gets minimum size of TextArea
paramString()	Gets string of parameters for TextArea
preferredSize(int, int)	Gets specified rows and columns of TextArea
preferredSize()	Gets specified rows and columns of TextArea
replaceText(String, int, int)	Replaces text from start to end

Create a new project in the Java WorkShop now, calling it **TextA**. Add this code to the **TextA.java** file:

```
import Java.applet.Applet;
import Java.awt.*;
```

```
public class TextA extends Applet {
        .
        .
        .
```

Next, instead of declaring a textfield as we have done, we set up a TextArea object named textarea1:

```
import Java.applet.Applet;
import Java.awt.*;

public class TextA extends Applet {

-->         TextArea textarea1;
        .
        .
        .
```

And we create and add that object to our applet in the init() function:

```
import Java.applet.Applet;
import Java.awt.*;

public class TextA extends Applet {

        TextArea textarea1;
        Button button1;

-->     public void init(){
-->             textarea1 = new TextArea(5, 20);
-->             add(textarea1);
-->             button1 = new Button("Click Me");
-->             add(button1);
-->     }        .
                 .
                 .
                 .
```

Then, in the action() method, we check to see if the **Click Me** button, button1, was pushed:

```
import Java.applet.Applet;
import Java.awt.*;

public class TextA extends Applet {

        TextArea textarea1;
        Button button1;

        public void init(){
                textarea1 = new TextArea(5, 20);
                add(textarea1);
                button1 = new Button("Click Me");
                add(button1);
        }

        public boolean action (Event e, Object o){
-->             if(e.target.equals(button1)){
                                .
                                .
                                .
```

If so, we want to put the message "Hello World!" into the textarea. Looking at Table 2.4, we see we can use the insertText() method, which we do this way (the second argument, 0, indicates that we want to place this text at the very beginning of the textarea):

```
import Java.applet.Applet;
import Java.awt.*;

public class TextA extends Applet {

        TextArea textarea1;
        Button button1;

        public void init(){
                textarea1 = new TextArea(5, 20);
                add(textarea1);
                button1 = new Button("Click Me");
                add(button1);
        }

        public boolean action (Event e, Object o){
```

```
-->                    String msg = "Hello World!";
                       if(e.target.equals(button1)){
-->                            textarea1.insertText(msg, 0);
                       }
                       return true;
               }
       }
```

That's it. Now we can place text into a multiline textarea control; the result appears in Figure 2.10. Our TextArea applet is a success.

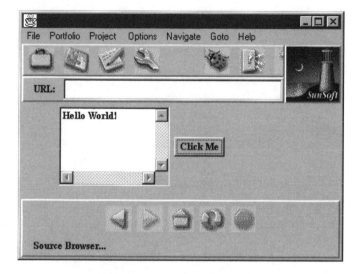

Figure 2.10 Our TextArea applet.

That's it for the TextArea applet—and for this chapter. We've come far in this chapter. We got an overview of the Java WorkShop and built our first applet, seeing it work. We've examined several controls: textfields, buttons, and textareas. And we'll continue to explore what the Java WorkShop has to offer in the next chapter, where we start working with two new controls—radio buttons and check boxes—and more powerful Java techniques.

CHAPTER THREE

CHECK BOXES, RADIO BUTTONS, AND MANAGING MULTIPLE CONTROLS

In this chapter, we will explore the use of two new controls: check boxes and radio buttons. Check boxes (square controls that can display check marks) allow the user to specify a set of options, and radio buttons (round controls that can display a dot when selected) allow the user to select one option from a number of choices. Radio buttons are coordinated, that is, you can select only one among them at a time. This raises a new question. How do we let separate groups of such controls operate independently? We'll see the importance of this issue as we start to deal with more controls in our applets. We'll also see the importance of *laying out* the controls in our applets. Let's start with an example that will show us the importance of control layout.

A Calculator Applet

Let's set up an applet calculator like this so that it can perform simple additions:

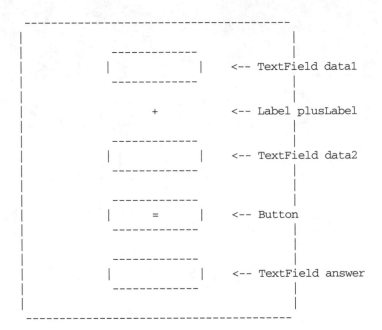

The user can enter an integer into the top textfield and another integer into the second textfield and then click the button marked **=** to see the sum of the two integers in the bottom textfield:

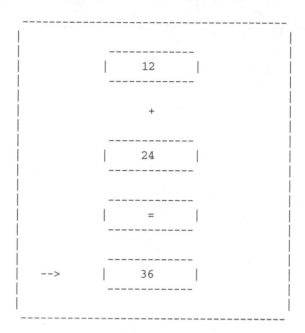

Let's put this applet together now. We begin by setting up the first textfield, which will hold the first number to add. This textfield will be named data1:

```
        import java.applet.Applet;
        import java.awt.*;

        public class Calc extends Applet {

-->         TextField data1;

            public void init(){
-->             data1 = new TextField(20);
-->             add(data1);
                    .
                    .
                    .
```

Now we need to have a plus sign, (+) appear in our applet like this:

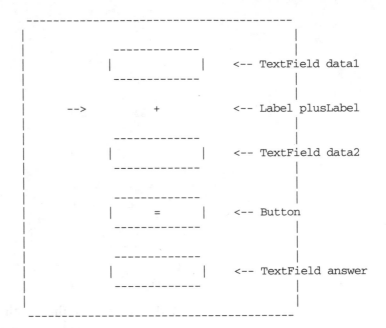

We can do that with a *label* control, which displays a single line of read-only text. That is just what we need here, so we add a new label with the text "+":

```
import java.applet.Applet;
import java.awt.*;

public class Calc extends Applet {

        TextField data1;
-->     Label plusLabel;

        public void init(){
                data1 = new TextField(20);
                add(data1);
-->             plusLabel = new Label("+");
-->             add(plusLabel);
                .
                .
                .
```

The Label class's constructors and methods appear in Table 3.1.

Table 3.1 Label Constructors and Methods

```
        java.lang.Object
               |
        +----java.awt.Component
               |
            +----java.awt.Label
```

Label()	Constructs a label (which will be empty)
Label(String)	Constructs a label with specified text
Label(String, int)	Constructs a label with specified text and the specified alignment (RIGHT, CENTER, or LEFT)
addNotify()	Creates peer for label
getAlignment()	Gets current alignment of label
getText()	Gets the text of the label
paramString()	Returns parameter string of label
setAlignment(int)	Sets alignment for label
setText(String)	Sets text in label

Next, we add the rest of the components: a new textfield control named data2, the button displaying an equals sign, and the bottom textfield named answer.

```
        import java.applet.Applet;
        import java.awt.*;

        public class Calc extends Applet {

   -->          TextField data1, data2, answer;
                Label plusLabel;
   -->          Button equalButton;

                public void init(){
                        data1 = new TextField(20);
                        add(data1);
                        plusLabel = new Label("+");
```

```
                              add(plusLabel);
    -->                       data2 = new TextField(20);
    -->                       add(data2);
    -->                       equalButton = new Button("=");
    -->                       add(equalButton);
    -->                       answer = new TextField(20);
    -->                       add(answer);
    -->           }               .
                                  .
                                  .
```

That completes the addition of our controls.

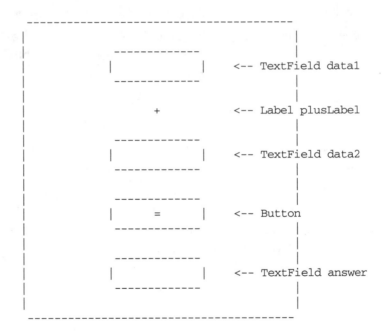

Now we set up the action() method to catch events from the = button.

```
import java.applet.Applet;
import java.awt.*;

public class Calc extends Applet {

        TextField data1, data2, answer;
```

```
        Label plusLabel;
        Button equalButton;

        public void init(){
                data1 = new TextField(20);
                add(data1);
                plusLabel = new Label("+");
                add(plusLabel);
                data2 = new TextField(20);
                add(data2);
                equalButton = new Button("=");
                add(equalButton);
                answer = new TextField(20);
                add(answer);
        }

-->     public boolean action (Event e, Object o){
-->             String caption = (String)o;
-->             if(e.target.equals(equalButton)){
                        .
                        .
                        .
```

The next step is to retrieve the two numbers from the textfields data1 and data2 and add those two numbers together. However, when we use the TextField getText() method, we'll retrieve a string from the textfields, not a number, and we'll have to convert that string into an integer. We do that by using the Integer class, and we pass the string we want to convert to an integer to the class's parseInt() method like this: `Integer.parseInt(data1.getText())`. All that remains is to add the two integers together, placing the result in a new integer named, for example, sum:

```
import java.applet.Applet;
import java.awt.*;

public class Calc extends Applet {

        TextField data1, data2, answer;
        Label plusLabel;
        Button equalButton;
```

```
        public void init(){
                .
                .
                .

        }


        public boolean action (Event e, Object o){
                String caption = (String)o;
                if(e.target.equals(equalButton)){
-->             int sum = Integer.parseInt(data1.getText()) +
-->                     Integer.parseInt(data2.getText());
                .
                .
                .
```

We can display the integer in sum, which gives us the opposite problem that
we just solved. Now we have to convert an integer into a string. We do that by
creating a new String object and using the String class's ValueOf() method this
way:

```
import java.applet.Applet;
        import java.awt.*;

        public class Calc extends Applet {

                TextField data1, data2, answer;
                Label plusLabel;
                Button equalButton;

                public void init(){
                        .
                        .
                        .

                }

                public boolean action (Event e, Object o){
                        String caption = (String)o;
                        if(e.target.equals(equalButton)){
                                int sum = Integer.parseInt(data1.getText()) +
                                        Integer.parseInt(data2.getText());
```

```
    -->                         answer.setText(String.valueOf(sum));
                    }
                    return true;
            }
    }
```

Our applet is ready to use. It works, as shown in Figure 3.1, but the alignment is all wrong. As you can see, the = button appears next to a textfield, and nothing is aligned as it should be. What went wrong?

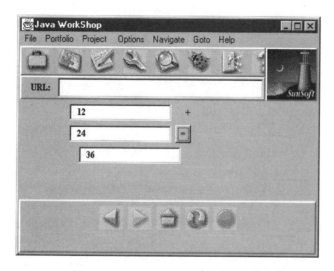

Figure 3.1 Our Calc applet needs some work on layout.

The answer is that we are using Java's default *layout manager*, the FlowLayout Manager. This manager oversees the layout of our controls in the applet and simply puts controls into the applet as they are added, left to right and then top to bottom, much as if you were adding text to a typewritten page. However, as we can see here, that is a problem for us. Now that we are handling multiple controls, we should examine some of the other layout managers available to give us more control over the placement of controls in our applets. We'll take a look at layout managers in both this and the next chapter, and we'll begin with the Grid Layout.

Grid Layout: The Flippit Game

Our first layout example will be the two-player Flippit game. This game is similar to tic-tac-toe, except that we have four rows of four buttons, marked alternately with *x* or *o* in this way:

```
-------------------------------------
|   ---      ---      ---      ---    |
|  | x |    | o |    | x |    | o |   |
|   ---      ---      ---      ---    |
|   ---      ---      ---      ---    |
|  | o |    | x |    | o |    | x |   |
|   ---      ---      ---      ---    |
|   ---      ---      ---      ---    |
|  | o |    | x |    | o |    | x |   |
|   ---      ---      ---      ---    |
|   ---      ---      ---      ---    |
|  | x |    | o |    | x |    | o |   |
|   ---      ---      ---      ---    |
-------------------------------------
```

To play the game, each player clicks buttons. When clicked, the button captions switch from *x* to *o* or *o* to *x*. The game is over when one player has four of their pieces in a row, like this, where the *x* player has four *x*es lined up in the first column.

```
-------------------------------------
|   ---      ---      ---      ---    |
|  | x |    | o |    | x |    | o |   |
|   ---      ---      ---      ---    |
|   ---      ---      ---      ---    |
|  | x |    | x |    | o |    | x |   |
|   ---      ---      ---      ---    |
|   ---      ---      ---      ---    |
|  | x |    | o |    | o |    | o |   |
|   ---      ---      ---      ---    |
|   ---      ---      ---      ---    |
|  | x |    | o |    | x |    | o |   |
|   ---      ---      ---      ---    |
-------------------------------------
```

Clearly, putting together the Flippit game will introduce us to control layout in Java. We start our new applet by declaring all 16 buttons—b1 to b16:

```
import java.applet.Applet;
import java.awt.*;

public class Flippit extends Applet {

        Button b1, b2, b3, b4;
        Button b5, b6, b7, b8;
        Button b9, b10, b11, b12;
        Button b13, b14, b15, b16;
            .
            .
            .
```

Next, we create the new button objects, giving them the correct captions:

```
import java.applct.Applet;
import java.awt.*;

public class Flippit extends Applet {

        Button b1, b2, b3, b4;
        Button b5, b6, b7, b8;
        Button b9, b10, b11, b12;
        Button b13, b14, b15, b16;

        public void init() {

-->             b1 = new Button("x");
-->             b2 =. new Button("o");
-->             b3 = new Button("x");
-->             b4 = new Button("o");
-->             b5 = new Button("o");
-->             b6 = new Button("x");
-->             b7 = new Button("o");
-->             b8 = new Button("x");
-->             b9 = new Button("o");
-->             b10 = new Button("x");
-->             b11 = new Button("o");
-->             b12 = new Button("x");
-->             b13 = new Button("x");
```

```
-->          b14 = new Button("o");
-->          b15 = new Button("x");
-->          b16 = new Button("o");
                      .
                      .
                      .
```

Finally, we add these buttons to our applet as usual:

```
import java.applet.Applet;
import java.awt.*;

public class Flippit extends Applet {

        Button b1, b2, b3, b4;
        Button b5, b6, b7, b8;
        Button b9, b10, b11, b12;
        Button b13, b14, b15, b16;

        public void init() {

                setLayout(new GridLayout(4, 4));

                b1 = new Button("x");
                      .
                      .
                      .
                b16 = new Button("o");

-->          add(b1);
-->          add(b2);
-->          add(b3);
-->          add(b4);
-->          add(b5);
-->          add(b6);
-->          add(b7);
-->          add(b8);
-->          add(b9);
-->          add(b10);
-->          add(b11);
-->          add(b12);
-->          add(b13);
```

```
-->        add(b14);
-->        add(b15);
-->        add(b16);
    }          .
               .
               .
               .
```

Now we can set up the action() method. Here, we want to flip the clicked button's caption from *x* to *o* or *o* to *x*. First, we check if the caption was *x*:

```
public boolean action(Event e, Object o){
        String caption = (String)o;
        if(caption == "x"){



                  .
                  .
```

If so, we can change it to *o* with the Button class's setLabel() method:

```
public boolean action(Event e, Object o){
        String caption = (String)o;
        if(caption == "x"){
-->                ((Button)e.target).setLabel("o");
        }          .
                   .
                   .
```

On the other hand, if the caption is *o*, we want to set it to *x*:

```
public boolean action(Event e, Object o){
        String caption = (String)o;
        if(caption == "x"){
                ((Button)e.target).setLabel("o");
        }
        if(caption == "o"){
                ((Button)e.target).setLabel("x");
        }
        return true;
    }
}
```

Our Flippit applet is ready, except that, as things stand now, we are still using the default FlowLayout Manager. We change that now to use a new layout manager called the GridLayout Manager.

The GridLayout Manager is perfect for our Flippit applet, because it arranges controls in a grid: `GridLayout(rows, cols)`. In this case, we'll use a grid layout of four rows and four columns like this:

```
-------------------------------------------
|    ---       ---       ---       ---     |
|   | x |     | o |     | x |     | o |    |
|    ---       ---       ---       ---     |
|    ---       ---       ---       ---     |
|   | o |     | x |     | o |     | x |    |
|    ---       ---       ---       ---     |
|    ---       ---       ---       ---     |
|   | o |     | x |     | o |     | x |    |
|    ---       ---       ---       ---     |
|    ---       ---       ---       ---     |
|   | x |     | o |     | x |     | o |    |
|    ---       ---       ---       ---     |
-------------------------------------------
```

To install this new layout manager, we use the setLayout() method:

```java
import java.applet.Applet;
import java.awt.*;

public class Flippit extends Applet {

        Button b1, b2, b3, b4;
        Button b5, b6, b7, b8;
        Button b9, b10, b11, b12;
        Button b13, b14, b15, b16;

        public void init() {

-->             setLayout(new GridLayout(4, 4));

                b1 = new Button("x");
                b2 = new Button("o");
```

```
b3 = new Button("x");
b4 = new Button("o");
b5 = new Button("o");
b6 = new Button("x");
b7 = new Button("o");
b8 = new Button("x");
          .
          .
          .
```

Now our buttons are enlarged and fit into the applet as shown in Figure 3.2. The layout of the buttons is just as we want it; our Flippit applet is a success. The code for this applet appears in Listing 3.1.

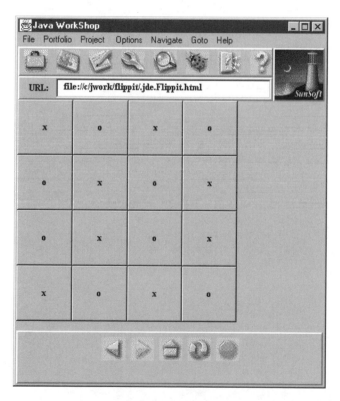

Figure 3.2 The Flippit game.

Listing 3.1 Flippit.java

```java
import java.applet.Applet;
import java.awt.*;

public class Flippit extends Applet {

        Button b1, b2, b3, b4;
        Button b5, b6, b7, b8;
        Button b9, b10, b11, b12;
        Button b13, b14, b15, b16;

        public void init() {

                setLayout(new GridLayout(4, 4));

                b1 = new Button("x");
                b2 = new Button("o");
                b3 = new Button("x");
                b4 = new Button("o");
                b5 = new Button("o");
                b6 = new Button("x");
                b7 = new Button("o");
                b8 = new Button("x");
                b9 = new Button("o");
                b10 = new Button("x");
                b11 = new Button("o");
                b12 = new Button("x");
                b13 = new Button("x");
                b14 = new Button("o");
                b15 = new Button("x");
                b16 = new Button("o");

                add(b1);
                add(b2);
                add(b3);
                add(b4);
                add(b5);
                add(b6);
                add(b7);
                add(b8);
                add(b9);
```

```
                add(b10);
                add(b11);
                add(b12);
                add(b13);
                add(b14);
                add(b15);
                add(b16);
        }
        public boolean action(Event e, Object o){
                String caption = (String)o;
                if(caption == "x"){
                        ((Button)e.target).setLabel("o");
                }
                if(caption == "o"){
                        ((Button)e.target).setLabel("x");
                }
                return true;
        }
}
```

We can use GridLayout Manager throughout this chapter to arrange our controls. This enables us to handle multiple controls in our applets, which means that we can start working with controls that are meant to be used in groups, like check boxes and radio buttons.

Check Boxes

Let's look at check boxes first. For example, we might set up three check boxes and a textfield like this:

```
-----------------------------------------------------------
|                                                         |
|   [ ] Checkbox 1   [ ] Checkbox 2    [ ] Checkbox 3     |
|                                                         |
|                   --------------------                  |
|                   |                  |                  |
|                   --------------------                  |
|                                                         |
|                                                         |
|                                                         |
-----------------------------------------------------------
```

When the user clicks a check box, a check mark appears in the check box, and we can indicate what check box was clicked in the textfield:

```
 ---------------------------------------------------------
|                                                         |
|  [v] Checkbox 1   [ ] Checkbox 2    [ ] Checkbox 3      |
|                                                         |
|               ----------------------                    |
|              | Checkbox 1 clicked |                     |
|               ----------------------                    |
|                                                         |
|                                                         |
 ---------------------------------------------------------
```

Let's put this applet together. We'll begin by declaring three check boxes this way:

```
        import java.applet.Applet;
        import java.awt.*;

        public class Checks extends Applet {

 -->            Checkbox check1, check2, check3;
                      .
                      .
                      .
```

The Java Checkbox class's constructors and methods appear in Table 3.2.

Table 3.2 Check Box Constructors and Methods

```
        java.lang.Object
            |
            +----java.awt.Component
                     |
                     +----java.awt.Checkbox
```

Checkbox()	Constructs check box with no label
Checkbox(String)	Constructs check box with specified text, but no Checkbox group, and initialized false

Checkbox(String, CheckboxGroup, boolean)	Constructs check box with specified text, specified check box group, and specified boolean state (true or false)
addNotify()	Creates peer of check box
getCheckboxGroup()	Returns check box group
getLabel()	Gets label of check box
getState()	Returns boolean state of check box
paramString()	Returns parameter string of check box
setCheckboxGroup(CheckboxGroup)	Sets CheckboxGroup to specified group
setLabel(String)	Sets check box's text to the specified text
setState(boolean)	Sets check box to specified boolean state

Next, we set up the check boxes as we might standard buttons, giving each one its own caption. (Note that we also add the textfield we'll need at the end.)

```
import java.applet.Applet;
import java.awt.*;

public class Checks extends Applet {

        Checkbox check1, check2, check3;
-->     TextField text1;

-->     public void init(){
-->             check1 = new Checkbox("Checkbox 1");
-->             add(check1);
-->             check2 = new Checkbox("Checkbox 2");
-->             add(check2);
-->             check3 = new Checkbox("Checkbox 3");
-->             add(check3);
```

```
-->                        text1 = new TextField(30);
-->                        add(text1);
-->              }            .
                             .
                             .
```

We can also set up the action() method just as we might for buttons, where we examine which check box was clicked with the equals() button and place the corresponding text in the textfield this way:

```
import java.applet.Applet;
import java.awt.*;

public class Checks extends Applet {

        Checkbox check1, check2, check3;
        TextField text1;

        public void init(){
                check1 = new Checkbox("Checkbox 1");
                add(check1);
                check2 = new Checkbox("Checkbox 2");
                add(check2);
                check3 = new Checkbox("Checkbox 3");
                add(check3);
                text1 = new TextField(30);
                add(text1);
        }

        public boolean action (Event e, Object o){
-->             if(e.target.equals(check1)){
-->                     text1.setText("Checkbox 1 clicked");
-->             }
-->             if(e.target.equals(check2)){
-->                     text1.setText("Checkbox 2 clicked");
-->             }
-->             if(e.target.equals(check3)){
-->                     text1.setText("Checkbox 3 clicked");
-->             }
-->             return true;
        }
    }
```

The result appears in Figure 3.3; our check box applet is a success.

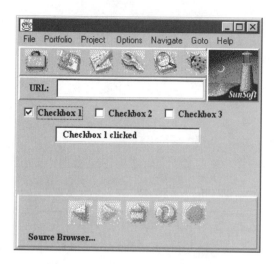

Figure 3.3 Our check box example.

Note, however, that users can click as many check boxes as they like but we'll display only the results of clicking the last one.

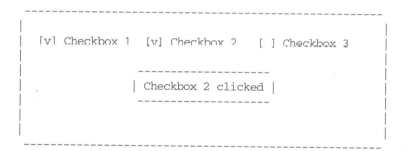

Using a single textfield like this is more appropriate for radio buttons, which allow only one radio button in a group to be selected. Let's take a look at radio buttons.

Radio Buttons

In our radio button example, we can place three radio buttons in the applet, along with a textfield.

```
 -----------------------------------------------------------
|                                                           |
|   ( ) Radio 1      ( ) Radio 2       ( ) Radio 3          |
|                                                           |
|                 --------------------                      |
|                |                    |                     |
|                 --------------------                      |
|                                                           |
|                                                           |
 -----------------------------------------------------------
```

When the user selects a radio button, we can indicate which one was clicked:

```
 -----------------------------------------------------------
|                                                           |
|   (*) Radio 1      ( ) Radio 2       ( ) Radio 3          |
|                                                           |
|                 --------------------                      |
|                | Radio 1 clicked    |                     |
|                 --------------------                      |
|                                                           |
|                                                           |
 -----------------------------------------------------------
```

And when the user clicks another radio button, that button appears selected, and the first one is automatically deselected:

```
---------------------------------------------------------
|                                                       |
|   ( ) Radio 1      (*) Radio 2        ( ) Radio 3     |
|                                                       |
|                  ---------------------                |
|                  | Radio 2 clicked   |                |
|                  ---------------------                |
|                                                       |
|                                                       |
---------------------------------------------------------
```

Let's put this together now. To coordinate the actions of the three radio buttons, we have to put them together into a special *CheckboxGroup* object like this:

```
                  ---------------------------------------------------------
                  | ------------------------------------------------------- |
CheckboxGroup-->| ( ) Radio 1      ( ) Radio 2        ( ) Radio 3     | |
                  | ------------------------------------------------------- |
                  |                  ---------------------                  |
                  |                  |                   |                  |
                  |                  ---------------------                  |
                  |                                                         |
                  ---------------------------------------------------------
```

You may have expected this object to be called a RadiobuttonGroup instead, but Java doesn't discriminate between radio buttons and check boxes. When you add check boxes to a CheckboxGroup object, Java turns them into radio buttons (i.e., from square to round) automatically. That means all we'll have to do to set up our radio button example is to include a new CheckboxGroup object:

```
        import java.applet.Applet;
        import java.awt.*;

        public class Radios extends Applet {

-->             CheckboxGroup checkboxgroup1;
                Checkbox check1, check2, check3;
                TextField text1;
                   .
                   .
                   .
```

The Java CheckboxGroup class's constructors and methods appear in Table 3.3.

Table 3.3 CheckboxGroup Constructors and Methods

```
java.lang.Object
    |
    +----java.awt.CheckboxGroup
```

CheckboxGroup()	Creates a CheckboxGroup
getCurrent()	Gets current choice
setCurrent(Checkbox)	Sets current choice to specified check box
toString()	Returns string of CheckboxGroup's values

Next, we create that CheckboxGroup object:

```
        import java.applet.Applet;
        import java.awt.*;

        public class Radios extends Applet {

                CheckboxGroup checkboxgroup1;
                Checkbox check1, check2, check3;
                TextField text1;

                public void init(){
-->                     checkboxgroup1 = new CheckboxGroup();
                             .
                             .
                             .
```

Finally, when we add each check box, we can turn it into a radio button by giving the name of our CheckboxGroup, checkboxgroup1, and also by giving each radio button an initial value (true = set, false = not set):

```
        import java.applet.Applet;
        import java.awt.*;
```

```
public class Radios extends Applet {

        CheckboxGroup checkboxgroup1;
        Checkbox check1, check2, check3;
        TextField text1;

        public void init(){
                checkboxgroup1 = new CheckboxGroup();
-->             check1 = new Checkbox("Radio 1", checkboxgroup1, false);
                add(check1);
-->             check2 = new Checkbox("Radio 2", checkboxgroup1, false);
                add(check2);
-->             check3 = new Checkbox("Radio 3", checkboxgroup1, false);
                add(check3);
                text1 = new TextField(30);
                add(text1);
        }

        public boolean action (Event e, Object o){
                if(e.target.equals(check1)){
                        text1.setText("Radio 1 clicked");
                }
                if(e.target.equals(check2)){
                        text1.setText("Radio 2 clicked");
                }
                if(e.target.equals(check3)){
                        text1.setText("Radio 3 clicked");
                }
                return true;
        }
}
```

Our radio buttons appear, as shown in Figure 3.4, and they are coordinated as well. When the user clicks one, it is selected, and we indicate which one it was in the textfield. If the user clicks another radio button, the first one is deselected, the new appears selected, and we print out the new result in the textfield.

Figure 3.4 Our radio button example.

Now we can handle check boxes and radio boxes, both of which are usually meant to be handled in groups. We're almost ready to bring together radio buttons, check boxes, and the GridLayout Manager into a larger applet, but there is one more layout item we should cover first—Java panels.

Panels

So far in this chapter, we've seen how a layout manager (and we'll see more layout managers in the next chapter) can handle all the controls in our applet, but it may also happen that you want to use different layout managers for different groups of controls. That is, while one section of your applet should use a GridLayout Manager, another should use, perhaps, the FlowLayout Manager. How do we handle that in Java?

The answer is that we set up Java panels. The Java Panel class, like the Java Applet class, is a *container* class; in fact, the Applet class is derived from the Panel class like this:

```
java.lang.Object
   |
   +----java.awt.Component
            |
            +----java.awt.Container
                     |
                     +----java.awt.Panel
                              |
                              +----java.applet.Applet
```

Each panel (in fact, each container object) is capable of having its own layout manager. This means that if you can divide your applet into rectangular panels, you can design the layout of each panel separately. Let's look at panels now, since they are a common Java programming technique. In this example, we might create three panels, each with two textfields like this (note that although we outline each panel here to give you an idea what is going on, panels are actually invisible).

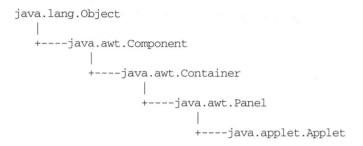

Let's put this three-panel example together now. Keep in mind that the Applet class itself is derived from the Panel class, so we can't just define our panels in the main applet-based class we'll be setting up. Instead, we'll need a whole new class. Let's call that new panel-based class textfieldPanel:

```
class textfieldPanel extends Panel {
      .
      .
      .
```

We leave this class private so that we can use it in the current file only, and we indicate that Panel is our base class. Next, we add the two textfields to our textfieldPanel class:

```
        class textfieldPanel extends Panel {
  -->           TextField text1, text2;
                        .
                        .
                        .
```

Now we can set up the textfields in our textfieldPanel class's constructor:

```
        class textfieldPanel extends Panel {
                TextField text1, text2;

  -->           textfieldPanel(){
                        .
                        .
                        .
```

We create the first textfield as usual, giving it the text "Hello":

```
        class textfieldPanel extends Panel {
                TextField text1, text2;

                textfieldPanel(){
                        text1 = new TextField("Hello");
                                .
                                .
                                .
```

Next, we add that to our panel with the add() method [add() is a method of the Java container class]:

```
        class textfieldPanel extends Panel {
                TextField text1, text2;

                textfieldPanel(){
                        text1 = new TextField("Hello");
```

```
-->                   add(text1);
                          .
                          .
                          .
```

Then we add the second textfield:

```
class textfieldPanel extends Panel {
        TextField text1, text2;

        textfieldPanel(){
                text1 = new TextField("Hello");
                add(text1);
-->             text2 = new TextField("World!");
-->             add(text2);
        }
}
```

And that's it for our new textfieldPanel class. We can start on the applet itself by first declaring three panels of class textfieldPanel (this is the same file that contains our textfieldPanel class):

```
import java.applet.Applet;
import java.awt.*;

public class Panels extends Applet {

-->         textfieldPanel panel1, panel2, panel3;
                  .
                  .
                  .
```

In the applet's init() function, we can set up a grid layout of our panels, asking for one row of three panels this way:

```
import java.applet.Applet;
import java.awt.*;

public class Panels extends Applet {

        textfieldPanel panel1, panel2, panel3;
```

```
        public void init(){
  -->           setLayout(new GridLayout(1, 3));
                      .
                      .
                      .
```

Then we create the new panel objects:

```
import java.applet.Applet;
import java.awt.*;

public class Panels extends Applet {

        textfieldPanel panel1, panel2, panel3;

        public void init(){
                setLayout(new GridLayout(1, 3));
  -->           panel1 = new textfieldPanel();
  -->           panel2 = new textfieldPanel();
  -->           panel3 = new textfieldPanel();
                      .
                      .
                      .
```

And finally, we add the panels to our applet:

```
import java.applet.Applet;
import java.awt.*;

public class Panels extends Applet {

        textfieldPanel panel1, panel2, panel3;

        public void init(){
                setLayout(new GridLayout(1, 3));
                panel1 = new textfieldPanel();
                panel2 = new textfieldPanel();
                panel3 = new textfieldPanel();
  -->           add(panel1);
  -->           add(panel2);
  -->           add(panel3);
                }       .
        }               .
                        .
```

Now our panels are ready to go. As you can see in Figure 3.5, our three panels each display two textfields, just as they should. Our Panel applet is a success. The code for this applet appears in Listing 3.2.

Figure 3.5 A Panel class example.

Listing 3.2 Panels.java

```
import java.applet.Applet;
import java.awt.*;

public class Panels extends Applet {

        textfieldPanel panel1, panel2, panel3;

        public void init(){
                setLayout(new GridLayout(1, 3));
                panel1 = new textfieldPanel();
                panel2 = new textfieldPanel();
                panel3 = new textfieldPanel();
                add(panel1);
                add(panel2);
                add(panel3);
        }


}
```

```
class textfieldPanel extends Panel {
        TextField text1, text2;

        textfieldPanel(){
                text1 = new TextField("Hello");
                add(text1);
                text2 = new TextField("World!");
                add(text2);
        }
}
```

The Panels applet works as expected, which means that now we are ready to bring together check boxes, radio buttons, the GridLayout Manager, and panels into a single example.

The Fly-by-Night Travel Company, Inc., Example

In this example, we'll bring all the techniques and controls of this chapter together. If we want to show users the prices of various tour packages of Fly-by-Night Travel Company, Inc., we might set up an applet like this:

```
-----------------------------------------------------
|                                                   |
|    ( ) Tour Package 1       [ ] Vacation Spot 1   |
|                                                   |
|    ( ) Tour Package 2       [ ] Vacation Spot 2   |
|                                                   |
|    ( ) Tour Package 3       [ ] Vacation Spot 3   |
|                                                   |
|    -----------------        [ ] Vacation Spot 4   |
|    |               |                              |
|    -----------------                              |
-----------------------------------------------------
```

Now users can select one (but only one) tour package by clicking a radio button. When they do, we can set the check boxes to match, showing them what tour destinations are in that tour and how much the tour costs.

```
-------------------------------------------------------
|                                                       |
|    ( ) Tour Package 1        [ ] Vacation Spot 1      |
|                                                       |
|    (*) Tour Package 2        [ ] Vacation Spot 2      |
|                                                       |
|    ( ) Tour Package 3        [v] Vacation Spot 3      |
|                                                       |
|    -----------------         [v] Vacation Spot 4      |
|    | Price: $2000.  |                                 |
|    -----------------                                  |
-------------------------------------------------------
```

This way, we can check the check boxes that correspond to the selected tour package. If called for, we can even check all tour destinations at once:

```
-------------------------------------------------------
|                                                       |
|    ( ) Tour Package 1        [v] Vacation Spot 1      |
|                                                       |
|    ( ) Tour Package 2        [v] Vacation Spot 2      |
|                                                       |
|    (*) Tour Package 3        [v] Vacation Spot 3      |
|                                                       |
|    -----------------         [v] Vacation Spot 4      |
|    | Price: $4000.  |                                 |
|    -----------------                                  |
-------------------------------------------------------
```

To do this, we'll set up two new panels and place the correct controls in them:

```
            Panel1                    Panel2
-------------------------------------------------------
| -------------------      -------------------- |
| | ( ) Tour Package 1 |    | [ ] Vacation Spot 1 |  |
| |                    |    |                     |  |
| | ( ) Tour Package 2 |    | [ ] Vacation Spot 2 |  |
| |                    |    |                     |  |
| | ( ) Tour Package 3 |    | [ ] Vacation Spot 3 |  |
| |                    |    |                     |  |
| | ----------------   |    | [ ] Vacation Spot 4 |  |
| | |              ||   |    |                     |  |
| | ----------------   |    |                     |  |
| -------------------      -------------------- |
-------------------------------------------------------
```

Let's start with the panel that displays the available tour packages as a set of radio buttons. We set that panel up as a new Panel class named PackagePanel:

```
class PackagePanel extends Panel {
    .
    .
    .
```

Next, we add the controls we'll need:

```
        class PackagePanel extends Panel {
    -->         CheckboxGroup CGroup;
    -->         Checkbox Tour1, Tour2, Tour3;
    -->         TextField Pricebox;
                    .
                    .
                    .
```

And in the panel's constructor, we set up these check box controls—Tour1 to Tour 3—in a CheckboxGroup object of their own, CGroup, and add the textfield to display the total price of the tour at the bottom. Let's call the textfield Pricebox:

```
        class PackagePanel extends Panel {
                CheckboxGroup CGroup;
                Checkbox Tour1, Tour2, Tour3;
                TextField Pricebox;

    -->         PackagePanel(){
    -->             CGroup = new CheckboxGroup();
    -->             add(Tour1 = new Checkbox("Tour Package 1", CGroup,
    -->                 false));
    -->             add(Tour2 = new Checkbox("Tour Package 2", CGroup,
    -->                 false));
    -->             add(Tour3 = new Checkbox("Tour Package 3", CGroup,
    -->                 false));
    -->             Pricebox = new TextField(15);
    -->             add(Pricebox);
    -->         }
            }
```

Now we can set up the Panel with the names of the vacation cities each tour selects from:

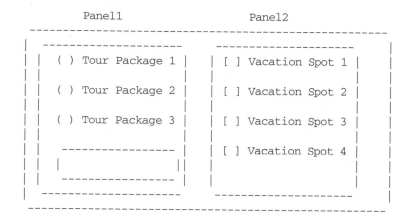

Let's call this panel CityPanel. Here, we just set up the check boxes as required—City1 to City4—and that's all we need:

```
class CityPanel extends Panel {
        Checkbox City1, City2, City3, City4;

        CityPanel(){
                add(City1 = new Checkbox("Vacation Spot 1"));
                add(City2 = new Checkbox("Vacation Spot 2"));
                add(City3 = new Checkbox("Vacation Spot 3"));
                add(City4 = new Checkbox("Vacation Spot 4"));
        }
}
```

Now we're ready to set up the applet-based class itself. We start by including our two panels:

```
import java.applet.Applet;
import java.awt.*;

public class Flyby extends Applet {
```

```
-->          PackagePanel Panel1;
-->          CityPanel Panel2;
                  .
                  .
                  .
```

We can arrange the panels in a grid layout of one row with two columns as we add the panels to the applet this way:

```
import java.applet.Applet;
import java.awt.*;

public class Flyby extends Applet {

        PackagePanel Panel1;
        CityPanel Panel2;

        public void init(){
-->             setLayout(new GridLayout(1, 2));
-->             Panel1 = new PackagePanel();
-->             Panel2 = new CityPanel();
-->             add(Panel1);
-->             add(Panel2);
        }       .
                .
                .
```

The next question is How do we determine if a radio button in our PackagePanel is clicked, such as Tour1 here?

```
------------------------------------------------------
|                                                    |
|     (*) Tour Package 1       [v] Vacation Spot 1   |
|                                                    |
|     ( ) Tour Package 2       [v] Vacation Spot 2   |
|                                                    |
|     ( ) Tour Package 3       [ ] Vacation Spot 3   |
|                                                    |
|     ------------------       [ ] Vacation Spot 4   |
|     | Price: $2000.  |                             |
|     ------------------                             |
------------------------------------------------------
```

That radio button is named Tour1, so normally our action() method would just use a line like this:

```
            public boolean action (Event e, Object o){
   -->               if(e.target.equals(Tour1)){
                            .
                            .
                            .
```

However, that won't work, since the Tour1 button is not a part of our main applet class. Instead, Tour1 is part of the PackagePanel class, and we do have a PackagePanel object in our main applet class Panel1:

```
      import java.applet.Applet;
      import java.awt.*;

      public class Flyby extends Applet {

   -->          PackagePanel Panel1;
               CityPanel Panel2;

               public void init(){
                       setLayout(new GridLayout(1, 2));
                       Panel1 = new PackagePanel();
                            .
                            .
                            .
```

That means that we can refer to the Tour1 button as Panel1.Tour1 (i.e., Tour1 is a member object of our Panel1 object), and we do that like this:

```
      import java.applet.Applet;
      import java.awt.*;

      public class Flyby extends Applet {

               PackagePanel Panel1;
               CityPanel Panel2;

               public void init(){
                       setLayout(new GridLayout(1, 2));
```

```
                    Panel1 = new PackagePanel();
                    Panel2 = new CityPanel();
                    add(Panel1);
                    add(Panel2);
            }

            public boolean action (Event e, Object o){
-->                 if(e.target.equals(Panel1.Tour1)){
                         .
                         .
                         .
```

If **Tour1** was clicked, we set the matching city check boxes in Panel2 in a similar way:

```
    import java.applet.Applet;
    import java.awt.*;

    public class Flyby extends Applet {

            PackagePanel Panel1;
            CityPanel Panel2;
                    .
                    .
                    .

            public boolean action (Event e, Object o){
                    if(e.target.equals(Panel1.Tour1)){
-->                     Panel2.City1.setState(true);
-->                     Panel2.City2.setState(true);
-->                     Panel2.City3.setState(false);
-->                     Panel2.City4.setState(false);
-->                     Panel1.Pricebox.setText("Price: $2000.");
                    }               .
                                    .
                                    .
```

We do the same for Tour2, setting the matching cities check boxes appropriately for this tour:

```
            public boolean action (Event e, Object o){
                    if(e.target.equals(Panel1.Tour1)){
                        Panel2.City1.setState(true);
                        Panel2.City2.setState(true);
```

```
                    Panel2.City3.setState(false);
                    Panel2.City4.setState(false);
                    Panel1.Pricebox.setText("Price: $2000.");
             }
             if(e.target.equals(Panel1.Tour2)){
  -->              Panel2.City1.setState(false);
  -->              Panel2.City2.setState(false);
  -->              Panel2.City3.setState(true);
  -->              Panel2.City4.setState(true);
  -->              Panel1.Pricebox.setText("Price: $2000.");
             }                     .

                                   .

                                   .
```

And the same for package 3 (corresponding to the Tour3 radio button), where we check all check boxes:

```
        public boolean action (Event e, Object o){
                              .

                              .

             if(e.target.equals(Panel1.Tour2)){
                    Panel2.City1.setState(false);
                    Panel2.City2.setState(false);
                    Panel2.City3.setState(true);
                    Panel2.City4.setState(true);
                    Panel1.Pricebox.setText("Price: $2000.");
             }
             if(e.target.equals(Panel1.Tour3)){
  -->              Panel2.City1.setState(true);
  -->              Panel2.City2.setState(true);
  -->              Panel2.City3.setState(true);
  -->              Panel2.City4.setState(true);
  -->              Panel1.Pricebox.setText("Price: $4000.");
             }
             return true;
        }
    }
```

Now all the panels, check boxes, radio buttons, and textfield have all been set up, and the applet is fully functional, as we see in Figure 3.6. When the user clicks various radio button tour packages, the applet displays automatically what cities are in the tour and that tour's price. Our applet is a success. The code for this applet appears in Listing 3.3.

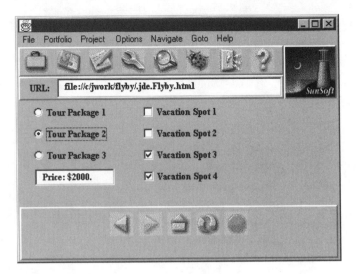

Figure 3.6 The Fly-by-Night Company, Inc., travel example.

Listing 3.3 Flyby.java

```java
import java.applet.Applet;
import java.awt.*;

public class Flyby extends Applet {

        PackagePanel Panel1;
        CityPanel Panel2;

        public void init(){
            setLayout(new GridLayout(1, 2));
            Panel1 = new PackagePanel();
            Panel2 = new CityPanel();
            add(Panel1);
            add(Panel2);
        }

        public boolean action (Event e, Object o){
```

```
            if(e.target.equals(Panel1.Tour1)){
                Panel2.City1.setState(true);
                Panel2.City2.setState(true);
                Panel2.City3.setState(false);
                Panel2.City4.setState(false);
                Panel1.Pricebox.setText("Price: $2000.");
            }
            if(e.target.equals(Panel1.Tour2)){
                Panel2.City1.setState(false);
                Panel2.City2.setState(false);
                Panel2.City3.setState(true);
                Panel2.City4.setState(true);
                Panel1.Pricebox.setText("Price: $2000.");
            }
            if(e.target.equals(Panel1.Tour3)){
                Panel2.City1.setState(true);
                Panel2.City2.setState(true);
                Panel2.City3.setState(true);
                Panel2.City4.setState(true);
                Panel1.Pricebox.setText("Price: $4000.");
            }
            return true;
        }
}


class PackagePanel extends Panel {
        CheckboxGroup CGroup;
        Checkbox Tour1, Tour2, Tour3;
        TextField Pricebox;

        PackagePanel(){
            CGroup = new CheckboxGroup();
            add(Tour1 = new Checkbox("Tour Package 1", CGroup,
                false));
            add(Tour2 = new Checkbox("Tour Package 2", CGroup,
                false));
            add(Tour3 = new Checkbox("Tour Package 3", CGroup,
                false));
            Pricebox = new TextField(15);
            add(Pricebox);
        }
}

class CityPanel extends Panel {
        Checkbox City1, City2, City3, City4;
```

```
        CityPanel(){
            add(City1 = new Checkbox("Vacation Spot 1"));
            add(City2 = new Checkbox("Vacation Spot 2"));
            add(City3 = new Checkbox("Vacation Spot 3"));
            add(City4 = new Checkbox("Vacation Spot 4"));
        }
    }
```

In this chapter, we saw more multiple-control techniques, along with two new controls: radio buttons and check boxes. We also saw how panels work and learned a little about layout managers. In the next chapter, we'll continue our exploration of Java controls and layout managers.

CHAPTER FOUR

SCROLLBARS, CHOICE CONTROLS, AND SCROLLING LISTS

In this chapter, we'll explore several new controls: scrollbars, choice controls, and scrolling lists (also called list boxes), as well as two new Java layouts—border and gridbag. In this way, we'll extend our expertise in putting together Java applets and placing in them the controls we want. Scrollbars and scrolling lists in particular are very common controls, and knowing how they work is important for Java programmers, so let's begin with them.

133

Scrollbars

Let's start this chapter with a scrollbar example where we have a textfield and two scrollbars, one vertical and one horizontal:

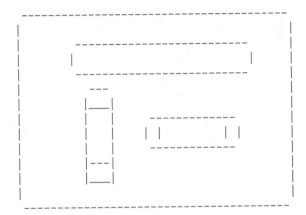

Scrollbars have minimum and maximum values that we can set. If we set a scrollbar's minimum to 1 and maximum to 100, then when the user scrolls scrollbar, it will return values from 1 to 100. We can display which scrollbar was used in the textfield and what the scrollbar's new value is like this:

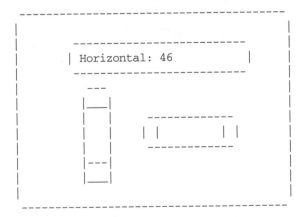

We start our new applet when we add the textfield and the two scrollbars—hScroll will be the horizontal scrollbar and vScroll the vertical scrollbar:

```
import java.applet.Applet;
import java.awt.*;

public class Scroll extends Applet {

-->    TextField text1;
-->    Scrollbar hScroll, vScroll;
          .
          .
          .
```

The Scrollbar class's constructors and methods appear in Table 4.1.

Table 4.1 Scrollbar Constructors and Methods

```
java.lang.Object
    |
    +----java.awt.Component
            |
            +----java.awt.Scrollbar
```

Method	Means
Scrollbar()	Constructs a vertical scrollbar
Scrollbar(int)	Constructs a scrollbar with specified orientation: Scrollbar.HORIZONTAL or Scrollbar.VERTICAL
Scrollbar(int, int, int, int, int)	Constructs a scrollbar with specified orientation, value, scroll thumb size, minimum and maximum values
addNotify()	Creates scrollbar's peer
getLineIncrement()	Gets line increment for scrollbar
getMaximum()	Returns maximum value of Scrollbar

getMinimum()	Returns minimum value of Scrollbar
getOrientation()	Returns orientation of Scrollbar
getPageIncrement()	Returns page increment for Scrollbar
getValue()	Returns current value of Scrollbar
getVisible()	Returns the visible amount of Scrollbar
paramString()	Returns string parameters for Scrollbar
setLineIncrement(int)	Sets line increment for Scrollbar
setPageIncrement(int)	Sets page increment for Scrollbar
setValue(int)	Sets value of Scrollbar to specified value
setValues(int, int, int, int)	Sets values for Scrollbar

Next, we set up the textfield in the applet's init() function:

```
        import java.applet.Applet;
        import java.awt.*;

        public class Scroll extends Applet {

  -->           TextField text1;
                Scrollbar hScroll, vScroll;

                public void init(){
  -->                   text1 = new TextField(45);
  -->                   add(text1);
                          .
                          .
                          .
```

Now we're ready to construct our new scrollbars. We do that like this for the vertical scrollbar vScroll, where we indicate that we want it to be vertical by passing the built-in Scrollbar class constant Scrollbar.VERTICAL. We also set the scrollbar's initial value to 1, giving the scroll box (also called the thumb) a height of 10 pixels (the size of the thumb can indicate how much of a document is currently showing). Finally, we give the scrollbar a minimum possible value of 1 and a maximum possible value of 100 this way:

```
      import java.applet.Applet;
      import java.awt.*;

      public class Scroll extends Applet {

             TextField text1;
             Scrollbar hScroll, vScroll;

             public void init(){
                    text1 = new TextField(45);
                    add(text1);
-->                 vScroll = new Scrollbar(Scrollbar.VERTICAL, 1, 10,
-->                     1, 100);
-->                 add(vScroll);
                        .
                        .
                        .
```

And we do the same for the horizontal scrollbar, indicating that we want it to be horizontal by passing a value of Scrollbar.HORIZONTAL:

```
      import java.applet.Applet;
      import java.awt.*;

      public class Scroll extends Applet {

             TextField text1;
             Scrollbar hScroll, vScroll;

             public void init(){
                    text1 = new TextField(45);
                    add(text1);
                    vScroll = new Scrollbar(Scrollbar.VERTICAL, 1, 10,
                        1, 100);
                    add(vScroll);
-->                 hScroll = new Scrollbar(Scrollbar.HORIZONTAL, 1, 10,
-->                     1, 100);
-->                 add(hScroll);
             }          .
                        .
                        .
```

Now our scrollbars are installed. To actually use them, you might think we would set up the action() method, but in fact we use a new method for scrollbars— handleEvent():

```
public boolean handleEvent(Event e){
                    .
                    .
                    .
```

As with the action() method, we can check which control—the vertical or horizontal scrollbar—caused the event with the equals() method like this, where we check for the vertical scrollbar:

```
public boolean handleEvent(Event e){
        if(e.target.equals(vScroll)){
                    .
                    .
                    .
```

At this point, we could determine which action took place by checking the ID member of the Event e, which can take on these values: e.ID = SCROLL_ABSOLUTE, SCROLL_LINE_DOWN, SCROLL_LINE_UP, SCROLL_PAGE_DOWN, or SCROLL_PAGE_UP (depending on whether the user dragged the thumb or scrolled by a line or a page). In this case, we'll display the new setting of the scrollbar in the textfield. We do that by using the Scrollbar method getValue() to get the current setting of the scrollbar, using the String class's valueOf() function to convert the scrollbar's setting to a string and displaying that string in the textfield with setText():

```
        public boolean handleEvent(Event e){
                if(e.target.equals(vScroll)){
-->                       text1.setText("Vertical: " +
-->
String.valueOf(((Scrollbar)e.target).getValue()));
                    }       .
                            .
                            .
```

Then we do the same for the horizontal scrollbar:

```
            public boolean handleEvent(Event e){
                    if(e.target.equals(vScroll)){
                            text1.setText("Vertical: " +

String.valueOf(((Scrollbar)e.target).getValue()));
                    }
-->                 if(e.target.equals(hScroll)){
-->                         text1.setText("Horizontal: " +
-->
String.valueOf(((Scrollbar)e.target).getValue()));
-->                 }                   .
                                        .
                                        .
```

At the end of the action() method, we return true if we handle the action and
false otherwise. Here, however, we pass the scrollbar action back to the
Scrollbar class's own event handler so it can respond appropriately. However,
that raises a problem: we are overriding the Scrollbar class's handleEvent()
method here to add our own functionality. Now that we've displayed the
scrollbar settings in our textfield, we want to call the original handleEvents().
Both methods are called handleEvents(), so if we call that method, we'll just
call our own function. It turns out that we can call the original Scrollbar class
handleEvents() like this: super.handleEvent(e) (where super stands for
superclass), and that looks like this in our code:

```
            public boolean handleEvent(Event e){
                    if(e.target.equals(vScroll)){
                            text1.setText("Vertical: " +

String.valueOf(((Scrollbar)e.target).getValue()));
                    }
                    if(e.target.equals(hScroll)){
                            text1.setText("Horizontal: " +

String.valueOf(((Scrollbar)e.target).getValue()));
                    }
-->                 return super.handleEvent(e);
            }
        }
```

Now our scrollbars are active, as shown in Figure 4.1. Our scrollbar example is
a success. The code for this applet appears in Listing 4.1.

Figure 4.1 Our first scrollbar example.

Listing 4.1 Scroll.java

```java
import java.applet.Applet;
import java.awt.*;

public class Scroll extends Applet {

    TextField text1;
    Scrollbar hScroll, vScroll;

    public void init(){
        text1 = new TextField(45);
        add(text1);
        vScroll = new Scrollbar(Scrollbar.VERTICAL, 1, 10,
            1, 100);
        add(vScroll);
        hScroll = new Scrollbar(Scrollbar.HORIZONTAL, 1, 10,
            1, 100);
        add(hScroll);
    }

    public boolean handleEvent(Event e){
        if(e.target.equals(vScroll)){
            text1.setText("Vertical: " +
```

```
String.valueOf(((Scrollbar)e.target).getValue()));
                    }
                if(e.target.equals(hScroll)){
                        text1.setText("Horizontal: " +
String.valueOf(((Scrollbar)e.target).getValue()));
                    }
                return super.handleEvent(e);
            }
        }
```

Note that the scrollbars in Figure 4.1 are an inconvenient size; there's practically no room to scroll the thumb. We could resize the scrollbar using its resize() method if we wished. However, there's another way of sizing and placing scrollbars correctly, and we'll see that now as we examine the Border Layout Manager.

Putting Scrollbars to Work: The Scroller Example

The Java Border Layout Manager allows us to arrange five controls in our applet: one stretched to take up each of the four edges and one in the center. This layout manager is perfect for scrollbars, because they are supposed to appear at the edges of applets. In this case, we want to set up four scrollbars at the edges of our applet and have a textfield in a panel in the center:

```
    -------------------------------------------
   |-|---------------------------------------|-|
   | |                                       | |
   | |      ---------------                  | |
   | |     | I'm scrolling! |                | |
   | |      ---------------                  | |
   | |                                       | |
   | |                                       | |
   | |                                       | |
   | |                                       | |
   | |                                       | |
   | |                                       | |
   | |                                       | |
   | |                                       | |
   |-|---------------------------------------|-|
    -------------------------------------------
```

When the user scrolls the scrollbars, we can move the textfield around in the panel to match:

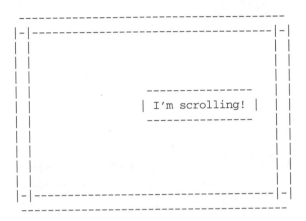

We start with four new scrollbars, two horizontal and two vertical:

```
import java.applet.Applet;
import java.awt.*;

public class Scroller extends Applet {

-->         Scrollbar hScroll1, hScroll2, vScroll1, vScroll2;
              .
              .
              .
```

Next, we indicate that we want a border layout:

```
import java.applet.Applet;
import java.awt.*;

public class Scroller extends Applet {

          Scrollbar hScroll1, hScroll2, vScroll1, vScroll2;
```

```
          public void init(){
-->            setLayout(new BorderLayout());
                  .
                  .
                  .
```

Now we set up our first horizontal scrollbar, giving it a range of 1 to 200:

```
import java.applet.Applet;
import java.awt.*;

public class Scroller extends Applet {

    Scrollbar hScroll1, hScroll2, vScroll1, vScroll2;

    public void init(){
        setLayout(new BorderLayout());

-->     hScroll1 = new Scrollbar(Scrollbar.HORIZONTAL, 1, 1,
-->         1, 200);
                  .
                  .
                  .
```

We add the new scrollbar to our layout next. We specify the five possible positions in a border layout as north, south, east, west, and center like this:

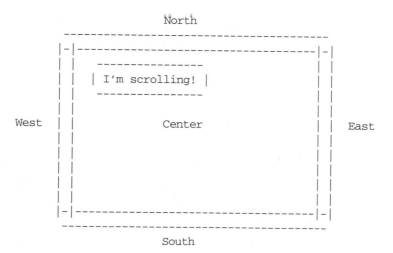

That means we add our horizontal scrollbar to the top of our applet, making it the north control:

```
import java.applet.Applet;
import java.awt.*;

public class Scroller extends Applet {

        Scrollbar hScroll1, hScroll2, vScroll1, vScroll2;

        public void init(){
                setLayout(new BorderLayout());

                hScroll1 = new Scrollbar(Scrollbar.HORIZONTAL, 1, 1,
                        1, 200);
-->             add("North", hScroll1);
                                .
                                .
                                .
```

In the same way, we add the three other scrollbars:

```
import java.applet.Applet;
import java.awt.*;

public class Scroller extends Applet {

        Scrollbar hScroll1, hScroll2, vScroll1, vScroll2;

        public void init(){
                setLayout(new BorderLayout());

                hScroll1 = new Scrollbar(Scrollbar.HORIZONTAL, 1, 1,
                        1, 200);
                add("North", hScroll1);

-->             vScroll1 = new Scrollbar(Scrollbar.VERTICAL, 1, 1,
-->                     1, 200);
-->             add("West", vScroll1);

-->             hScroll2 = new Scrollbar(Scrollbar.HORIZONTAL, 1,
-->                     1, 1, 200);
```

```
-->              add("South", hScroll2);

-->              vScroll2 = new Scrollbar(Scrollbar.VERTICAL, 1, 1,
-->                  1, 200);
-->              add("East", vScroll2);
                    .
                    .
                    .
```

All that remains is to set up a new panel class (this panel will include the textfield that we will move around on demand) and add that to our applet. We will call our new panel class textPanel, and we add it this way, making it the center control:

```
import java.applet.Applet;
import java.awt.*;

public class Scroller extends Applet {

        Scrollbar hScroll1, hScroll2, vScroll1, vScroll2;
-->     textPanel Panel1;

        public void init(){
                setLayout(new BorderLayout());

                hScroll1 = new Scrollbar(Scrollbar.HORIZONTAL, 1, 1,
                    1, 200);
                add("North", hScroll1);
                    .

                    .

                vScroll2 = new Scrollbar(Scrollbar.VERTICAL, 1, 1,
                    1, 200);
                add("East", vScroll2);

-->             Panel1 = new textPanel();
-->             add("Center", Panel1);
-->             Panel1.Text1.move(0, 0);
        }           .

                    .

                    .
```

Now let's design our panel class. We start like this:

```
class textPanel extends Panel {
    .
    .
    .
```

Next, we add the textfield that we want to move around, calling it Text1:

```
      class textPanel extends Panel {
-->          TextField Text1;
                .
                .
                .
```

All that remains is to create the new textfield and give it some text. Let's give it the text "I'm scrolling!" in the panel's constructor:

```
      class textPanel extends Panel {
             TextField Text1;

-->          textPanel(){
-->                  Text1 = new TextField("I'm scrolling!");
-->                  add(Text1);
-->          }
```

Now we set up the handleEvent() method, which we'll need to handle scrollbar movements:

```
          public boolean handleEvent(Event e){
                  .
                  .
                  .
```

Let's work scrollbar by scrollbar, starting with the top scrollbar, hScroll1:

```
          public boolean handleEvent(Event e){
                  if(e.target.equals(hScroll1)){
                          .
                          .
                          .
```

If we arrive at this point, the user has moved the top scrollbar. You might not expect a scrollbar to behave in this manner, but it will not leave the thumb at the position the user scrolled it to by itself (because the user may have scrolled to some area you consider forbidden). In order to reposition the thumb at the new position, use the scrollbar's setValue() method, setting its value to the value the user placed it at. (If we don't do this, the thumb will spring back to its original position when the user releases it.)

```
        public boolean handleEvent(Event e){
            if(e.target.equals(hScroll1)){
-->             hScroll1.setValue(hScroll1.getValue());
                            .
                            .
                            .
```

We should also move the bottom horizontal scrollbar hScroll2 to match the top scrollbar:

```
        public boolean handleEvent(Event e){
            if(e.target.equals(hScroll1)){
                hScroll1.setValue(hScroll1.getValue());
-->             hScroll2.setValue(hScroll1.getValue());
                            .
                            .
                            .
```

Next, we can move the textfield in the textPanel to match the new position of the scrollbars. We do that with the move() method (which is part of the Java component class, so it's built into all controls):

```
        public boolean handleEvent(Event e){
            if(e.target.equals(hScroll1)){
                hScroll1.setValue(hScroll1.getValue());
                hScroll2.setValue(hScroll1.getValue());
-->             Panel1.Text1.move(hScroll1.getValue(),
-->                 vScroll1.getValue());
            }           .
                        .
                        .
```

Now when the user scrolls the top scrollbar, we move the bottom one to match and reposition the textfield in the center accordingly. Let's add similar code to make the other scrollbars active:

```
        public boolean handleEvent(Event e){
                if(e.target.equals(hScroll1)){
                        hScroll1.setValue(hScroll1.getValue());
                        hScroll2.setValue(hScroll1.getValue());
                        Panel1.Text1.move(hScroll1.getValue(),
                            vScroll1.getValue());
                }
-->             if(e.target.equals(vScroll1)){
-->                     vScroll1.setValue(vScroll1.getValue());
-->                     vScroll2.setValue(vScroll1.getValue());
-->                     Panel1.Text1.move(hScroll1.getValue(),
-->                         vScroll1.getValue());
-->             }
-->             if(e.target.equals(hScroll2)){
-->                     hScroll2.setValue(hScroll2.getValue());
-->                     hScroll1.setValue(hScroll2.getValue());
-->                     Panel1.Text1.move(hScroll1.getValue(),
-->                         vScroll1.getValue());
-->             }
-->             if(e.target.equals(vScroll2)){
-->                     vScroll2.setValue(yScroll2.getValue());
-->                     vScroll1.setValue(vScroll2.getValue());
-->                     Panel1.Text1.move(hScroll1.getValue(),
-->                         vScroll1.getValue());
-->             }
-->             return super.handleEvent(e);
        }
```

That's it for our Scroller applet; you can see the result in Figure 4.2. When the user moves any scrollbar, both it and the corresponding scrollbar move, and the textfield moves to match. Our applet is a success. The code for this applet appears in Listing 4.2.

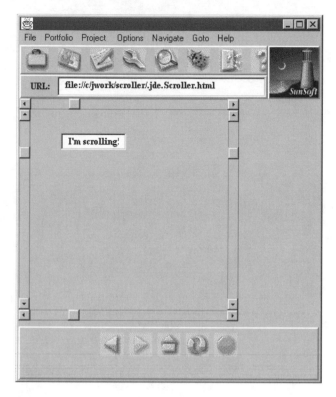

Figure 4.2 Our Scroller applet moves a textfield around.

Listing 4.2 Scroller.java

```
import java.applet.Applet;
import java.awt.*;

public class Scroller extends Applet {

        Scrollbar hScroll1, hScroll2, vScroll1, vScroll2;
        textPanel Panel1;

        public void init(){
                setLayout(new BorderLayout());

                hScroll1 = new Scrollbar(Scrollbar.HORIZONTAL, 1, 1,
                        1, 200);
```

```
            add("North", hScroll1);

            vScroll1 = new Scrollbar(Scrollbar.VERTICAL, 1, 1,
                1, 200);
            add("West", vScroll1);

            hScroll2 = new Scrollbar(Scrollbar.HORIZONTAL, 1,
                1, 1, 200);
            add("South", hScroll2);

            vScroll2 = new Scrollbar(Scrollbar.VERTICAL, 1, 1,
                1, 200);
            add("East", vScroll2);

            Panel1 = new textPanel();
            add("Center", Panel1);
            Panel1.Text1.move(0, 0);
    }


    public boolean handleEvent(Event e){
            if(e.target.equals(hScroll1)){
                    hScroll1.setValue(hScroll1.getValue());
                    hScroll2.setValue(hScroll1.getValue());
                    Panel1.Text1.move(hScroll1.getValue(),
                        vScroll1.getValue());
            }
            if(e.target.equals(vScroll1)){
                    vScroll1.setValue(vScroll1.getValue());
                    vScroll2.setValue(vScroll1.getValue());
                    Panel1.Text1.move(hScroll1.getValue(),
                        vScroll1.getValue());
            }
            if(e.target.equals(hScroll2)){
                    hScroll2.setValue(hScroll2.getValue());
                    hScroll1.setValue(hScroll2.getValue());
                    Panel1.Text1.move(hScroll1.getValue(),
                        vScroll1.getValue());
            }
            if(e.target.equals(vScroll2)){
                    vScroll2.setValue(vScroll2.getValue());
                    vScroll1.setValue(vScroll2.getValue());
                    Panel1.Text1.move(hScroll1.getValue(),
                        vScroll1.getValue());
            }
```

```
                    return super.handleEvent(e);
        }

    }

class textPanel extends Panel {
        TextField Text1;

        textPanel(){
                Text1 = new TextField("I'm scrolling!");
                add(Text1);
        }
    }
```

Let's examine choice controls next. A choice control functions much like a drop-down list box: it presents a drop-down list of options the user can select from. After that, we'll combine choice controls and scrollbars when we explore scrolling lists.

Choice Controls

In this example, we can place a choice control in an applet and add a textfield like this:

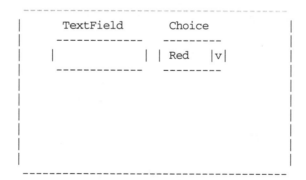

When the user clicks the downward pointing arrow in the choice control, it opens to a selection of choices where we allow the user to select between **Red**, **Green**, and **Blue**:

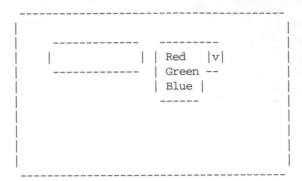

When the user selects one of the choices, we can display it in the textfield:

We start by declaring a new object of class Choice, colors:

```
import java.applet.Applet;
import java.awt.*;

public class Choices extends Applet {

-->        Choice colors;
               .
               .
               .
```

The Choice control's constructors and methods appear in Table 4.2.

Table 4.2 Choice Control's Constructors and Methods

```
java.lang.Object
   |
   +----java.awt.Component
           |
           +----java.awt.Choice
```

Method	Means
Choice()	Constructs a choice control
addItem(String)	Adds item to choice control
addNotify()	Creates choice's peer
countItems()	Returns number of items in choice
getItem(int)	Returns string at specified index in choice control
getSelectedIndex()	Returns index of currently selected item
getSelectedItem()	Returns string representation of current choice control
paramString()	Returns parameter string of choice control
select(int)	Selects item at specified position
select(String)	Selects item with specified text

Next, we declare and create our textfield:

```
       import java.applet.Applet;
       import java.awt.*;

       public class Choices extends Applet {

               Choice colors;
-->            TextField text1;

               public void init(){
-->                    text1 = new TextField(20);
-->                    add(text1);
                        .
                        .
                        .
```

Now we create the Choice object itself:

```
import java.applet.Applet;
import java.awt.*;

public class Choices extends Applet {

        Choice colors;
        TextField text1;

        public void init(){
                text1 = new TextField(20);
                add(text1);
-->             colors = new Choice();
                .
                .
                .
```

To install the three choices **Red, Green,** and **Blue,** we use the Choice control's addItem() method:

```
import java.applet.Applet;
import java.awt.*;

public class Choices extends Applet {

        Choice colors;
        TextField text1;

        public void init(){
                text1 = new TextField(20);
                add(text1);
                colors = new Choice();
                colors.addItem("Red");
                colors.addItem("Green");
                colors.addItem("Blue");
                .
                .
                .
```

Now we can add the new choice control to our applet:

```
import java.applet.Applet;
import java.awt.*;

public class Choices extends Applet {

        Choice colors;
        TextField text1;

        public void init(){
                text1 = new TextField(20);
                add(text1);
                colors = new Choice();
                colors.addItem("Red");
                colors.addItem("Green");
                colors.addItem("Blue");
-->             add(colors);
        }               .
                        .
                        .
```

The Choice control appears in the applet with three choices. Next, we can make the Choice control active, which we do in the action() method:

```
        public boolean action (Event c, Object o){
                .
                .
                .
```

First, we check to see if the control that caused the event was indeed our Choice control:

```
                public boolean action (Event e, Object o){
-->                     if(e.target.equals(colors)){
                                .
                                .
                                .
```

If so, we can place the user's color selection into the textfield. To do that, we first get the text of the selection this way:

```
         public boolean action (Event e, Object o){
-->              String caption = (String)o;
                 if(e.target.equals(colors)){
                          .
                          .
                          .
```

After we get the selected text, we can place it into the textfield this way:

```
         public boolean action (Event e, Object o){
                 String caption = (String)o;
                 if(e.target.equals(colors)){
-->                      text1.setText(caption);
                 }
                 return true;
         }
```

Our Choice control is installed and ready to use. When the user makes a selection in the Choice control, we'll see the result in the textfield, as in Figure 4.3. Our applet is a success. The code for this applet appears in Listing 4.3.

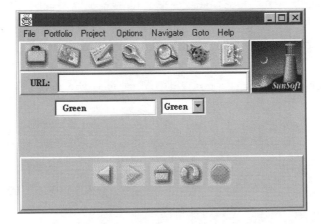

Figure 4.3 Our Choice control example.

Listing 4.3 Colors.java

```java
import java.applet.Applet;
import java.awt.*;

public class Choices extends Applet {

        Choice colors;
        TextField text1;

        public void init(){
                text1 = new TextField(20);
                add(text1);
                colors = new Choice();
                colors.addItem("Red");
                colors.addItem("Green");
                colors.addItem("Blue");
                add(colors);
        }

        public boolean action (Event e, Object o){
                String caption = (String)o;
                if(e.target.equals(colors)){
                        text1.setText(caption);
                }
                return true;
        }
}
```

We can put Choice controls and Scrollbar controls together when we look at the List control.

Scrolling Lists

Our next example will set up a scrolling list in an applet. Such a control presents a list (which doesn't have to scroll if you don't want it to) of options to the user. For example, if we wanted to modify our colors example, the three choices **Red**, **Green**, and **Blue** would appear in a list. If not all the choices were visible, we could have a vertical scrollbar as part of the control so the user could see all the options by scrolling:

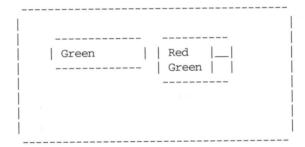

```
 -------------------------------------------
|                                           |
|   -------------    ----------             |
|  |             |  | Red    |_|            |
|   -------------   | Green |  |            |
|                    ----------             |
|                                           |
|                                           |
|                                           |
 -------------------------------------------
```

Then, when the user made a selection, we could display the result of that in a textfield:

```
 --------------------------------------------
|                                            |
|   -------------    ----------              |
|  | Green       |  | Red    |_|             |
|   -------------   | Green |  |             |
|                    ----------              |
|                                            |
|                                            |
|                                            |
 --------------------------------------------
```

Let's put this to work by modifying our Choices example. First, we replace the Choice control named colors with a List control of the same name:

```
import java.applet.Applet;
import java.awt.*;

public class Scrlist extends Applet {

-->        List colors;
           TextField text1;
                  .
                  .
                  .
```

The List control's constructors and methods appear in Table 4.3.

Table 4.3 List Control's Constructors and Methods

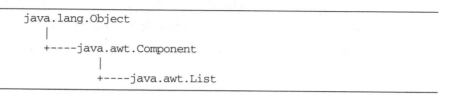

```
java.lang.Object
    |
    +----java.awt.Component
            |
            +----java.awt.List
```

Method	Means
List()	Creates scrolling list with no visible lines
List(int, boolean)	Creates scrolling list with specified number of lines; boolean indicates whether multiple selections are allowed
addItem(String)	Adds specified item to end of scrolling list
addItem(String, int)	Adds specified item to specified position in scrolling list
addNotify()	Creates peer for the list
allowsMultipleSelections()	Returns true if list allows multiple selections
clear()	Clears all entries in list
countItems()	Returns number of items in list
delItem(int)	Deletes item from list
delItems(int, int)	Deletes a number of items from list
deselect(int)	Deselects item at specified index
getItem(int)	Returns item at specified index
getRows()	Returns number of visible lines in list
getSelectedIndex()	Returns selected item (−1 if no item is selected)
getSelectedIndexes()	Returns selected indexes on the list
getSelectedItem()	Returns selected item; null if no item is selected
getSelectedItems()	Returns selected items
getVisibleIndex()	Returns index of item that was last made visible

isSelected(int)	Returns true if the item at specified index is selected
makeVisible(int)	Makes item at specified index visible
minimumSize(int)	Returns minimum dimensions for number of rows
specifiedminimumSize()	Returns minimum dimensions needed for list
paramString()	Returns parameter string of list
preferredSize(int)	Returns preferred dimensions for list with the specified number of rows
preferredSize()	Returns preferred dimensions for list
removeNotify()	Removes peer for list
replaceItem(String, int)	Replaces item at given index
select(int)	Selects item at specified index
setMultipleSelections(boolean)	Sets whether or not list should allow multiple selections

Next, we set up our textfield:

```
import java.applet.Applet;
import java.awt.*;

public class Scrlist extends Applet {

        List colors;
        TextField text1;

        public void init(){
-->             text1 = new TextField(20);
-->             add(text1);
                .
                .
                .
```

Now we can create our List control. We indicate that we want only two choices visible at once in the Choice control, and we also indicate (by passing a value of true) that we want the List control to allow multiple selections (passing false would mean the Choice control should handle only single selections):

```java
import java.applet.Applet;
import java.awt.*;

public class Scrlist extends Applet {

        List colors;
        TextField text1;

        public void init(){
                text1 = new TextField(20);
                add(text1);
-->             colors = new List(2, true);
                        .
                        .
                        .
```

Now we add our **Red, Green,** and **Blue** choices to the List just as we did with the Choice control and then add the new List to the applet:

```java
import java.applet.Applet;
import java.awt.*;

public class Scrlist extends Applet {

        List colors;
        TextField text1;

        public void init(){
                text1 = new TextField(20);
                add(text1);
                colors = new List(2, true);
-->             colors.addItem("Red");
-->             colors.addItem("Green");
-->             colors.addItem("Blue");
-->             add(colors);
        }       .
                .
                .
```

We'll need to make these modifications to our Choices applet. The action() method stays the same as before:

```
public boolean action (Event e, Object o){
        String caption = (String)o;
        if(e.target.equals(colors)){
                text1.setText(caption);
        }
        return true;
}
```

We've combined scollbars and choice controls into a List control, as shown in Figure 4.4. Our List example is a success. The code for this applet appears in Listing 4.4.

Figure 4.4 Our List example.

Listing 4.4 Scrlist.java

```
import java.applet.Applet;
import java.awt.*;

public class Scrlist extends Applet {
```

```
        List colors;
        TextField text1;

        public void init(){
                text1 = new TextField(20);
                add(text1);
                colors = new List(2, true);
                colors.addItem("Red");
                colors.addItem("Green");
                colors.addItem("Blue");
                add(colors);
        }

        public boolean action (Event e, Object o){
                String caption = (String)o;
                if(e.target.equals(colors)){
                        text1.setText(caption);
                }
                return true;
        }
    }
```

We've introduced several new controls in this chapter: choices, scrollbars, and lists. Given this profusion of controls, this is a good time to look at the most powerful layout manager—the GridBag Layout Manager.

GridBag Layout

The GridBag Layout Manager is the most versatile and complex of all the Java layout managers. With it, you can specify just about any arrangement of controls; of course, that also means that GridBag Layout Manager is the hardest layout manager to use.

Let's put the GridBag Layout Manager to work now as we create a simple applet:

```
----------------------------------------
|         |           |           |
| Red Text | Green Text | Blue Text |
|         |           |           |
|----------------------------------------|
|                                        |
|                                        |
|                                        |
|                                        |
|                                        |
|                                        |
|                                        |
|                                        |
----------------------------------------
```

Here, we've placed three buttons—marked **Red Text**, **Blue Text**, and **Green Text**—above a textarea. These buttons allow users to select the text color in the textarea; when they click **Blue**, for example, and type, the text will appear in blue:

```
----------------------------------------
|         |           |           |
| Red Text | Green Text | Blue Text |
|         |           |           |
|----------------------------------------|
| This is a test...                      |
|                                        |
|                                        |
|                                        |
|                                        |
|                                        |
|                                        |
----------------------------------------
```

First, let's declare the buttons (redButton, greenButton, and blueButton) and the textarea (Text1) we'll need:

```
import java.applet.Applet;
import java.awt.*;

public class Gridbag extends Applet {
```

```
-->          Button redButton, greenButton, blueButton;
-->          TextArea Text1;
                 .
                 .
                 .
```

Next, we indicate that we want a GridBag layout:

```
        import java.applet.Applet;
        import java.awt.*;

        public class Gridbag extends Applet {

                Button redButton, greenButton, blueButton;
                TextArea Text1;

                public void init(){
-->                     GridBagLayout gbLayout = new GridBagLayout();
                            .
                            .
                            .
```

Now we install the new GridBag layout with setLayout():

```
        import java.applet.Applet;
        import java.awt.*;

        public class Gridbag extends Applet {

                Button redButton, greenButton, blueButton;
                TextArea Text1;

                public void init(){
                        GridBagLayout gbLayout = new GridBagLayout();
-->                     setLayout(gbLayout);
                            .
                            .
                            .
```

We can start specifying our button's layout now. The way we specify the relative sizes of controls in a row is the weightx and weighty data members. For example, if we want all the controls to be the same width, we give them all the same weightx:

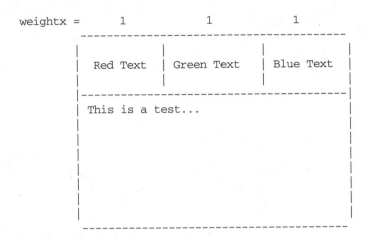

If we want one control to be twice as wide, we give it a weightx twice as large as the others:

```
weightx =        1            1            2
           ------------------------------------------
          |       |         |         |              |
          | Red Text|Green Text|     Blue Text       |
          |       |         |         |              |
          |-----------------------------------------|
          | This is a test...                        |
          |                                          |
          |                                          |
          |                                          |
          |                                          |
          |                                          |
          |                                          |
           ------------------------------------------
```

To control their relative heights, use weighty. These variables, weightx and weighty, are actually members of the GridBagConstraints class (not the GridBag class), so we add a new object of that class now like this:

```
        import java.applet.Applet;
        import java.awt.*;

        public class Gridbag extends Applet {

                Button redButton, greenButton, blueButton;
                TextArea Text1;

                public void init(){
                        GridBagLayout gbLayout = new GridBagLayout();
-->                     GridBagConstraints gbConstraints = new
-->                         GridBagConstraints();
                        setLayout(gbLayout);
                                .
                                .
                                .
```

Since we want all our controls to be the same height, we place a 1 in the weighty data member:

```
        import java.applet.Applet;
        import java.awt.*;

        public class Gridbag extends Applet {

                Button redButton, greenButton, blueButton;
                TextArea Text1;

                public void init(){
                        GridBagLayout gbLayout = new GridBagLayout();
                        GridBagConstraints gbConstraints = new
                            GridBagConstraints();
                        setLayout(gbLayout);
-->                     gbConstraints.weighty = 1;
                                .
                                .
                                .
```

In addition, we want our buttons to fill the space the layout manager gives to them, rather than to appear as standard buttons:

```
-------------------------------------------
|            |             |              |
| Red Text   | Green Text  | Blue Text    |
|            |             |              |
|-----------------------------------------|
| This is a test...                       |
|                                         |
|                                         |
|                                         |
|                                         |
|                                         |
|                                         |
|                                         |
-------------------------------------------
```

We do this with the *fill* member of the GridBagConstraints class. This member can be set to the constants GridBagConstraints.VERTICAL to stretch the control vertically, GridBagConstraints.HORIZONTAL to stretch it horizontally, and GridBagConstraints.BOTH to stretch the control in both dimensions. Let's use GridBagConstraints.BOTH here (not placing anything in the fill member would leave the buttons looking like standard buttons, shaped to fit the text of their captions):

```
        import java.applet.Applet;
        import java.awt.*;

        public class Gridbag extends Applet {

                Button redButton, greenButton, blueButton;
                TextArea Text1;

                public void init(){
                        GridBagLayout gbLayout = new GridBagLayout();
                        GridBagConstraints gbConstraints = new
                            GridBagConstraints();
                        setLayout(gbLayout);
                        gbConstraints.weighty = 1;
  -->                   gbConstraints.fill = GridBagConstraints.BOTH;
                                  .
                                  .
                                  .
```

Now let's add our first button, the Red Text button. We give it a weightx value of 1 and create the button this way:

```
import java.applet.Applet;
import java.awt.*;

public class Gridbag extends Applet {

        Button redButton, greenButton, blueButton;
        TextArea Text1;

        public void init(){
                GridBagLayout gbLayout = new GridBagLayout();
                GridBagConstraints gbConstraints = new
                    GridBagConstraints();
                setLayout(gbLayout);
                gbConstraints.weighty = 1;
                gbConstraints.fill = GridBagConstraints.BOTH;

-->             gbConstraints.weightx = 1;
-->             redButton = new Button("Red Text");
                        .
                        .
                        .
```

We then install this button's GridBag constraints with the setConstraints() method:

```
import java.applet.Applet;
import java.awt.*;

public class Gridbag extends Applet {

        Button redButton, greenButton, blueButton;
        TextArea Text1;

        public void init(){
            GridBagLayout gbLayout = new GridBagLayout();
            GridBagConstraints gbConstraints = new
                GridBagConstraints();
            setLayout(gbLayout);
            gbConstraints.weighty = 1;
```

```
                  gbConstraints.fill = GridBagConstraints.BOTH;

                  gbConstraints.weightx = 1;
                  redButton = new Button("Red Text");
        -->       gbLayout.setConstraints(redButton, gbConstraints);
                      .
                      .
                      .
```

Then we add the button to the layout with the add() method:

```
        import java.applet.Applet;
        import java.awt.*;

        public class Gridbag extends Applet {

                Button redButton, greenButton, blueButton;
                TextArea Text1;

                public void init(){
                    GridBagLayout gbLayout = new GridBagLayout();
                        .
                        .
                        .
                    gbConstraints.weightx = 1;
                    redButton = new Button("Red Text");
                    gbLayout.setConstraints(redButton, gbConstraints);
        -->         add(redButton);
                        .
                        .
                        .
```

Now our Red Text button is installed. We can do the same for the Green Text button:

```
        import java.applet.Applet;
        import java.awt.*;

        public class Gridbag extends Applet {

                Button redButton, greenButton, blueButton;
                TextArea Text1;
```

```
        public void init(){
            GridBagLayout gbLayout = new GridBagLayout();
                            .
                            .
                            .
-->         gbConstraints.weightx = 1;
-->         greenButton = new Button("Green Text");
-->         gbLayout.setConstraints(greenButton, gbConstraints);
-->         add(greenButton);
                            .
                            .
                            .
```

We want to do the same things with the Blue Text button, but we also want to tell the layout manager that we are finished with the current row of buttons and want to go to the next row (where the textarea will be). We do that by setting the GridBagConstraint's gridWidth member to GridBagConstraints.REMAINDER:

```
import java.applet.Applet;
import java.awt.*;

public class Gridbag extends Applet {

        Button redButton, greenButton, blueButton;
        TextArea Text1;

        public void init(){
            GridBagLayout gbLayout = new GridBagLayout();
                            .
                            .
                            .
            gbConstraints.weightx = 1;
            blueButton = new Button("Blue Text");
-->         gbConstraints.gridwidth = GridBagConstraints.REMAINDER;
            gbLayout.setConstraints(blueButton, gbConstraints);
                add(blueButton);
                            .
                            .
                            .
```

Now our three buttons are set up. All that remains is to add the textarea. Since there is only one control in the textarea's row, we don't have to specify weightx values here; all we need to do is indicate that we're done defining the row when we set up our textarea, which we do with GridBagConstraints.REMAINDER:

```
import java.applet.Applet;
import java.awt.*;

public class Gridbag extends Applet {

        Button redButton, greenButton, blueButton;
        TextArea Text1;

        public void init(){
                GridBagLayout gbLayout = new GridBagLayout();
                      .

                      .

                gbConstraints.weightx = 1;
                blueButton = new Button("Blue Text");
                gbConstraints.gridwidth = GridBagConstraints.REMAINDER;
                gbLayout.setConstraints(blueButton, gbConstraints);
                add(blueButton);

                Text1 = new TextArea();
    -->         gbConstraints.gridwidth = GridBagConstraints.REMAINDER;
                gbLayout.setConstraints(Text1, gbConstraints);
                add(Text1);
        }     .

              .

              .
```

Our layout is complete. The next step is to make the buttons active. We do that in the action() method:

```
              public boolean action(Event e, Object o){
                      .

                      .

                      .
```

First we check to see if, for example, the **Red Text** button was clicked:

```
         public boolean action(Event e, Object o){
  -->           if(e.target.equals(redButton)){
                                  .
                                  .
                                  .
```

If so, we want to change the text color in the TextArea to red. We set up a Color object and pass it to the TextArea's setForeGround() method, which sets the textarea's foreground drawing color. The Color class allows us to handle colors with red, blue, and green settings. Much like an HTML color setting, we can create a new color in Java by passing the red, blue, and green values we want (in that order; the values are integers varying from 0 to 255) to the Color class's constructor, which looks like this for red:

```
       public boolean action(Event e, Object o){
             if(e.target.equals(redButton)){
  -->               Text1.setForeground(new Color(255, 0, 0));
             }          .
                        .
                        .
```

We do the same for the **Green Text** and **Blue Text** buttons:

```
       public boolean action(Event e, Object o){
             if(e.target.equals(redButton)){
                    Text1.setForeground(new Color(255, 0, 0));
             }
  -->        if(e.target.equals(greenButton)){
  -->               Text1.setForeground(new Color(0, 255, 0));
  -->        }
  -->        if(e.target.equals(blueButton)){
  -->               Text1.setForeground(new Color(0, 0, 255));
  -->        }
             return true;
       }
```

The results appear in Figure 4.5. As you can see, our layout appears as we wanted it. When the user selects a text color, the text they type appears in that color. Our GridBag applet is a success. The code for this applet appears in Listing 4.5.

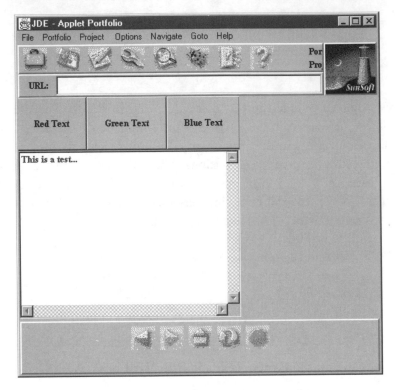

Figure 4.5 Our GridBag Layout example.

Listing 4.5 Gridbag.java

```java
import java.applet.Applet;
import java.awt.*;

public class Gridbag extends Applet {

        Button redButton, greenButton, blueButton;
        TextArea Text1;

        public void init(){
                GridBagLayout gbLayout = new GridBagLayout();
                GridBagConstraints gbConstraints = new
                    GridBagConstraints();
                setLayout(gbLayout);
                gbConstraints.weighty = 1;
```

```
            gbConstraints.fill = GridBagConstraints.BOTH;

            gbConstraints.weightx = 1;
            redButton = new Button("Red Text");
            gbLayout.setConstraints(redButton, gbConstraints);
            add(redButton);

            gbConstraints.weightx = 1;
            greenButton = new Button("Green Text");
            gbLayout.setConstraints(greenButton, gbConstraints);
            add(greenButton);

            gbConstraints.weightx = 1;
            blueButton = new Button("Blue Text");
            gbConstraints.gridwidth = GridBagConstraints.REMAINDER;
            gbLayout.setConstraints(blueButton, gbConstraints);
            add(blueButton);

            Text1 = new TextArea();
            gbConstraints.gridwidth = GridBagConstraints.REMAINDER;
            gbLayout.setConstraints(Text1, gbConstraints);
            add(Text1);
        }


public boolean action(Event e, Object o){
        if(e.target.equals(redButton)){
                Text1.setForeground(new Color(255, 0, 0));
        }
        if(e.target.equals(greenButton)){
                Text1.setForeground(new Color(0, 255, 0));
        }
        if(e.target.equals(blueButton)){
                Text1.setForeground(new Color(0, 0, 255));
        }
        return true;
    }
}
```

In this chapter, we've seen new controls: choice controls, scrollbars, and list controls. In addition, we were introduced to the Border and GridBag Layout Managers. All in all, we added a great deal of power to our Java arsenal. In the next chapter, we'll go on to even more powerful techniques as we examine windows, menus, and dialog boxes.

CHAPTER FIVE

WINDOWS, MENUS, AND DIALOG BOXES

In this chapter, we'll explore some important Java objects: pop-up windows, menus, and dialog boxes. It's possible for our applet to support all these things; as you can see, there's a tremendous amount of programming power here. When we finish this chapter, we'll be able to pop up new windows in our applets and display a menu with all kinds of extras, including check marks next to selected items, submenus, and separator bars, as well as display dialog boxes. In addition, we'll also see a new layout manager—the CardLayout Manager. Let's start at once by seeing how to pop up a new window from our applet.

Pop-up Windows

The first applet in this chapter displays two buttons: **Show Window** and **Hide Window**:

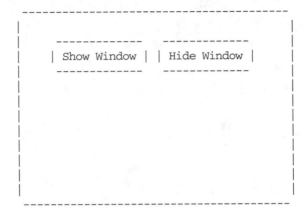

When the user clicks the **Show Window** button, we'll pop a new window on the screen with our "Hello World!" message in it.

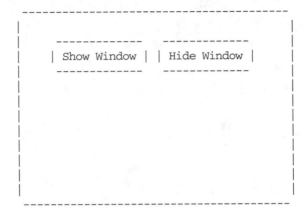

The Frame Class

Let's set up an object of the Java class named Frame (for frame window). After we create this class, we'll be able to create an object of that class in our applet and use the show() method to show the window and the hide() menu to hide it.

We might call our new window class windowFrame. Let's begin that class this way:

```
class windowFrame extends Frame {
         .
         .
         .
```

This indicates that we want to derive our frameWindow class from the Java Frame class. The Frame class's constructors and methods appear in Table 5.1.

Table 5.1 Frame Class's Constructors and Methods

```
java.lang.Object
    |
    +----java.awt.Component
              |
              +----java.awt.Container
                        |
                        +----java.awt.Window
                                  |
                                  +----java.awt.Frame
```

Frame()	Constructs a frame, initially invisible
Frame(String)	Constructs initially invisible frame with specified title
addNotify()	Creates Frame's peer
dispose()	Disposes of Frame
getCursorType()	Returns cursor type
getIconImage()	Returns icon image for Frame
getMenuBar()	Returns menu bar for Frame

getTitle()	Returns title of Frame
isResizable()	Returns true if user can resize Frame
paramString()	Returns parameter string of Frame
remove(MenuComponent)	Removes specified menu bar from Frame
setCursor(int)	Sets cursor to a predefined cursor
setIconImage(Image)	Sets image to show when Frame is iconized
setMenuBar(MenuBar)	Sets menu bar for this Frame
setResizable(boolean)	Sets resizable flag
setTitle(String)	Sets title for Frame to specified title

The first thing to do in the new windowFrame class is to set up the class's constructor, which is called when we create an object of this class. In this case, we'll give the constructor one parameter: a String object that we can pass to the Frame class's constructor to give our window a title:

```
class windowFrame extends Frame {

        windowFrame(String title){
            .
            .
            .
```

To pass this string back to the Java class Frame's constructor, we just call the function super(), which is how you reach the base class's constructor. In code, that looks like this:

```
class windowFrame extends Frame {

            windowFrame(String title){
-->               super(title);
                .
                .
                .
```

Next, we place a textfield in our new window, and place the text "Hello World!" in it. We can stretch that textfield to cover the window's client area with a GridLayout this way:

```
      class windowFrame extends Frame {
              TextField DisplayText;
              windowFrame(String title){
                      super(title);
-->                   setLayout(new GridLayout(1, 1));
-->                   DisplayText = new TextField("Hello World!");
-->                   add(DisplayText);
              }
      }
```

That completes our new window class windowFrame. We now add the applet code (to the same file), starting it this way, where we add our **Show Window** and **Hide Window** buttons:

```
      import java.applet.Applet;
      import java.awt.*;

      public class Wnd extends Applet {

-->           Button button1, button2;
                      .
                      .
                      .
```

Next, we create an object of our windowFrame class named, for example, popWindow:

```
      import java.applet.Applet;
      import java.awt.*;

      public class Wnd extends Applet {

              Button button1, button2;
-->           windowFrame popWindow;
                      .
                      .
                      .
```

Now we create and add the buttons, giving them the correct captions:

```
import java.applet.Applet;
import java.awt.*;

public class Wnd extends Applet {

        Button button1, button2;
        windowFrame popWindow;

        public void init(){
-->             button1 = new Button("Show window");
-->             add(button1);
-->             button2 = new Button("Hide window");
-->             add(button2);
                         .
                         .
                         .
```

We create the new window, giving it the title "Hello World!" and resizing it to 100 pixels by 100 pixels:

```
import java.applet.Applet;
import java.awt.*;

public class Wnd extends Applet {

        Button button1, button2;
        windowFrame popWindow;

        public void init(){
                button1 = new Button("Show window");
                add(button1);
                button2 = new Button("Hide window");
                add(button2);

-->             popWindow = new windowFrame("Hello World!");
-->             popWindow.resize(100, 100);
        }
```

At this point, all we have to do is make the buttons active, showing or hiding the window. We do that in the action() method:

```
public boolean action (Event e, Object o){
              .
              .
              .
```

First, let's handle the **Show Window** button, button1:

```
public boolean action (Event e, Object o){
        if(e.target.equals(button1)){
                .
                .
                .
```

If the user pressed the **Show Window** button, we just use the window object's show() method to pop the window onto the screen:

```
public boolean action (Event e, Object o){
        if(e.target.equals(button1)){
                popWindow.show();
        }            .
                     .
                     .
```

We also make active button2, which hides the window. When the user wants to hide the window, we just use the Frame class's hide() method:

```
       public boolean action (Event e, Object o){
               if(e.target.equals(button1)){
                       popWindow.show();
               }
  -->          if(e.target.equals(button2)){
  -->                  popWindow.hide();
  -->          }
               return true;
       }
```

Now when we run the applet, our two buttons appear, as shown in Figure 5.1. When we click the **Show Window** button, our new window pops up, as shown in Figure 5.2. (You can move and resize the window with the move() and resize() methods.) Our applet is a success, and the code appears in Listing 5.1.

Figure 5.1 Our Wnd applet will pop up a window.

Figure 5.2 Our first pop-up window.

Listing 5.1 Wnd.java

```java
import java.applet.Applet;
import java.awt.*;

public class Wnd extends Applet {

        Button button1, button2;
        windowFrame popWindow;

        public void init(){
                button1 = new Button("Show window");
                add(button1);
                button2 = new Button("Hide window");
                add(button2);

                popWindow = new windowFrame("Hello World!");
                popWindow.resize(100, 100);
        }

        public boolean action (Event e, Object o){
                if(e.target.equals(button1)){
                        popWindow.show();
                }
                if(e.target.equals(button2)){
                        popWindow.hide();
                }
                return true;
        }
    }

class windowFrame extends Frame {
        TextField DisplayText;
        windowFrame(String title){
                super(title);
                setLayout(new GridLayout(1, 1));
                DisplayText = new TextField("Hello World!");
                add(DisplayText);
        }
    }
```

Now that we've seen how to create pop-up windows, let's move on to menus.

Menus

In this next example, we'll create a menu with two items: **Hello** and **World!**:

```
-------------------------------------
| File                              |
| | Hello |                         |
| | World! |                        |
|  --------                         |
|                                   |
|                                   |
|                                   |
|                                   |
|                                   |
|                                   |
|                                   |
-------------------------------------
```

When the user selects either item, we can have that word appear in the window (e.g., selecting **Hello** makes the word *Hello* appear in the window).

It turns out that you can in Java add menus only to Frame windows, so we'll need a Frame window. We might call our window MenuFrame and derive it from the Frame class like this:

```
class MenuFrame extends Frame {
        .
        .
        .
```

Then we can set up our window as before, with a textfield that displays the words Hello World!:

```
class MenuFrame extends Frame {

        MenuFrame(String title){
                super(title);
                DisplayText = new TextField("Hello World!");
                setLayout(new GridLayout(1, 1));
```

```
                            add(DisplayText);
                                 .
                                 .
                                 .
```

Now we can add a menu system to this window. That process starts with a menu bar (we'll add the individual menus to this menu bar). We create a new object of class MenuBar named, for example, MenuBar1 this way:

```
          class MenuFrame extends Frame {

  -->             MenuBar Menubar1;
                  TextField DisplayText;

                  MenuFrame(String title){
                        super(title);
                        DisplayText = new TextField("Hello World!");
                        setLayout(new GridLayout(1, 1));
                        add(DisplayText);
  -->                   Menubar1 = new MenuBar();
                             .
                             .
                             .
```

The MenuBar class's constructors and methods appear in Table 5.2.

Table 5.2 MenuBar Constructors and Methods

```
      java.lang.Object
         |
      +----java.awt.MenuComponent
               |
               +----java.awt.MenuBar
```

MenuBar()	Creates a menu bar
add(Menu)	Adds specified menu to menu bar
addNotify()	Creates menu bar's peer
countMenus()	Returns number of menus in menu bar
getHelpMenu()	Returns help menu in menu bar

getMenu(int)	Returns specified menu
remove(int)	Removes menu at specified index from menu bar
remove(MenuComponent)	Removes specified menu from menu bar
removeNotify()	Removes menu bar's peer
setHelpMenu(Menu)	Sets help menu to specified menu in menu bar

Now that we've added the menu bar, we can add menus to it. In particular, let's add the File menu. We do that with a Menu object, which we might call Menu1, and which we create this way, giving this menu the title "File":

```
        class MenuFrame extends Frame {

-->         Menu Menu1;
            MenuBar Menubar1;
            TextField DisplayText;
                    .
                    .
                    .
                Menubar1 = new MenuBar();
-->             Menu1 = new Menu("File");
                    .
                    .
                    .
```

The Menu class's constructors and methods appear in Table 5.3.

Table 5.3 Menu Constructors and Methods

```
        java.lang.Object
           |
        +----java.awt.MenuComponent
                 |
              +----java.awt.MenuItem
                      |
                   +----java.awt.Menu
```

Menu(String)	Constructs Menu with specified label
Menu(String, boolean)	Constructs Menu with specified label, enabled if boolean if true

add(MenuItem)	Adds specified item to Menu
add(String)	Adds item with specified label to Menu
addNotify()	Creates Menu's peer
addSeparator()	Adds separator line to Menu
countItems()	Returns number of elements in Menu
getItem(int)	Returns item at specified index of Menu
isTearOff()	Returns true if Menu is a tear-off menu
remove(int)	Removes item from Menu at specified index
remove(MenuComponent)	Removes specified item from Menu
removeNotify()	Removes Menu's peer

We want two menu items in the File menu, **Hello** and **World!**:

```
------------------------------------------
| File                                   |
| | Hello  |                             |
| | World! |                             |
|  --------                              |
|                                        |
|                                        |
|                                        |
|                                        |
|                                        |
|                                        |
|                                        |
|                                        |
 ----------------------------------------
```

Each menu item is actually an object of class MenuItem, and we add our two items to the File menu this way:

```
class MenuFrame extends Frame {
                .
                .
                .
        Menubar1 = new MenuBar();
        Menu1 = new Menu("File");
-->     Menu1.add(new MenuItem("Hello"));
```

```
-->              Menu1.add(new MenuItem("World!"));
                        .
                        .
                        .
```

Now our File menu is prepared, and we add it to the menu bar with the add()
method:

```
class MenuFrame extends Frame {
                        .
                        .
                        .
                 Menubar1 = new MenuBar();
                 Menu1 = new Menu("File");
                 Menu1.add(new MenuItem("Hello"));
                 Menu1.add(new MenuItem("World!"));
-->              Menubar1.add(Menu1);
                        .
                        .
                        .
```

At this point, we could add other menus (e.g., Edit) to the menu bar, but here
we have only our File menu, so the menu bar is entirely set up. To display it in
our window, we use the setMenuBar() method:

```
class MenuFrame extends Frame {
                        .
                        .
                        .
                 Menubar1 = new MenuBar();
                 Menu1 = new Menu("File");
                 Menu1.add(new MenuItem("Hello"));
                 Menu1.add(new MenuItem("World!"));
                 Menubar1.add(Menu1);
                 Menubar1.setHelpMenu(Menu1);
-->              setMenuBar(Menubar1);
         }
```

Now our menu-supporting window class (MenuFrame) is almost complete.
The remaining step, of course, is to respond when the user has clicked the

individual menu items. We do that with an action() method in the MenuFrame class, where we first check to see if the clicked object is of class MenuItem:

```
                public boolean action (Event e, Object o){
                        String caption = (String)o;
    -->                 if(e.target instanceof MenuItem){
                                    .
                                    .
                                    .
```

If so, we check the clicked item's caption. If it's **Hello**, we place that word in the textfield, which covers the window's client area:

```
                public boolean action (Event e, Object o){
                        String caption = (String)o;
                        if(e.target instanceof MenuItem){
    -->                         if(caption == "Hello"){
    -->                                 DisplayText.setText("Hello");
                                }           .
                                            .
                                            .
                                            .
```

And if the user clicks the **World!** menu item, we place that in the textfield instead:

```
                public boolean action (Event e, Object o){
                        String caption = (String)o;
                        if(e.target instanceof MenuItem){
                                if(caption == "Hello"){
                                        DisplayText.setText("Hello");
                                }
    -->                         if(caption == "World!"){
    -->                                 DisplayText.setText("World!");
    -->                         }
                        }
                        return true;
                }
        }
```

We just need to modify the applet code to display and enable two buttons: **Show menu window** and **Hide menu window,** as we did in our pop-up window example. We set up the two buttons like this:

```
        import java.applet.Applet;
        import java.awt.*;

        public class Menus extends Applet {

-->             Button button1, button2;
                MenuFrame menuWindow;

                public void init(){
-->                     button1 = new Button("Show menu window");
-->                     add(button1);
-->                     button2 = new Button("Hide menu window");
-->                     add(button2);

                        menuWindow = new MenuFrame("Hello World!");
                        menuWindow.resize(100, 100);
                }            .
                             .
                             .
```

Now we enable those buttons in the action() method, allowing the user to show a window of our MenuFrame class (which includes our new menu):

```
        import java.applet.Applet;
        import java.awt.*;

        public class Menus extends Applet {

                Button button1, button2;
                MenuFrame menuWindow;
                    .
                    .
                    .
-->             public boolean action (Event e, Object o){
```

```
-->                  if(e.target.equals(button1)){
-->                          menuWindow.show();
-->                  }
-->                  if(e.target.equals(button2)){
-->                          menuWindow.hide();
-->                  }
-->                  return true;
-->          }
      }
```

When we run the applet and click the **Show menu window** button, our new window pops up with a File menu that includes two items, as shown in Figure 5.3. When you click, for example, the **Hello** item, the corresponding text appears in the window, as shown in Figure 5.4. Our menu applet is a success. The code for this applet appears in Listing 5.2.

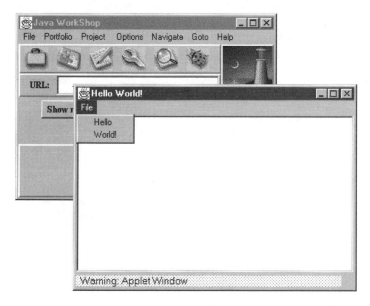

Figure 5.3 Our first menu example.

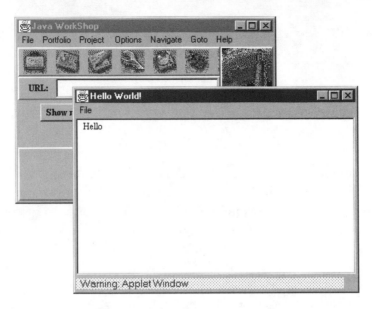

Figure 5.4 Our menu example at work.

Listing 5.2 Menus.java

```
import java.applet.Applet;
import java.awt.*;

public class Menus extends Applet {

        Button button1, button2;
        MenuFrame menuWindow;

        public void init(){
                button1 = new Button("Show menu window");
                add(button1);
                button2 = new Button("Hide menu window");
                add(button2);

                menuWindow = new MenuFrame("Hello World!");
                menuWindow.resize(100, 100);
        }

        public boolean action (Event e, Object o){
```

```
                    if(e.target.equals(button1)){
                           menuWindow.show();
                    }
                    if(e.target.equals(button2)){
                           menuWindow.hide();
                    }
                    return true;
             }
      }

class MenuFrame extends Frame {

      Menu Menu1;
      MenuBar Menubar1;
      TextField DisplayText;

      MenuFrame(String title){
             super(title);
             DisplayText = new TextField("Hello World!");
             setLayout(new GridLayout(1, 1));
             add(DisplayText);
             Menubar1 = new MenuBar();
             Menu1 = new Menu("File");
             Menu1.add(new MenuItem("Hello"));
             Menu1.add(new MenuItem("World!"));
             Menubar1.add(Menu1);
             Menubar1.setHelpMenu(Menu1);
             setMenuBar(Menubar1);
      }

      public boolean action (Event e, Object o){
             String caption = (String)o;
             if(e.target instanceof MenuItem){
                    if(caption == "Hello"){
                           DisplayText.setText("Hello");
                    }
                    if(caption == "World!"){
                           DisplayText.setText("World!");
                    }
             }
             return true;
      }
   }
```

We can do a lot more with menus, and we'll explore some of that now.

Adding Powerful Menus

Besides simple menu items, we can also support menu separators (horizontal spacer bars), submenus (menus that pop up from the menu itself), and check box items:

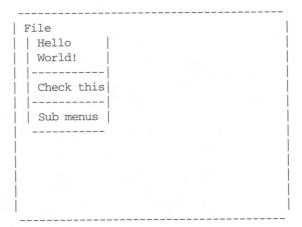

When we click the check box item **Check this**, for example, we can have a check mark appear in front of it:

```
          ----------------------------------------
          | File                                  |
          | | Hello     |                         |
          | | World!    |                         |
          | |-----------|                         |
    -->   | |vCheck this|                         |
          | |-----------|                         |
          | | Sub menus |                         |
          |  -----------                          |
          |                                       |
          |                                       |
          |                                       |
          |                                       |
          ----------------------------------------
```

Selecting that item again can toggle the check mark off. In addition, selecting the **Sub menus** item brings up a submenu like this:

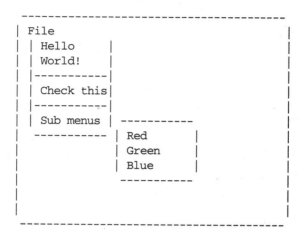

```
-------------------------------------------
| File                                    |
| | Hello    |                            |
| | World!   |                            |
| |----------|                            |
| | Check this|                           |
| |----------|                            |
| | Sub menus |  ----------               |
|   ----------  | Red      |              |
|               | Green    |              |
|               | Blue     |              |
|                ----------               |
|                                         |
|                                         |
-------------------------------------------
```

The user can select from these new items. Let's start this applet, by adding these new items to our menu example. We can add a separator bar, which visually separates menu items into groups, just by adding a dash (-) as a menu item. Java knows enough to make this a separator:

```
class menuFrame extends Frame {

    Menu Menu1, SubMenu;
    MenuBar Menubar1;
    TextField DisplayText;

    menuFrame(String title){
        super(title);
        DisplayText = new TextField("Hello World!");
        setLayout(new GridLayout(1, 1));
        add(DisplayText);
        Menubar1 = new MenuBar();
        Menu1 = new Menu("File");
        Menu1.add(new MenuItem("Hello"));
        Menu1.add(new MenuItem("World!"));
-->     Menu1.add(new MenuItem("-"));
                      .
                      .
                      .
```

Next, we can set up our submenu, which is itself just a new Menu object:

```
class menuFrame extends Frame {
                    .
                    .
                    .
                Menu1.add(new MenuItem("-"));
-->             SubMenu = new Menu("Sub menus");
                    .
                    .
                    .
```

Now we add the **Red**, **Green**, and **Blue** items to the submenu:

```
class menuFrame extends Frame {
                    .
                    .
                    .
                Menu1.add(new MenuItem("-"));
                SubMenu = new Menu("Sub menus");
-->             SubMenu.add(new MenuItem("Red"));
-->             SubMenu.add(new MenuItem("Green"));
-->             SubMenu.add(new MenuItem("Blue"));
                    .
                    .
                    .
```

Finally, we add the new menu with the title "Sub menus" to the File menu:

```
class menuFrame extends Frame {
                    .
                    .
                    .
                Menu1.add(new MenuItem("-"));
                SubMenu = new Menu("Sub menus");
                SubMenu.add(new MenuItem("Red"));
                SubMenu.add(new MenuItem("Green"));
                SubMenu.add(new MenuItem("Blue"));
-->             Menu1.add(SubMenu);
                    .
                    .
                    .
```

To make this submenu active, you just add code to the action() method as we've done with the other menu items. Next, let's add our check box menu item, which we name "Check this." This will be a new item of the Java class CheckboxMenuItem:

```
class menuFrame extends Frame {
                      .
                      .
                      .
                Menu1.add(new MenuItem("-"));
-->             Menu1.add(new CheckboxMenuItem("Check this"));
                Menu1.add(new MenuItem("-"));
                SubMenu = new Menu("Sub menus");
                SubMenu.add(new MenuItem("Red"));
                SubMenu.add(new MenuItem("Green"));
                SubMenu.add(new MenuItem("Blue"));
                Menu1.add(SubMenu);
                Menubar1.add(Menu1);
                setMenuBar(Menubar1);
        }
```

To add the check mark in front of the **Check this** item when it's selected, we first determine whether that was indeed the menu item selected:

```
public boolean action (Event e, Object o){
        String caption = (String)o;
        if(e.target instanceof MenuItem){
                if(caption == "Hello"){
                        DisplayText.setText("Hello");
                }
                if(caption == "World!"){
                        DisplayText.setText("World!");
                }
        }
-->     if(e.target instanceof CheckboxMenuItem){
-->             if(caption == "Check this"){
                        .
                        .
                        .
```

If so, we can toggle the check mark on and off with the CheckboxMenuItem methods getState() and setState(), which work with boolean values:

```
public boolean action (Event e, Object o){
        String caption = (String)o;
        if(e.target instanceof MenuItem){
                if(caption == "Hello"){
                        DisplayText.setText("Hello");
                }
                if(caption == "World!"){
                        DisplayText.setText("World!");
                }
        }
        if(e.target instanceof CheckboxMenuItem){
                if(caption == "Check this"){
  -->                    ((CheckboxMenuItem)e.target).
                        setState(!((CheckboxMenuItem)
                        e.target).getState());
                }
        }
        return true;
    }
}
```

Now our check box menu item works, as shown in Figure 5.5, and the submenu also works, as shown in Figure 5.6. (Note the menu separators in these figures.) Our new menu applet is a success. The code for this applet appears in Listing 5.3.

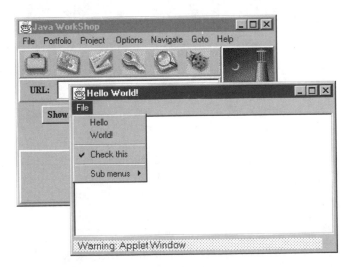

Figure 5.5 Our menu example with a check box item.

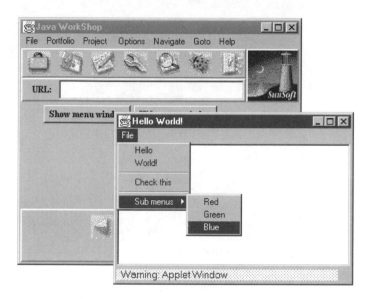

Figure 5.6 Our menu example with a submenu.

Listing 5.3 Menus2.java

```
import java.applet.Applet;
import java.awt.*;

public class Menus2 extends Applet {

        Button button1, button2;
        Frame frameWindow;

        public void init(){
                button1 = new Button("Show menu window");
                add(button1);
                button2 = new Button("Hide menu window");
                add(button2);

                frameWindow = new menuFrame("Hello World!");
                frameWindow.resize(100, 100);
        }
```

```java
        public boolean action (Event e, Object o){
                if(e.target.equals(button1)){
                        frameWindow.show();
                }
                if(e.target.equals(button2)){
                        frameWindow.hide();
                }
                return true;
        }
}

class menuFrame extends Frame {

        Menu Menu1, SubMenu;
        MenuBar Menubar1;
        TextField DisplayText;

        menuFrame(String title){
                super(title);
                DisplayText = new TextField("Hello World!");
                setLayout(new GridLayout(1, 1));
                add(DisplayText);
                Menubar1 = new MenuBar();
                Menu1 = new Menu("File");
                Menu1.add(new MenuItem("Hello"));
                Menu1.add(new MenuItem("World!"));
                Menu1.add(new MenuItem("-"));
                Menu1.add(new CheckboxMenuItem("Check this"));
                Menu1.add(new MenuItem("-"));
                SubMenu = new Menu("Sub menus");
                SubMenu.add(new MenuItem("Red"));
                SubMenu.add(new MenuItem("Green"));
                SubMenu.add(new MenuItem("Blue"));
                Menu1.add(SubMenu);
                Menubar1.add(Menu1);
                setMenuBar(Menubar1);
        }

        public boolean action (Event e, Object o){
                String caption = (String)o;
                if(e.target instanceof MenuItem){
                        if(caption == "Hello"){
                                DisplayText.setText("Hello");
                        }
```

```
                                    if(caption == "World!"){
                                            DisplayText.setText("World!");
                                    }
                            }
                            if(e.target instanceof CheckboxMenuItem){
                                    if(caption == "Check this"){
                                            ((CheckboxMenuItem)e.target).
                                            setState(!((CheckboxMenuItem)
                                            e.target).getState());
                                    }
                            }
                            return true;
                    }
            }
```

We can do more here, as we'll see when we look into dialog boxes.

Dialog Boxes

Java also supports dialog boxes. To add them to our Java arsenal, we might, for example, add an **Open dialog...** menu item to our applet like this:

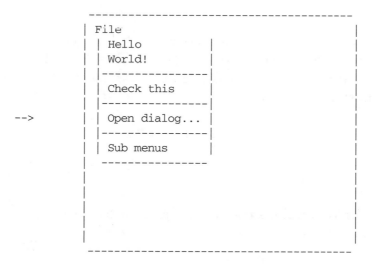

```
        ---------------------------------------
        | File                                |
        | | Hello        |                    |
        | | World!       |                    |
        | |--------------|                    |
        | | Check this   |                    |
        | |--------------|                    |
  -->   | | Open dialog... |                  |
        | |--------------|                    |
        | | Sub menus    |                    |
        |  --------------                     |
        |                                     |
        |                                     |
        |                                     |
        |                                     |
        |                                     |
        ---------------------------------------
```

When the user selects this item, we can open a dialog box with two buttons: **OK** and **Cancel**:

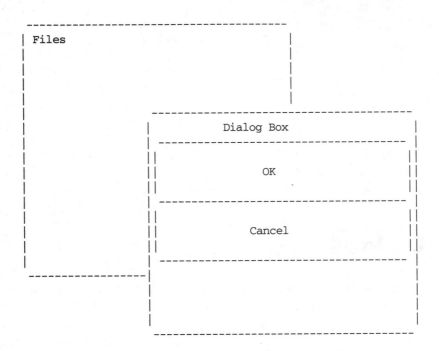

When the user selects one of these buttons, we can hide the dialog box again. Let's start now by creating our dialog box. Java provides the Dialog class for this purpose. We can derive our dialog box class named, for example, OKDialog, from that class this way:

```
class OKDialog extends Dialog {
        .
        .
        .
```

The Dialog class's constructors and methods appear in Table 5.4.

Table 5.4 Dialog Constructors and Methods

```
java.lang.Object
   |
   +----java.awt.Component
            |
            +----java.awt.Container
                     |
                     +----java.awt.Window
                              |
                              +----java.awt.Dialog
```

Dialog(Frame, boolean)	Constructs initially invisible Dialog, modal if boolean is true
Dialog(Frame, String, boolean)	Constructs initially invisible Dialog with title, modal if boolean is true
addNotify()	Creates frame's peer
getTitle()	Returns title of Dialog
isModal()	Returns true if Dialog is modal
isResizable()	Returns true if user can resize Dialog
paramString()	Returns parameter string of Dialog
setResizable(boolean)	Sets resizable flag
setTitle(String)	Sets title of Dialog

Next, we add our two buttons, the **OK** button and the **Cancel** button:

```
class OKDialog extends Dialog {

        Button OKButton, CancelButton;
            .
            .
            .
```

Now we can write our dialog box's constructor:

```
class OKDialog extends Dialog {

        Button OKButton, CancelButton;

-->     OKDialog(Frame hostFrame, String title, boolean dModal){
            .
            .
            .
```

The constructor of our base class Dialog requires that the following items be passed to it: the current Frame window, the title of the dialog box, and a boolean argument that is true if the dialog box should be modal and false otherwise. The first thing to do in our constructor is to pass these arguments back to the Dialog class's constructor by calling super():

```
class OKDialog extends Dialog {

        Button OKButton, CancelButton;

        OKDialog(Frame hostFrame, String title, boolean dModal){
-->             super(hostFrame, title, dModal);
            .
            .
            .
```

Then we just create and add our two new buttons in a grid layout:

```
class OKDialog extends Dialog {

        Button OKButton, CancelButton;

        OKDialog(Frame hostFrame, String title, boolean dModal){
                super(hostFrame, title, dModal);

-->             setLayout(new GridLayout(4, 2));
-->             OKButton = new Button("OK");
-->             add(OKButton);
```

```
    -->                    CancelButton = new Button("Cancel");
    -->                    add(CancelButton);
              }               .
                              .
                              .
```

Now we can make the buttons active by adding an action() method to our new OKDialog class:

```
    class OKDialog extends Dialog {

            Button OKButton, CancelButton;

            OKDialog(Frame hostFrame, String title, boolean dModal){
               .
               .
               .

            }

    -->     public boolean action (Event e, Object o){
                 .
                 .
                 .
```

In the action() method, we check to see if the **OK** button was pushed:

```
            public boolean action (Event e, Object o){
    -->            String caption = (String)o;
    -->            if(e.target instanceof Button){
    -->                if(caption == "OK"){
                          .
                          .
                          .
```

In this case, you can read data the user typed into a textfield or examine the state of check boxes if you have designed your dialog box to include those items. Here, we simply make the dialog box disappear:

```
            public boolean action (Event e, Object o){
                   String caption = (String)o;
                   if(e.target instanceof Button){
```

```
                                        if(caption == "OK"){
         -->                                    hide();
                                        }               .
                                                        .
                                                        .
```

We do the same thing for the **Cancel** button:

```
        public boolean action (Event e, Object o){
                String caption = (String)o;
                if(e.target instanceof Button){
                        if(caption == "OK"){
                                hide();
                        }
         -->            if(caption == "Cancel"){
         -->                    hide();
         -->            }
                }
                return true;
        }
```

We've designed our dialog box. Now we can add it to our Frame window. In that window's class, we will create a dialog box object of our new class OKDialog named dialogBox. First, we have to call our OKDialog's constructor, which takes three arguments: the current Frame window, the title of the dialog box, and a boolean value indicating if this dialog box should be modal. That all sounds easy except for passing the constructor the current Frame window. How do we do that?

The this Pointer

Java supports a pointer named *this*, which points to the current object. We simply pass this pointer to OKDialog's constructor like this:

```
class menuFrame extends Frame {

        Menu Menu1, SubMenu;
        MenuBar Menubar1;
        TextField DisplayText;
```

```
-->      OKDialog dialogBox;

         menuFrame(String title){
                              .
                              .
                              .
                 SubMenu.add(new MenuItem("Red"));
                 SubMenu.add(new MenuItem("Green"));
                 SubMenu.add(new MenuItem("Blue"));
                 Menu1.add(new MenuItem("Open Dialog..."));
                 Menu1.add(SubMenu);
                 Menubar1.add(Menu1);
                 setMenuBar(Menubar1);
-->              dialogBox = new OKDialog(this, "Dialog Box", true);
         }
```

All that remains is to pop it on the screen when asked, which we do when the user selects the **Open Dialog...** menu item:

```
         public boolean action (Event e, Object o){
                 String caption = (String)o;
                 if(e.target instanceof MenuItem){
                         if(caption == "Hello"){
                                 DisplayText.setText("Hello");
                         }
                         if(caption == "World!"){
                                 DisplayText.setText("World!");
                         }
-->                      if(caption == "Open Dialog..."){
-->                              dialogBox.show();
-->                      }
```

When you run the applet and select the **Open Dialog...** menu item, the dialog box, with an **OK** button and a **Cancel** button, appears on the screen, as shown in Figure 5.7. When you click either button, the dialog box disappears. Our applet is a success. The code for this applet appears in Listing 5.4.

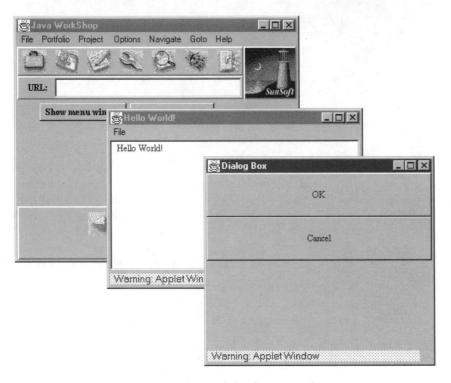

Figure 5.7 Our dialog box example.

Listing 5.4 Dialogs.java

```
import java.applet.Applet;
import java.awt.*;

public class Dialogs extends Applet {

        Button button1, button2;
        menuFrame frameWindow;

        public void init(){
                button1 = new Button("Show menu window");
                add(button1);
                button2 = new Button("Hide menu window");
                add(button2);
```

```
                    frameWindow = new menuFrame("Hello World!");
                    frameWindow.resize(100, 100);
        }

        public boolean action (Event e, Object o){
                if(e.target.equals(button1)){
                        frameWindow.show();
                }
                if(e.target.equals(button2)){
                        frameWindow.hide();
                }
                return true;
        }
}

class menuFrame extends Frame {

        Menu Menu1, SubMenu;
        MenuBar Menubar1;
        TextField DisplayText;
        OKDialog dialogBox;

        menuFrame(String title){
                super(title);
                DisplayText = new TextField("Hello World!");
                setLayout(new GridLayout(1, 1));
                add(DisplayText);
                Menubar1 = new MenuBar();
                Menu1 = new Menu("File");
                Menu1.add(new MenuItem("Hello"));
                Menu1.add(new MenuItem("World!"));
                Menu1.add(new MenuItem("-"));
                Menu1.add(new CheckboxMenuItem("Check this"));
                Menu1.add(new MenuItem("-"));
                SubMenu = new Menu("Sub menus");
                SubMenu.add(new MenuItem("Red"));
                SubMenu.add(new MenuItem("Green"));
                SubMenu.add(new MenuItem("Blue"));
                Menu1.add(new MenuItem("Open Dialog..."));
                Menu1.add(SubMenu);
                Menubar1.add(Menu1);
                setMenuBar(Menubar1);
                dialogBox = new OKDialog(this, "Dialog Box", true);
        }
```

```
public boolean action (Event e, Object o){
        String caption = (String)o;
        if(e.target instanceof MenuItem){
                if(caption == "Hello"){
                        DisplayText.setText("Hello");
                }
                if(caption == "World!"){
                        DisplayText.setText("World!");
                }
                if(caption == "Open Dialog..."){
                        dialogBox.show();
                }

        }
        if(e.target instanceof CheckboxMenuItem){
                if(caption == "Check this"){
                        ((CheckboxMenuItem)e.target).
                        setState(!((CheckboxMenuItem)
                        e.target).getState());
                }
        }
        return true;
    }
}

class OKDialog extends Dialog {

    Button OKButton, CancelButton;

    OKDialog(Frame hostFrame, String title, boolean dModal){

        super(hostFrame, title, dModal);

        setLayout(new GridLayout(4, 2));
        OKButton = new Button("OK");
        add(OKButton);
        CancelButton = new Button("Cancel");
        add(CancelButton);
    }

    public boolean action (Event e, Object o){
        String caption = (String)o;
        if(e.target instanceof Button){
```

```
                        if(caption == "OK"){
                                hide();
                        }
                        if(caption == "Cancel"){
                                hide();
                        }
                }
                return true;
        }
}
```

In this chapter, we introduced pop-up windows that allow us to place windows of information on the screen. There is actually a new layout manager. It acts in much the same way, dividing its display into *cards* that you can create and flash on the screen as needed. We'll look at the last of the Java layout managers next.

CardLayout Manager

Using the CardLayout Manager is like setting up new Frame windows to pop on the screen. Using it, you can create new cards and pop them on the screen as you like. For example, if we set up three cards, each with two textfields, we can pop them on the screen as needed. In particular, we can add text to the textboxes so that we know which card is showing, like this:

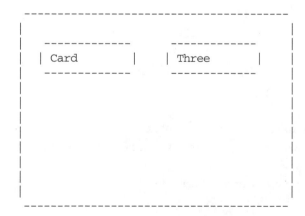

Let's put this to work. As you might expect, cards are actually panels, which means that we can begin by deriving a new class, called, for example, cardPanel, from the Panel class and adding our two textfields:

```
      class cardPanel extends Panel {
-->           TextField textfield1, textfield2;
                      .
                      .
                      .
```

Now we write the new class's constructor:

```
      class cardPanel extends Panel {
              TextField textfield1, textfield2;

-->           cardPanel(){
                      .
                      .
                      .
```

Here, we just add our two textfields, textfield1 and textfield2, and initialize the top textfield to show the word *Card*:

```
      class cardPanel extends Panel {
              TextField textfield1, textfield2;

              cardPanel(){
-->                   textfield1 = new TextField("Card");
-->                   add(textfield1);
-->                   textfield2 = new TextField("");
-->                   add(textfield2);
              }
```

Now that we have our new cardPanel class, we can use it in an applet like this, where we declare three such cards and create a new CardLayout Manager:

```
      import java.applet.Applet;
      import java.awt.*;
```

```
         public class Cards extends Applet {

-->            cardPanel panel1, panel2, panel3;

               public void init(){
-->                    CardLayout cLayout = new CardLayout();
-->                    setLayout(cLayout);
                             .
                             .
                             .
```

The CardLayout Manager's constructors and methods appear in Table 5.5.

Table 5.5 CardLayout Constructors and Methods

```
         java.lang.Object
            |
            +----java.awt.CardLayout
```

CardLayout()	Creates new card layout
CardLayout(int, int)	Creates card layout with specified gaps
addLayoutComponent(String, Component)	Adds specified component with specified name
first(Container)	Flips to first card
last(Container)	Flips to last card
layoutContainer(Container)	Lays out specified container
minimumLayoutSize(Container)	Returns minimum size for container
next(Container)	Flips to next card
preferredLayoutSize(Container)	Returns preferred size for specified container
previous(Container)	Flips to previous card
removeLayoutComponent(Component)	Removes specified component from layout

show(Container, String)　　　　　　　　　Flips to specified component

toString()　　　　　　　　　　　　　　　Returns string representation of
　　　　　　　　　　　　　　　　　　　　CardLayout's values

Now we can create and add our three new cards. We create the first card this way:

```
import java.applet.Applet;
import java.awt.*;

public class Cards extends Applet {

        cardPanel panel1, panel2, panel3;

        public void init(){
                CardLayout cLayout = new CardLayout();
                setLayout(cLayout);
-->             panel1 = new cardPanel();
                        .
                        .
                        .
```

Our idea here is to show which card is which by placing *One*, *Two*, or *Three* in the second textfield this way:

```
-------------------------------------------
|                                         |
|    --------------      -------------     |
|   | Card         |    | Three       |    |
|    --------------      -------------     |
|                                         |
|                                         |
|                                         |
|                                         |
|                                         |
|                                         |
|                                         |
 -----------------------------------------
```

In other words, we should initialize each card as we create it, placing text in the second textbox, which we can refer to as panel1.textfield2, to match the card number:

```
import java.applet.Applet;
import java.awt.*;

public class Cards extends Applet {

        cardPanel panel1, panel2, panel3;

        public void init(){
                CardLayout cLayout = new CardLayout();
                setLayout(cLayout);
                panel1 = new cardPanel();
-->             panel1.textfield2.setText("One");
                    .
                    .
                    .
```

And we do the same for the other cards:

```
import java.applet.Applet;
import java.awt.*;

public class Cards extends Applet {

        cardPanel panel1, panel2, panel3;

        public void init(){
                CardLayout cLayout = new CardLayout();
                setLayout(cLayout);
                panel1 = new cardPanel();
                panel1.textfield2.setText("One");
-->             panel2 = new cardPanel();
-->             panel2.textfield2.setText("Two");
-->             panel3 = new cardPanel();
-->             panel3.textfield2.setText("Three");
                    .
                    .
                    .
```

We can now add these new cards to the CardLayout Manager with the add()
method. We indicate their order with the arguments "first", "second", and
"third" this way:

```
import java.applet.Applet;
import java.awt.*;

public class Cards extends Applet {

        cardPanel panel1, panel2, panel3;

        public void init(){
                CardLayout cLayout = new CardLayout();
                setLayout(cLayout);
                panel1 = new cardPanel();
                panel1.textfield2.setText("One");
                panel2 = new cardPanel();
                panel2.textfield2.setText("Two");
                panel3 = new cardPanel();
                panel3.textfield2.setText("Three");
-->             add("first", panel1);
-->             add("second", panel2);
-->             add("third", panel3);
                          .
                          .
                          .
```

Now our cards are set up and installed. To show a card, you simply use the
CardLayout Manager's show() method this way:

```
import java.applet.Applet;
import java.awt.*;

public class Cards extends Applet {

        cardPanel panel1, panel2, panel3;

        public void init(){
                CardLayout cLayout = new CardLayout();
                setLayout(cLayout);
```

```
                         panel1 = new cardPanel();
                         panel1.textfield2.setText("One");
                         panel2 = new cardPanel();
                         panel2.textfield2.setText("Two");
                         panel3 = new cardPanel();
                         panel3.textfield2.setText("Three");
                         add("first", panel1);
                         add("second", panel2);
                         add("third", panel3);
    -->                  cLayout.show(this, "third");
             }


         }
```

In this case, we display the third card in the applet, as shown in Figure 5.8. You can flip through the cards using the CardLayout Manager's next() and previous() methods in code if you like and use the first() and last() methods to skip to the first and last cards, respectively. Using these methods and adding buttons marked **First**, **Last**, **Next**, and **Previous**, you can create a cardfile applet. Our applet is a success. The code for this applet appears in Listing 5.5.

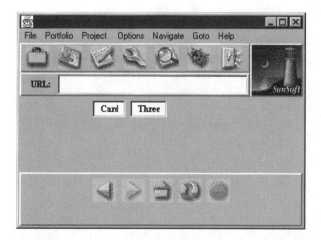

Figure 5.8 Our CardLayout Manager example.

Listing 5.5 Cards.java

```java
import java.applet.Applet;
import java.awt.*;

public class Cards extends Applet {

        cardPanel panel1, panel2, panel3;

        public void init(){
                CardLayout cLayout = new CardLayout();
                setLayout(cLayout);
                panel1 = new cardPanel();
                panel1.textfield2.setText("One");
                panel2 = new cardPanel();
                panel2.textfield2.setText("Two");
                panel3 = new cardPanel();
                panel3.textfield2.setText("Three");
                add("first", panel1);
                add("second", panel2);
                add("third", panel3);
                cLayout.show(this, "third");
        }

}

class cardPanel extends Panel {
        TextField textfield1, textfield2;

        cardPanel(){
                textfield1 = new TextField("Card");
                add(textfield1);
                textfield2 = new TextField("");
                add(textfield2);
        }
}
```

We've come far in this chapter, seeing how to create and use pop-up windows, menus, and dialog boxes, as well as how to use the CardLayout Manager. In the next chapter, we'll continue our tour by starting to examine how to work with graphics.

CHAPTER SIX

DRAWING LINES, CIRCLES, RECTANGLES, AND MORE

Welcome to the exciting world of Java graphics! In this chapter, we'll examine the fundamentals of drawing graphics, including lines, rectangles, and ovals. In the next chapter, we'll explore using image files, imagemaps, fonts, and more. In Chapter 8, we'll explore graphics animation in detail. Let's start with a small applet that illustrates the heart of graphics programming in Java.

Welcome to Graphics: The paint() Method

In our first graphics example, we'll put together a small applet that draws directly on the applet's background to see how graphics programming works in Java. This is the first time we've directly drawn in our applets. Until now, we've let the controls handle that. For this first example, we'll simply place the "Hello World!" text in our applet directly (with no textfields, no textareas):

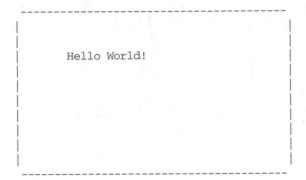

How do we do that? A paint *event* is built into Java applets. It occurs when the applet needs to be (re)drawn (i.e., when it first appears or when its appearance needs to be updated). We can override this event ourselves and place code in it to produce graphics, using the member functions of the Java Graphics class. Let's see how this works.

We begin our example by including the Java Graphics class:

```
import java.applet.Applet;
import java.awt.Graphics;        <--
            .
            .
            .
```

Next, we set up our applet's public class and override the paint() method this way:

```
import java.applet.Applet;
import java.awt.Graphics;

public class Hello extends java.applet.Applet {

    --> public void paint (Graphics g) {
          .
          .
          .
```

This function will be called when the applet is (re)drawn. The Graphics object passed to us (which we call g) is full of useful methods for drawing graphics, as detailed in Table 6.1.

Table 6.1 Graphics Constructors and Methods

```
        java.lang.Object
           |
        +----java.awt.Graphics
```

Graphics()	Constructs new Graphics Object
clearRect(int, int, int, int)	Clears specified rectangle
clipRect(int, int, int, int)	Clips to this rectangle
copyArea(int, int, int, int, int, int)	Copies area of screen
create()	Creates new Graphics Object (copy of original)
create(int, int, int, int)	Creates new Graphics Object with specified parameters
dispose()	Disposes of graphics context
draw3DRect(int, int, int, int, boolean)	Draws 3-D rectangle
drawArc(int, int, int, int, int, int)	Draws arc bounded by specified rectangle
drawBytes(byte[], int, int, int, int)	Draws specified bytes using current color
drawChars(char[], int, int, int, int)	Draws specified characters using current font and color

drawImage(Image, int, int, ImageObserver)	Draws specified image
drawImage(Image, int, int, int, int, ImageObserver)	Draws specified image inside specified rectangle
drawImage(Image, int, int, Color, ImageObserver)	Draws specified image at specified (x, y)
drawImage (Image, int, int, int, int, Color, ImageObserver)	Draws specified image inside specified rectangle, with indicated background color
drawLine(int, int, int, int)	Draws a line between the (x1, y1) and (x2, y2)
drawOval(int, int, int, int)	Draws oval inside the specified rectangle
drawPolygon(int[], int[], int)	Draws a polygon defined by array of x points and y points
drawPolygon(Polygon)	Draws polygon defined by specified points
drawRect(int, int, int, int)	Draws outline of specified rectangle
drawRoundRect(int, int, int, int, int, int)	Draws outlined rounded rectangle
drawString(String, int, int)	Draws specified string
fill3DRect(int, int, int, int, boolean)	Paints highlighted 3-D rectangle
fillArc(int, int, int, int, int, int)	Fills arc using current color
fillOval(int, int, int, int)	Fills oval inside specified rectangle with the current color
fillPolygon(int[], int[], int)	Fills a polygon with current color
fillPolygon(Polygon)	Fills specified polygon with current color
fillRect(int, int, int, int)	Fills specified rectangle with current color
fillRoundRect(int, int, int, int, int, int)	Draws rounded rectangle filled with current color

finalize()	Disposes of graphics context when it is not referenced
getClipRect()	Returns bounding rectangle of current clipping area
getColor()	Returns current color
getFont()	Returns current font
getFontMetrics()	Returns current font metrics
getFontMetrics(Font)	Gets current font metrics for specified font
setColor(Color)	Sets current color to specified color
setFont(Font)	Sets font for all text operations
setPaintMode()	Sets paint mode to overwrite destination with current color
setXORMode(Color)	Sets paint mode to XOR
toString()	Returns string representing Graphic's value
translate(int, int)	Translates specified parameters into origin of this graphics context

We use the Graphic class drawString() method to put our message on the screen; we pass the string we want to display and the location ((x, y) in pixels) at which we want the message to appear like this:

```java
import java.applet.Applet;
import java.awt.Graphics;

public class Hello extends java.applet.Applet {
        public void paint (Graphics g) {
                g.drawString("Hello world!", 40, 40);
        }
}
```

Applets are set up this way in terms of pixel coordinates, with (0, 0) set to the upper left:

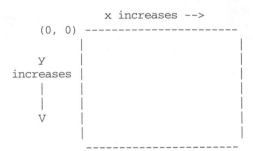

```
                        x increases -->
    (0, 0) ----------------------
            |                    |
    y       |                    |
increases   |                    |
    |       |                    |
    |       |                    |
    V       |                    |
            |                    |
            ----------------------
```

The result appears in Figure 6.1. As you can see, the message appears directly on the background of the applet, without any text controls. This is how we display our graphics in the paint() method. We don't have to wait for Java to call this method either; we can force it to call paint() and display our graphics with the repaint() method, which we can call at any time.

Figure 6.1 Our first graphics applet.

Let's go on now and develop a full-fledged graphics applet—a mouse-driven paint applet. The user will be able to drawn rectangles, ovals, and lines or just draw freehand using the mouse. Writing this applet will provide us with a good background in Java graphics. However, to put it together, we need to learn how to use the mouse directly (i.e., no longer relying on controls to handle the mouse for us). After we gain that expertise, we can put our paint applet together, so let's take a look at handling mouse events.

Using the Mouse

To become comfortable with the mouse, we'll write a short applet that displays the mouse's current status. It will tell us whether the mouse button is down or up, what its location is, and whether it's being dragged:

```
 ------------------------------------------
|                                          |
|      ------------------------------      |
|     |The left mouse button is down |     |
|      ------------------------------      |
|                                          |
|                                          |
|                                          |
|                                          |
|                                          |
|                                          |
|                                          |
 ------------------------------------------
```

Let's see how this works. We begin by setting up a textfield named MouseMsg so that we can easily display the status of the mouse:

```
        import java.applet.Applet;
        import java.awt.*;

        public class Mouser extends Applet {

-->             TextField MouseMsg;

                public void init(){
-->                     MouseMsg = new TextField(40);
-->                     add(MouseMsg);
                }           .
                            .
                            .
                            .
```

Let's handle the case in which the user presses the mouse button first.

Mouse Down Events

Now we can intercept mouse events with individual functions like MouseDown() to capture mouse down events where the user has pressed a mouse button. When we are passed an Event object and the location ((x,y) in pixels) at which the mouse went down (these are the same parameters passed to all mouse methods), we override that function like this:

```
public boolean mouseDown(Event e, int x, int y){
                .
                .
                .
```

The Event object e tells us a great deal about the mouse event. For example, if e.modifiers is equal to 0, the left mouse button was pressed, and we can display that in the MouseMsg textfield:

```
         public boolean mouseDown(Event e, int x, int y){
-->          if(e.modifiers == 0){
-->              MouseMsg.setText("The left mouse button is down");
-->          }        .
                      .
                      .
```

Otherwise, we need to inform the user that the right mouse button went down (you must modify this code for systems that use a one-button mouse):

```
         public boolean mouseDown(Event e, int x, int y){
             if(e.modifiers == 0){
                 MouseMsg.setText("The left mouse button is down");
             }
-->          else{
-->              MouseMsg.setText("The right mouse button is down");
-->          }        .
                      .
                      .
```

At the end of the function, we return a value of true to indicate that we have handled this event:

```
public boolean mouseDown(Event e, int x, int y){
        if(e.modifiers == 0){
            MouseMsg.setText("The left mouse button is down");
        }
        else{
            MouseMsg.setText("The right mouse button is down");
        }
-->     return true;
    }
```

That's all there is to it for mouse down events. Let's look at the mouse drag event next.

Mouse Drag Events

The mouse drag event occurs when the user holds a mouse button down and moves the mouse. You intercept that event by overriding the mouseDrag() method:

```
public boolean mouseDrag(Event e, int x, int y){
        .
        .
        .
```

We can indicate that this event occurred this way in the textfield MouseMsg:

```
        public boolean mouseDrag(Event e, int x, int y){
-->         MouseMsg.setText("The mouse button is dragged");
            return true;
        }
```

Notice also that we returned a value of true at the end of the function, as we will with all mouse event handling functions, to indicate that we handled the event. Let's look at the mouse up event next.

Mouse Up Events

You use the mouseUp() method to override mouse up events, which occur when the user releases the mouse button. We can indicate which button went up in much the same way as we indicated which button went down in the mouse down event:

```
public boolean mouseUp(Event e, int x, int y){
        if(e.modifiers == 0){
            MouseMsg.setText("The left mouse button is up");
        }
        else{
            MouseMsg.setText("The right mouse button is up");
        }
        return true;
}
```

That's all there is to the mouse up event. Let's look into mouse move events next.

Mouse Move Events

Mouse move events occur when the user simply drags the mouse (unlike mouse drag events, which occur only when the user moves the mouse with the mouse button down). We handle those events in the mouseMove() method this way:

```
public boolean mouseMove(Event e, int x, int y){
        .
        .
        .
```

We can display the new position of the mouse after the mouse move event this way in mouseMove():

```
         public boolean mouseMove(Event e, int x, int y){
-->          MouseMsg.setText("Mouse X: " + x + " Y: " + y);
-->          return true;
         }
```

We simply report the (x, y) value passed to us and return true at the end of the function as usual.

It is simple to handle mouse events. We just set up a matching mouse method like mouseDown(). Now we need to look at two more mouse event methods—mouseEnter() and mouseExit().

Mouse Enter Events

Mouse enter events occur when the mouse enters our applet's space in the Web page. We intercept them in the mouseEnter() method and indicate that such an event occurred like this:

```
public boolean mouseEnter(Event e, int x, int y){
        MouseMsg.setText("The mouse button is in");
        return true;
}
```

The last mouse method is mouseExit(), which we'll turn to now.

Mouse Exit Events

Mouse exit events occur when the mouse leaves our applet's space in the Web page. We can indicate that it has happened in the mouseExit() method this way:

```
public boolean mouseExit(Event e, int x, int y){
        MouseMsg.setText("The mouse button is out");
        return true;
}
```

Now we can examine what happens with the mouse as in Figure 6.2, where we indicate the mouse's current position. The code for this applet appears in Listing 6.1.

Figure 6.2 We explore mouse events.

Listing 6.1 Mouser.java

```
import java.applet.Applet;
import java.awt.*;

public class Mouser extends Applet {

        TextField MouseMsg;

        public void init(){
                MouseMsg = new TextField(40);
                add(MouseMsg);
        }

        public boolean mouseDown(Event e, int x, int y){
                if(e.modifiers == 0){
                    MouseMsg.setText("The left mouse button is down");
                }
                else{
                    MouseMsg.setText("The right mouse button is down");
                }
                return true;
        }

        public boolean mouseDrag(Event e, int x, int y){
```

```
                    MouseMsg.setText("The mouse button is dragged");
                    return true;
              }

       public boolean mouseUp(Event e, int x, int y){
              if(e.modifiers == 0){
                  MouseMsg.setText("The left mouse button is up");
              }
              else{
                  MouseMsg.setText("The right mouse button is up");
              }
              return true;
       }

       public boolean mouseMove(Event e, int x, int y){
              MouseMsg.setText("Mouse X: " + x + " Y: " + y);
              return true;
       }

       public boolean mouseEnter(Event e, int x, int y){
              MouseMsg.setText("The mouse button is in");
              return true;
       }

       public boolean mouseExit(Event e, int x, int y){
              MouseMsg.setText("The mouse button is out");
              return true;
       }
}
```

At this point, we have enough expertise with the mouse to write our mouse-driven paint applet. This applet allows us to get a good overview of using and creating graphics in Java.

Painter: A Mouse-Driven Paint Applet

Our paint applet, called Painter, will let the user draw lines, rectangles, ovals, 3-D rectangles, and rounded rectangles and draw freehand by just moving the mouse. The user needs to select a button only once, at the top of our applet like this:

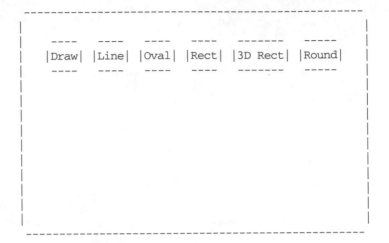

For example, if the user selects the **Rectangle** drawing tool, they could click the mouse at point A, drag it to point B, and then release the mouse. At that point, we'll draw the rectangle they outlined:

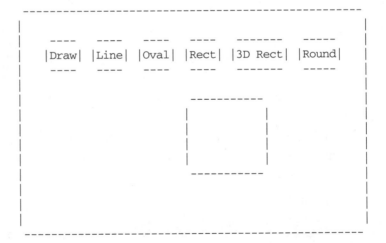

We begin by including the Java classes we'll need, including the Graphics class and the Math class, which we'll need for some math manipulations later:

```
import java.awt.Graphics;
import java.awt.*;
```

```
        import java.lang.Math;
        import java.applet.Applet;

    public class Painter extends Applet {
                 .
                 .
                 .
```

In addition, we set up our size buttons by declaring them this way:

```
        import java.awt.Graphics;
        import java.awt.*;
        import java.lang.Math;
        import java.applet.Applet;

    public class Painter extends Applet {

-->     Button buttonDraw, buttonLine, buttonOval, buttonRect, button3DRect;
-->     Button buttonRounded;
                 .
                 .
                 .
```

Next, we create and add the buttons, giving them the correct captions in the init() method:

```
        import java.awt.Graphics;
        import java.awt.*;
        import java.lang.Math;
        import java.applet.Applet;

    public class Painter extends Applet {

    Button buttonDraw, buttonLine, buttonOval, buttonRect, button3DRect;
    Button buttonRounded;

    public void init() {

-->         buttonDraw = new Button("Draw");
-->         buttonLine = new Button("Line");
-->         buttonOval = new Button("Oval");
-->         buttonRect = new Button("Rect");
```

```
-->        button3DRect = new Button("3D Rect");
-->        buttonRounded = new Button("Round");


-->        add(buttonDraw);
-->        add(buttonLine);
-->        add(buttonOval);
-->        add(buttonRect);
-->        add(button3DRect);
-->        add(buttonRounded);
     }
```

We need some way of determining which button the user clicked so we'll know what to draw—a line, an oval, or whatever. They can draw only one type of figure at a time, so we might add a set of boolean flags that indicate what the current drawing tool is:

```
import java.awt.Graphics;
import java.awt.*;
import java.lang.Math;
import java.applet.Applet;

public class Painter extends Applet {

    Button buttonDraw, buttonLine, buttonOval, buttonRect, button3DRect;
    Button buttonRounded;

-->  boolean bDrawFlag = false;
-->  boolean bLineFlag = false;
-->  boolean bOvalFlag = false;
-->  boolean bRectFlag = false;
-->  boolean b3DRectFlag = false;
-->  boolean bRoundedFlag = false;
            .
            .
            .
```

In addition, we can make the buttons active by setting the drawing flags correctly in an action() method:

```
public boolean action(Event e, Object o){
            .
            .
            .
```

For example, when the user clicks the **Draw** tool for freehand drawing, we can toggle that tool on or off. At the same time, we can turn off all the other drawing tools (by setting their flags to false) since the user can draw only one type of figure at a time:

```
    public boolean action(Event e, Object o){
-->         if(e.target.equals(buttonDraw)){
-->             bDrawFlag = !bDrawFlag;
-->             bLineFlag = false;
-->             bOvalFlag = false;
-->             bRectFlag = false;
-->             b3DRectFlag = false;
-->             bRoundedFlag = false;
-->         }            .
                         .
                         .
```

We make all the buttons active in that way, setting the matching tool flags:

```
    public boolean action(Event e, Object o){
-->         if(e.target.equals(buttonDraw)){
                bDrawFlag = !bDrawFlag;
                bLineFlag = false;
                bOvalFlag = false;
                bRectFlag - false;
                b3DRectFlag - false;
                bRoundedFlag = false;
            }
-->         if(e.target.equals(buttonLine)){
                bLineFlag = !bLineFlag;
                bDrawFlag = false;
                bOvalFlag = false;
                bRectFlag = false;
                b3DRectFlag = false;
                bRoundedFlag = false;
            }
-->         if(e.target.equals(buttonOval)){
                bOvalFlag = !bOvalFlag;
                bLineFlag = false;
                bDrawFlag = false;
                bRectFlag = false;
                b3DRectFlag = false;
                bRoundedFlag = false;
            }
```

```
-->        if(e.target.equals(buttonRect)){
                   bRectFlag = !bRectFlag;
                   bLineFlag = false;
                   bOvalFlag = false;
                   bDrawFlag = false;
                   b3DRectFlag = false;
                   bRoundedFlag = false;
           }
-->        if(e.target.equals(button3DRect)){
                   b3DRectFlag = !b3DRectFlag;
                   bLineFlag = false;
                   bOvalFlag = false;
                   bRectFlag = false;
                   bDrawFlag = false;
                   bRoundedFlag = false;
           }
-->        if(e.target.equals(buttonRounded)){
                   bRoundedFlag = !bRoundedFlag;
                   bLineFlag = false;
                   bOvalFlag = false;
                   bRectFlag = false;
                   b3DRectFlag = false;
                   bDrawFlag = false;
           }
           return true;
    }
```

Now we have six active flags: bDrawFlag, bLineFlag, bOvalFlag, bRectFlag, b3DRectFlag, and bRoundedFlag. When it is time to draw a graphics figure, these flags will tell us what figure to draw (and only one will be true at a time).

Now that we know what to draw, we must figure out *where* the user wants us to draw it. We do that with the mouse. For example, if we're supposed to draw a line, the user presses the mouse button at one point, which we can call the *Anchor point*:

```
Anchor Point x
```

Then the user moves the mouse to a new location and release the mouse button, at which point we are supposed to draw the line from the anchor point to the point we are at now, the *DrawTo point*:

```
Anchor Point x--------------------x DrawTo Point
```

For that reason, we should keep track of when the mouse button is up or down, and we should also store the Anchor point and the DrawTo point. That information, together with the drawing flags like bLineFlag, will tell us all we need to know to draw in our applet.

To determine the mouse's state, we set up a mouseDown() event handler; that is, the user presses the mouse button at the point where the graphics figure should start. In this function, we can set flags to match the mouse's pressed state and record the location of the Anchor point. To record the mouse's state, we add two new boolean flags to our applet—bMouseDownFlag (true if the mouse is down) and bMouseUpFlag (true if the mouse is up):

```
public class Painter extends Applet {

        Button buttonDraw, buttonLine, buttonOval, buttonRect, button3DRect;
        Button buttonRounded;

  -->   boolean bMouseDownFlag = false;
  -->   boolean bMouseUpFlag = false;
        boolean bDrawFlag = false;
        boolean bLineFlag = false;
          .
          .
          .
```

When we draw our graphics in the paint() method, we first check these mouse flags to make sure the user released the mouse. In the mouseDown function(), we set the bMouseDownFlag to true:

```
        public boolean mouseDown(Event e, int x, int y){
                bMouseDownFlag = true;
                  .
                  .
                  .
```

And we set the bMouseUpFlag flag to false:

```
     public boolean mouseDown(Event e, int x, int y){
            bMouseDownFlag = true;
-->         bMouseUpFlag = false;
                   .
                   .
                   .
```

In addition, the first point at which the mouse goes down marks one end of our graphics figure. We record that point, the Anchor point, like this:

```
     public boolean mouseDown(Event e, int x, int y){
            bMouseDownFlag = true;
            bMouseUpFlag = false;
-->         ptAnchor = new Point(x, y);
            return true;
     }
```

Here we use the Java Point class, which has two members x and y. We declare the two points we'll need, ptAnchor and ptDrawTo now:

```
     public class Painter extends Applet {

         Button buttonDraw, buttonLine, buttonOval, buttonRect, button3DRect;
         Button buttonRounded;

-->      Point ptAnchor, ptDrawTo;

         boolean bMouseDownFlag = false;
         boolean bMouseUpFlag = false;
         boolean bDrawFlag = false;
         boolean bLineFlag = false;
                .
                .
                .
```

Now when we need the x coordinate of the Anchor point, we can get it like this: ptAnchor.x. The y coordinate is ptAnchor.y.

Next, we handle the mouse up event. Here, we first set the mouse flags, indicating that the mouse is up:

```
public boolean mouseUp(Event e, int x, int y){
        bMouseDownFlag = false;
        bMouseUpFlag = true;
            .
            .
            .
```

Next, we want to record the location at which the mouse went up, calling that the DrawTo point. We'll draw our graphics between these two points, which looks like this for a line:

```
Anchor Point x--------------------x DrawTo Point
   (Mouse down point)           (Mouse up point)
```

Our drawing is bounded by ptAnchor and ptDrawTo. To make things simpler, we can set up these two points so that we make sure that the Anchor point is the top left of the figure we are to draw and the DrawTo point is the bottom right of the figure, which looks like this for a rectangle:

```
Anchor Point x--------------------
             |                   |
             |                   |
             |                   |
             |                   |
             |_____x DrawTo Point
```

To set up the ptAnchor and ptDrawTo points this way, we use the Math class min() method, which returns the minimum of two integers, and the max() method, which returns the maximum of two integers:

```
     public boolean mouseUp(Event e, int x, int y){
             bMouseDownFlag = false;
             bMouseUpFlag = true;

-->          ptDrawTo = new Point(Math.max(x, ptAnchor.x),
                 Math.max(y, ptAnchor.y));
```

```
-->              ptAnchor = new Point(Math.min(x, ptAnchor.x),
                    Math.min(y, ptAnchor.y));
                              .
                              .
                              .
```

Now we are ready to draw our graphics figure, and we do so by calling the repaint() function. This in turn causes the applet to call paint() (which is where we'll place the actual calls to the Graphics object's methods):

```
public boolean mouseUp(Event e, int x, int y){
        bMouseDownFlag = false;
        bMouseUpFlag = true;

        ptDrawTo = new Point(Math.max(x, ptAnchor.x),
            Math.max(y, ptAnchor.y));
        ptAnchor = new Point(Math.min(x, ptAnchor.x),
            Math.min(y, ptAnchor.y));
-->     repaint();
        return true;
    }
```

At last we are ready. We know where we should draw by examining the two points, ptAnchor and ptDrawTo, and we know what we should draw by checking to see which flag is true of these: bLineFlag, bOvalFlag, bRectFlag, b3DRectFlag, bRoundedFlag, or bDrawFlag. All that remains now is to draw the figure. Let's start with the process of drawing lines in the paint() method.

Drawing Lines

We start our paint() method like this:

```
public void paint (Graphics g) {
                  .
                  .
                  .
```

Here, we are passed a Graphics object that will be the foundation of our drawing activities. For example, to draw a line, we use the Graphics class drawLine() method. First, we check to make sure that we are really supposed to draw a line by checking bLineFlag and making sure that the mouse button went up (i.e., we are supposed to draw our graphics figure when the user releases the mouse button) and by checking the bMouseUp flag like this:

```
        public void paint (Graphics g) {

-->             if(bLineFlag && bMouseUpFlag){
                        .
                        .
                        .
```

Both bLineFlag and bMouseUp have to be true for us to proceed. If we are supposed to draw a line, it goes from the Anchor point to the DrawTo point:

```
        Anchor Point x--------------------x DrawTo Point
```

To draw that line, we just pass these coordinates to drawLine() like this:

```
        public void paint (Graphics g) {

                if(bLineFlag && bMouseUpFlag){
-->                     g.drawLine(ptAnchor.x, ptAnchor.y, ptDrawTo.x,
                            ptDrawTo.y);
                }       .
                        .
                        .
```

Now the user can draw lines using our applet, as shown in Figure 6.3. Let's look into the process of drawing ovals and circles next.

Figure 6.3 Drawing lines with our Painter applet.

Drawing Ovals and Circles

To draw ovals and circles, we first make sure that we are really supposed to draw these figures by checking the bOvalFlag flag (i.e., the user has selected the **Oval** drawing tool) and the bMouseUpFlag to make sure the mouse button went up:

```
        public void paint (Graphics g) {

               if(bLineFlag && bMouseUpFlag){
                      g.drawLine(ptAnchor.x, ptAnchor.y, ptDrawTo.x,
                          ptDrawTo.y);
               }
-->            if(bOvalFlag && bMouseUpFlag){
                               .
                               .
                               .
```

If so, we can draw the oval, using the two points ptAnchor and ptDrawTo. We actually draw the oval with the Graphics class drawOval() method, where we pass the upper left of the oval to this method, as well as the width and height we want our oval to have. (If the width is the same as the height, the result will be a circle.) To find the width, we find the difference of ptAnchor.x and ptDrawTo.x and store it in an integer named, for example, drawWidth. To find the height, we find the difference of ptAnchor.y and ptDrawTo.y and store that in, for example, an integer named drawHeight like this:

```
       public void paint (Graphics g) {
-->            int drawWidth, drawHeight;

               if(bLineFlag && bMouseUpFlag){
                      g.drawLine(ptAnchor.x, ptAnchor.y, ptDrawTo.x,
                          ptDrawTo.y);
               }
               if(bOvalFlag && bMouseUpFlag){
-->                   drawWidth = ptDrawTo.x - ptAnchor.x;
-->                   drawHeight = ptDrawTo.y - ptAnchor.y;
                          .
                          .
                          .
```

Recall that we have intentionally ordered our points so that ptDrawTo.x is larger than ptAnchor.x and ptDrawTo.y is larger than ptAnchor.y, so both our figure's width and height will be positive.

Next, we call drawOval(), passing it the location of the upper left of the box that bounds our oval, as well as that box's width and height:

```
       public void paint (Graphics g) {
               int drawWidth, drawHeight;

               if(bLineFlag && bMouseUpFlag){
                      g.drawLine(ptAnchor.x, ptAnchor.y, ptDrawTo.x,
                          ptDrawTo.y);
               }
               if(bOvalFlag && bMouseUpFlag){
                      drawWidth = ptDrawTo.x - ptAnchor.x;
```

```
             drawHeight = ptDrawTo.y - ptAnchor.y;
   -->       g.drawOval(ptAnchor.x, ptAnchor.y, drawWidth,
                 drawHeight);
   }                           .
                               .
                               .
```

Now we can draw ovals, as we see in Figure 6.4.

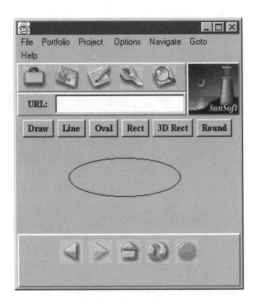

Figure 6.4 Our Painter applet draws ovals.

If the width of the oval was the same as the height, we would have drawn a circle. (If you want to draw circles, you must constrain the width to equal the height.) Let's look into drawing rectangles next.

Drawing Rectangles

We can draw rectangles with the Graphics class's drawRect() method. First, we make sure that we are supposed to draw a rectangle as we have done before, by checking the mouse up flag and the correct drawing tool's flag:

```
        public void paint (Graphics g) {
                int drawWidth, drawHeight;
                        .
                        .
                        .
-->             if(bRectFlag && bMouseUpFlag){
                        .
                        .
                        .
```

Then we use the Graphics class's drawRect() method, passing it the upper left point of the rectangle, as well as the rectangle's width and height (just as we did for ovals):

```
        public void paint (Graphics g) {
                int drawWidth, drawHeight;
                        .
                        .
                        .
                if(bRectFlag && bMouseUpFlag){
-->                     drawWidth = ptDrawTo.x - ptAnchor.x;
-->                     drawHeight = ptDrawTo.y - ptAnchor.y;
-->                     g.drawRect(ptAnchor.x, ptAnchor.y, drawWidth,
-->                             drawHeight);
                }               .
                                .
                                .
```

Now the user can draw rectangles with our Painter applet as shown in Figure 6.5.

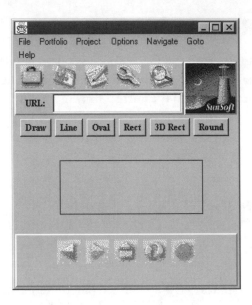

Figure 6.5 Drawing rectangles with the Painter applet.

However, there are actually three types of rectangles we can draw: normal rectangles as we have just drawn, 3-D rectangles, and rounded rectangles.

Drawing 3-D Rectangles

Let's draw 3-D rectangles, where the rectangle is supposed to appear raised from the page or lowered into it. We first check to make sure that the user clicked the **3D Rect** button and that the mouse button went up:

```
        public void paint (Graphics g) {
              int drawWidth, drawHeight;
                  .
                  .
                  .
-->           if(b3DRectFlag && bMouseUpFlag){
                  .
                  .
                  .
```

If so, then we can use the Graphics class method draw3DRect(), just as we did for drawRect(). However, we must add one more argument: a boolean argument set to true if you want the rectangle to appear raised from the page or false if you want it to appear lowered into it. Here we select a raised rectangle:

```
public void paint (Graphics g) {
        int drawWidth, drawHeight;
                .
                .
                .
        if(b3DRectFlag && bMouseUpFlag){
-->             drawWidth = ptDrawTo.x - ptAnchor.x;
-->             drawHeight = ptDrawTo.y - ptAnchor.y;
-->             g.draw3DRect(ptAnchor.x, ptAnchor.y, drawWidth,
                    drawHeight, true);
        }
                    .
                    .
                    .
```

Although this is the correct call, with the current Java Graphics class, the 3-D rectangle is indistinguishable from the standard rectangle. All that appears is the same rectangle as in Figure 6.5. However, this will probably change in the future. At this point, the best thing to do if you want 3-D rectangles is to watch future Java releases. Rounded rectangles do, however, function properly, so let's turn to drawing them.

Drawing Rounded Rectangles

A rounded rectangle is the same as a standard rectangle, except that it has rounded corners. We specify the normal arguments for a rectangle—the upper-left-hand corner and the width and height—but we also add two new parameters. They indicate how rounded the corners should be and give the width and height of a box in which the rounded part of the rectangle should fit. That is, if you specify these two parameters as 10 and 10, you'll get rounded corners where the rounded part has an x radius of 10 pixels and a y radius of 10 pixels. If you select 20 and 10, the rounded corners will be twice as wide as they are tall. We'll stick with 10 and 10 here. As before, we first check to make sure that we are supposed to be drawing a rounded rectangle and, if so, calculate the rectangle's width and height:

```
        public void paint (Graphics g) {
                int drawWidth, drawHeight;
                        .
                        .
                        .
-->             if(bRoundedFlag && bMouseUpFlag){
-->                     drawWidth = ptDrawTo.x - ptAnchor.x;
-->                     drawHeight = ptDrawTo.y - ptAnchor.y;
                }               .
                                .
                                .
```

To draw the rectangle, we use the Graphics class method drawRoundRect(), which looks like this (including our rounded corner specification of 10 pixels by 10 pixels):

```
        public void paint (Graphics g) {
                int drawWidth, drawHeight;
                        .
                        .
                        .
                if(bRoundedFlag && bMouseUpFlag){
                        drawWidth = ptDrawTo.x - ptAnchor.x;
                        drawHeight = ptDrawTo.y - ptAnchor.y;
-->                     g.drawRoundRect(ptAnchor.x, ptAnchor.y, drawWidth,
                                drawHeight, 10, 10);
                }               .
                                .
                                .
```

The result appears in Figure 6.6, complete with a rounded rectangle. Our Painter applet is a success so far.

Figure 6.6 Drawing rounded rectangles with the Painter applet.

The user can draw a variety of graphics figure now, from lines to rounded rectangles. Now we need to enable the **Freehand** drawing tool. Let's look into that next.

Drawing Freehand

Drawing freehand is a little different from the other drawing techniques we've seen, because we'll need to store lots of points as the mouse moves, not just two (i.e., where the mouse went up and down). After we have stored these points, we can display the mouse's path by connecting the points with lines. You might think we can just draw dots each time the mouse is moved to create a mouse trail as the mouse is dragged, but because there are only a certain number of mouse events a second, that would leave a trail of unconnected dots on the screen. Instead, we must connect the dots with lines (which are so short that they will appear to be continuous on the screen). We will also have to draw as the mouse moves, so we'll use the mouseDrag function.

First, we set aside the space we'll need for a hundred points in an array named pts[] of Point objects:

```
public class Painter extends Applet {

        Button buttonDraw, buttonLine, buttonOval, buttonRect, button3DRect;
        Button buttonRounded;

-->     Point pts[] = new Point[100];
        Point ptAnchor, ptDrawTo;
           .
           .
           .
```

We also need an index to keep track of the current location in the pts[] array so that we can add new points as the mouse moves. Let's call the pts[] array index ptindex and start it at 0:

```
public class Painter extends Applet {

        Button buttonDraw, buttonLine, buttonOval, buttonRect, button3DRect;
        Button buttonRounded;

-->     Point pts[] = new Point[100];
        Point ptAnchor, ptDrawTo;
-->     int ptindex = 0;
           .
           .
           .
```

Now we're ready for the mouseDrag() function. In this function, we record new points as the mouse moves. Then we call the repaint() function to draw the new points on the screen. We start like this in mouseDrag(), where we check to make sure that the user has clicked the Draw flag so that they are in fact drawing freehand:

```
        public boolean mouseDrag(Event e, int x, int y){
-->            if(bDrawFlag){
                   .
                   .
                   .
```

If so, we want to record the current (x, y) location of the mouse in the pts[] array so that we can "connect the dots" in the paint() method. We store the new mouse location like this in mouseDrag():

```
public boolean mouseDrag(Event e, int x, int y){
        if(bDrawFlag){
-->             pts[ptindex] = new Point(x, y);
                .
                .
                .
```

And we also increment the pts[] array index, ptindex, to be prepared for the next time the mouse moves:

```
public boolean mouseDrag(Event e, int x, int y){
        if(bDrawFlag){
                pts[ptindex] = new Point(x, y);
-->             ptindex++;
                .
                .
                .
```

Note that in a debugged applet we should also check to make sure that ptindex does not exceed the maximum possible value for our array, 99. Then we call repaint() to draw the collection of mouse points on the screen:

```
public boolean mouseDrag(Event e, int x, int y){
        if(bDrawFlag){
                pts[ptindex] = new Point(x, y);
                ptindex++;
-->             repaint();
        }
        return true;
}
```

Now let's turn to the paint() method. We begin by making sure that the user has clicked the **Draw** button this way (but we don't check to make sure that the mouse button has gone up, of course, because in this case the mouse is being dragged as the user draws):

```
         public void paint (Graphics g) {
                 int drawWidth, drawHeight;
                           .
                           .
                           .
   -->           if(bDrawFlag){
                           .
                           .
                           .

                 }
```

If so, then we should draw the mouse movements as recorded in our pts[] array. We do that simply by drawing a line between the points with drawLine(), which means that we must loop over all points in that array. That loop looks like this:

```
       public void paint (Graphics g) {
   -->          int loop_index;
                int drawWidth, drawHeight;
                          .
                          .
                          .
                if(bDrawFlag){
   -->                for(loop_index = 0; loop_index < ptindex; loop_index++){
                                .
                                .
                                .

                      }
                }
```

We connect the dots this way:

```
       public void paint (Graphics g) {
                int loop_index;
                int drawWidth, drawHeight;
                          .
                          .
                          .
                if(bDrawFlag){
                    for(loop_index = 0; loop_index < ptindex; loop_index++){
   -->                  g.drawLine(pts[loop_index].x, pts[loop_index].y,
                            pts[loop_index + 1].x, pts[loop_index + 1].y);
                      }
                }
```

Now we have enabled freehand drawing. When the user selects the **Draw** button, presses the mouse button, and drags the mouse, the mouse trail will be visible in our applet, as shown in Figure 6.7.

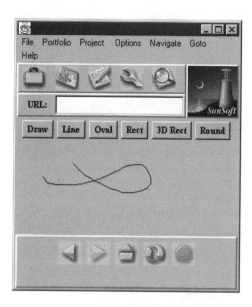

Figure 6.7 Drawing freehand with the Painter applet.

That's it for the Painter applet. This applet has given us a good introduction to graphics in Java. The listing for the Painter applet appears in Listing 6.2.

Listing 6.2 Painter.java

```
import java.awt.Graphics;
import java.awt.*;
import java.lang.Math;
import java.applet.Applet;

public class Painter extends Applet {

    Button buttonDraw, buttonLine, buttonOval, buttonRect, button3DRect;
    Button buttonRounded;

    Point pts[] = new Point[100];
```

```
Point ptAnchor, ptDrawTo;
int ptindex = 0;

boolean bMouseDownFlag = false;
boolean bMouseUpFlag = false;
boolean bDrawFlag = false;
boolean bLineFlag = false;
boolean bOvalFlag = false;
boolean bRectFlag = false;
boolean b3DRectFlag = false;
boolean bRoundedFlag = false;

public void init() {

        buttonDraw = new Button("Draw");
        buttonLine = new Button("Line");
        buttonOval = new Button("Oval");
        buttonRect = new Button("Rect");
        button3DRect = new Button("3D Rect");
        buttonRounded = new Button("Round");

        add(buttonDraw);
        add(buttonLine);
        add(buttonOval);
        add(buttonRect);
        add(button3DRect);
        add(buttonRounded);
}

public boolean mouseDown(Event e, int x, int y){
        bMouseDownFlag = true;
        bMouseUpFlag = false;
        ptAnchor = new Point(x, y);
        return true;
}

public boolean mouseUp(Event e, int x, int y){
        bMouseDownFlag = false;
        bMouseUpFlag = true;

        ptDrawTo = new Point(Math.max(x, ptAnchor.x), Math.max(y,
            ptAnchor.y));
        ptAnchor = new Point(Math.min(x, ptAnchor.x), Math.min(y,
            ptAnchor.y));
```

```
        repaint();
        return true;
}

public boolean mouseDrag(Event e, int x, int y){
        if(bDrawFlag){
                pts[ptindex] = new Point(x, y);
                ptindex++;
                repaint();
        }
        return true;
}

public void paint (Graphics g) {
        int loop_index;
        int drawWidth, drawHeight;

        if(bLineFlag && bMouseUpFlag){
                g.drawLine(ptAnchor.x, ptAnchor.y, ptDrawTo.x,
                    ptDrawTo.y);
        }
        if(bOvalFlag && bMouseUpFlag){
                drawWidth = ptDrawTo.x - ptAnchor.x;
                drawHeight = ptDrawTo.y - ptAnchor.y;
                g.drawOval(ptAnchor.x, ptAnchor.y, drawWidth,
                    drawHeight);
        }
        if(bRectFlag && bMouseUpFlag){
                drawWidth = ptDrawTo.x - ptAnchor.x;
                drawHeight = ptDrawTo.y - ptAnchor.y;
                g.drawRect(ptAnchor.x, ptAnchor.y, drawWidth,
                    drawHeight);
        }
        if(b3DRectFlag && bMouseUpFlag){
                drawWidth = ptDrawTo.x - ptAnchor.x;
                drawHeight = ptDrawTo.y - ptAnchor.y;
                g.draw3DRect(ptAnchor.x, ptAnchor.y, drawWidth,
                    drawHeight, true);
        }
        if(bRoundedFlag && bMouseUpFlag){
                drawWidth = ptDrawTo.x - ptAnchor.x;
                drawHeight = ptDrawTo.y - ptAnchor.y;
                g.drawRoundRect(ptAnchor.x, ptAnchor.y, drawWidth,
                    drawHeight, 10, 10);
        }
```

```
            if(bDrawFlag){
                for(loop_index = 0; loop_index < ptindex; loop_index++){
                    g.drawLine(pts[loop_index].x, pts[loop_index].y,
                        pts[loop_index + 1].x, pts[loop_index + 1].y);
                }
            }
    }

    public boolean action(Event e, Object o){
            if(e.target.equals(buttonDraw)){
                    bDrawFlag = !bDrawFlag;
                    bLineFlag = false;
                    bOvalFlag = false;
                    bRectFlag = false;
                    b3DRectFlag = false;
                    bRoundedFlag = false;
            }
            if(e.target.equals(buttonLine)){
                    bLineFlag = !bLineFlag;
                    bDrawFlag = false;
                    bOvalFlag = false;
                    bRectFlag = false;
                    b3DRectFlag = false;
                    bRoundedFlag = false;
            }
            if(e.target.equals(buttonOval)){
                    bOvalFlag = !bOvalFlag;
                    bLineFlag = false;
                    bDrawFlag = false;
                    bRectFlag = false;
                    b3DRectFlag = false;
                    bRoundedFlag = false;
            }
            if(e.target.equals(buttonRect)){
                    bRectFlag = !bRectFlag;
                    bLineFlag = false;
                    bOvalFlag = false;
                    bDrawFlag = false;
                    b3DRectFlag = false;
                    bRoundedFlag = false;
            }
            if(e.target.equals(button3DRect)){
                    b3DRectFlag = !b3DRectFlag;
                    bLineFlag = false;
                    bOvalFlag = false;
```

```
                bRectFlag = false;
                bDrawFlag = false;
                bRoundedFlag = false;
        }
        if(e.target.equals(buttonRounded)){
                bRoundedFlag = !bRoundedFlag;
                bLineFlag = false;
                bOvalFlag = false;
                bRectFlag = false;
                b3DRectFlag = false;
                bDrawFlag = false;
        }
        return true;
    }
}
```

We can also explore arcs in this chapter. Arcs are really just partial ovals, and we can specify what part of the oval we want. Arcs are too complex to handle with simple mouse down and mouse up events, so we'll set up a dedicated applet to see how drawing arcs works.

Drawing Arcs and Selecting Colors

To draw an arc, you use the Graphics class's drawArc() method, which you call like this (all dimensions are in pixels):

```
drawArc(xTopLeft, yTopLeft, Width, Height, Angle1, Angle2);
```

The first four parameters are just as we might use when we draw an oval. The first two parameters make up the location of the upper right of a rectangle enclosing the oval if we were to draw the oval fully, and the second two parameters are the width and height of that rectangle. So far, then, we've specified an oval, but as we know, arcs display only part of a full oval. How do we indicate what part we want?

We indicate how much of the oval we want to display in our arc with angles. To see how this works, imagine the following coordinate system placed in the exact middle of the oval from which we are going to create arcs. The measurements are in degrees, starting from the 3 o'clock position:

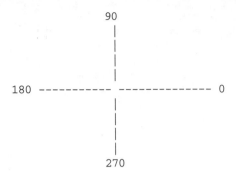

If we want to draw an arc corresponding to only the top of the oval, we specify a beginning angle of 0 and a finishing angle of 180. If we want only the left side of the oval, we specify 90 to 270 degrees. Of course, we can specify an integer value of degrees; we are not limited to numbers like 90 or 270. We can even specify negative degrees like this:

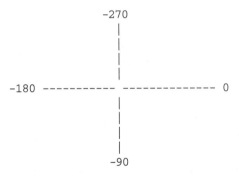

In this way, we can indicate exactly to the Graphics class how we want our arc to appear.

Drawing Arcs in Our Fillarc Applet

We start a new arc-displaying applet this way:

```
import java.applet.Applet;
import java.awt.*;
```

```
public class Fillarc extends java.applet.Applet {
                .
                .
                .
```

To draw an arc, we can override the paint() method this way:

```
import java.applet.Applet;
import java.awt.*;

public class Fillarc extends java.applet.Applet {

  -->     public void paint (Graphics g) {
                .
                .
                .
```

Our first arc consists of the top half of a circle beginning at location (10, 10); the top half of the arc is described by the angles 0 to 180 degrees. We draw an arc with the Graphics class drawArc() method, and our call looks like this:

```
import java.applet.Applet;
import java.awt.*;

public class Fillarc extends java.applet.Applet {

        public void paint (Graphics g) {
    -->         g.drawArc(10, 10, 100, 100, 0, 180);
                .
                .
                .
```

A filled arc (i.e., filled in with color) is just as easy to draw as an empty one, so let's see that now.

Filling Arcs with Color

We can also draw an arc filled with color, using fillArc(). Let's move our original arc over to the right and draw it now as a filled-in arc. We do that with the Graphics class's fillArc() method:

```
import java.applet.Applet;
import java.awt.*;

public class Fillarc extends java.applet.Applet {

        public void paint (Graphics g) {
                g.drawArc(10, 10, 100, 100, 0, 180);
   -->          g.fillArc(150, 10, 100, 100, 0, 180);
                 .
                 .
                 .
```

This draws an arc just as drawArc() did, but it fills it with the current drawing color, which is black by default. The result, which shows our two arcs, appears in Figure 6.8.

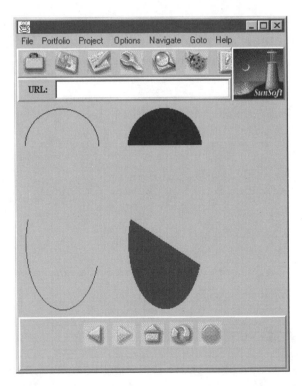

Figure 6.8 Our Fillarc applet can draw and fill arcs.

Another valuable graphics technique that we can examine here is changing the drawing color used in a Graphics object.

Selecting a Drawing Color

We can change the drawing color easily. For example, to change it to blue, we create a new Color object and pass the red, green, and blue values (0–255) we want to its constructor. We want pure blue, so we'll create our new Color object this way: `Color(0,0,255)`. We install our new color as the drawing color with the Graphics class's setColor() method:

```
import java.applet.Applet;
import java.awt.*;

public class Fillarc extends java.applet.Applet {
        public void paint (Graphics g) {
                g.drawArc(10, 10, 100, 100, 0, 180);
                g.fillArc(150, 10, 100, 100, 0, 180);
    -->         g.setColor(new Color(0, 0, 255));
                      .
                      .
                      .
```

Now anything we draw now will appear in blue. For example, we can draw another arc below the first two, making it go from –20 to –180 degrees in its oval and drawing it in blue:

```
import java.applet.Applet;
import java.awt.*;

public class Fillarc extends java.applet.Applet {

        public void paint (Graphics g) {
                g.drawArc(10, 10, 100, 100, 0, 180);
                g.fillArc(150, 10, 100, 100, 0, 180);
                g.setColor(new Color(0, 0, 255));
    -->         g.drawArc(10, 100, 100, 180, -20, -180);
                      .
                      .
                      .
```

This new arc appears in Figure 6.8. We can also draw the filled version of the same arc this way:

```
import java.applet.Applet;
import java.awt.*;

public class Fillarc extends java.applet.Applet {
        public void paint (Graphics g) {
                g.drawArc(10, 10, 100, 100, 0, 180);
                g.fillArc(150, 10, 100, 100, 0, 180);
                g.setColor(new Color(0, 0, 255));
                g.drawArc(10, 100, 100, 180, -20, -180);
    -->         g.fillArc(150, 100, 100, 180, -20, -180);
        }
}
```

This result also appears in Figure 6.8. Our arc applet is a success. In this way, we can draw arcs almost as easily as we can draw rectangles or other graphics figures.

In this chapter, we've seen how to work with the powerful Graphics class and how to use the mouse. We've also seen a great deal of graphics here, such as how to draw lines, circles, rectangles, rounded rectangles, arcs, and more. In the next chapter, we'll continue our exploration of graphics as we examine the use of images, imagemaps, and fonts.

CHAPTER SEVEN

GRAPHICS: FONTS, CANVASES, IMAGES, AND IMAGEMAPS

In this chapter, we'll continue our exploration of Java graphics. In particular, we'll examine the process of drawing text with different fonts, how to load images and store them in memory, and how to display and redimension images. We'll also create an *imagemap*, an image with spots you can click (called graphical buttons) in a Web browser to jump you to some new URL. We'll finish the chapter with an exploration of Java Canvases, which are controls that you can draw on and support all kinds of graphics. Let's start now with an examination of image handling as we see how to load images into our applets.

Handling Images: The Stretch Applet

Let's say that we have a graphics image that we store in a **.jpg** file called **figure.jpg**, as shown in Figure 7.1 (this file could be stored in your ISP).

Figure 7.1 Our figure.jpg file.

And let's also say that we wanted to load that **.jpg** file into our applet and display it like this:

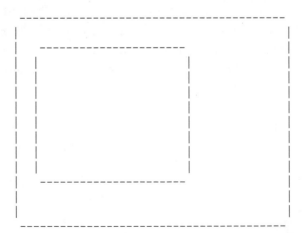

It turns out that we can load an image easily with the Graphics class getImage() method. And we can also display it easily with the drawImage() method. In fact, we can even draw the image stretched to a different shape:

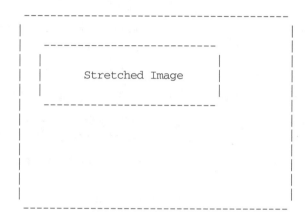

Let's write an example applet called Stretch that will let the user stretch our **figure.jpg** image and then display it. We might allow the user to outline with the mouse the rectangle in which the image is to appear. Then we'll fit our image into that rectangle, stretching it to fit.

We begin by declaring an object of class java.awt.Image named stretchImage in our applet:

```
import java.awt.*;
import java.lang.Math;
import java.applet.Applet;

public class Stretch extends Applet {

-->    Image stretchImage;
         .
         .
         .
```

This is where we'll store our image when we load it in from the **figure.jpg** file. The java.awt.Image class's constructors and methods appear in Table 7.1.

Table 7.1 Image Constructors and Methods

Image()	Constructs a new image
flush()	Flushes all resources used by Image object
getGraphics()	Returns a graphics object to draw in Image with
getHeight(ImageObserver)	Returns height of Image
getProperty(String, ImageObserver)	Returns a property of Image
getSource()	Returns object that produces pixels for the image
getWidth(ImageObserver)	Returns width of Image

To load the image, we just use the getImage() method like this:

```
import java.awt.*;
import java.lang.Math;
import java.applet.Applet;

public class Stretch extends Applet {

Image stretchImage;

public void init() {
-->        stretchImage = getImage(getCodeBase(), "figure.jpg");
}             .

           .

           .
```

Here we pass the location (i.e., the URL) and name of our image file **figure.jpg**. Notice in particular the getCodeBase() method, which returns the URL of the **.class** file for this applet (i.e., we make the assumption that the **figure.jpg** file is stored in the same place as the **Stretch.class** file).

Now our image is loaded into our Image object. The next step is to see how the user wants us to display it. When the user presses the mouse button, an Anchor point is set at one corner of the rectangle in which **figure.jpg** will fit. First, we add the mouseDown() method and set two flags, bMouseDownFlag and bMouseUp, to match the mouse's state (e.g., bMouseDownFlag = true if the mouse button is down):

```
        import java.awt.*;
        import java.lang.Math;
        import java.applet.Applet;

    public class Stretch extends Applet {

        Image stretchImage;
-->     boolean bMouseDownFlag = false;
-->     boolean bMouseUpFlag = false;

        public void init() {
                stretchImage = getImage(getCodeBase(), "figure.jpg");
        }

        public boolean mouseDown(Event e, int x, int y){
-->             bMouseDownFlag = true;
-->             bMouseUpFlag = false;
                    .
                    .
                    .
```

Next, we record the Anchor point in a new Java Point object named ptAnchor:

Here's how it looks in code:

```
        import java.awt.*;
        import java.lang.Math;
        import java.applet.Applet;

    public class Stretch extends Applet {
```

```
        Image stretchImage;
        boolean bMouseDownFlag = false;
        boolean bMouseUpFlag = false;
-->     Point ptAnchor;

        public void init() {
                stretchImage = getImage(getCodeBase(), "figure.jpg");
        }

        public boolean mouseDown(Event e, int x, int y){
                bMouseDownFlag = true;
                bMouseUpFlag = false;
-->             ptAnchor = new Point(x, y);
                return true;
        }               .
                        .
                        .
```

That's all the information we need from the mouse down event. The user then
moves the mouse to the other defining corner of the rectangle and releases the
mouse button, which causes a mouse up event. We can intercept that event in
the mouseUp() method like this, where we first set the mouse flags correctly:

```
        public boolean mouseDown(Event e, int x, int y){
                bMouseDownFlag = true;
                bMouseUpFlag = false;
                ptAnchor = new Point(x, y);
                return true;
        }

        public boolean mouseUp(Event e, int x, int y){
-->             bMouseDownFlag = false;
-->             bMouseUpFlag = true;
                        .
                        .
                        .
```

When the user releases the mouse button, the DrawTo point is defined. This
point, along with the Anchor point, defines our rectangle:

```
Anchor Point x--------------------
              |                   |
              |                   |
              |                   |
              |                   |
              |                   |
              |_____x DrawTo Point   <--
```

Let's record the DrawTo point in a new Point object named ptDrawTo this way:

```
    public class Stretch extends Applet {

        Image stretchImage;
        boolean bMouseDownFlag = false;
        boolean bMouseUpFlag = false;
-->     Point ptAnchor, ptDrawTo;
            .
            .
            .

        public boolean mouseDown(Event e, int x, int y){
            bMouseDownFlag = true;
            bMouseUpFlag = false;
            ptAnchor = new Point(x, y);
            return true;
        }


        public boolean mouseUp(Event e, int x, int y){
            bMouseDownFlag = false;
            bMouseUpFlag = true;

-->         ptDrawTo = new Point(Math.max(x, ptAnchor.x), Math.max(y,
                ptAnchor.y));
-->         ptAnchor = new Point(Math.min(x, ptAnchor.x), Math.min(y,
                ptAnchor.y));
                .
                .
                .
```

We have all the information we need to draw the rectangle that the user outlined and to draw **figure.jpg** in it. Now we can call repaint() to execute the drawing code, which we are about to place in the paint() method:

```
public class Stretch extends Applet {

    Image stretchImage;
    boolean bMouseDownFlag = false;
    boolean bMouseUpFlag = false;
    Point ptAnchor, ptDrawTo;
            .
            .
            .

    public boolean mouseUp(Event e, int x, int y){
            bMouseDownFlag = false;
            bMouseUpFlag = true;

            ptDrawTo = new Point(Math.max(x, ptAnchor.x), Math.max(y,
                ptAnchor.y));
            ptAnchor = new Point(Math.min(x, ptAnchor.x), Math.min(y,
                ptAnchor.y));
-->         repaint();
            return true;
    }
```

That's it for the mouse. Now let's look at the paint() method. Here, we should draw the rectangle that the user has outlined in our applet if the mouse button has gone up (i.e., if the user is done drawing). We first check to make sure that the mouse button has in fact gone up:

```
public void paint (Graphics g) {

-->         if(bMouseUpFlag){
                    .
                    .
                    .
```

Then we find the width (drawWidth) and height (drawHeight) of the rectangle we are to draw this way:

```
public void paint (Graphics g) {
        int drawWidth, drawHeight;
```

```
            if(bMouseUpFlag){
-->                 drawWidth = ptDrawTo.x - ptAnchor.x;
-->                 drawHeight = ptDrawTo.y - ptAnchor.y;
                         .
                         .
                         .
```

And then we simply draw the outlining rectangle with the Graphics class's drawRect() method:

```
        public void paint (Graphics g) {
                int drawWidth, drawHeight;

                if(bMouseUpFlag){
                        drawWidth = ptDrawTo.x - ptAnchor.x;
                        drawHeight = ptDrawTo.y - ptAnchor.y);
-->                     g.drawRect(ptAnchor.x, ptAnchor.y, drawWidth,
                            drawHeight);
                             .
                             .
                             .
```

The last step is to draw the image now stored in stretchImage. We do so with the Graphics class's drawImage() method this way:

```
        public void paint (Graphics g) {
                int drawWidth, drawHeight;

                if(bMouseUpFlag){
                        drawWidth = ptDrawTo.x - ptAnchor.x;
                        drawHeight = ptDrawTo.y - ptAnchor.y);
                        g.drawRect(ptAnchor.x, ptAnchor.y, drawWidth,
                            drawHeight);
-->                     g.drawImage(stretchImage, ptAnchor.x, ptAnchor.y,
                            drawWidth, drawHeight, this);
                }
        }
```

Notice the parameters we pass to drawImage(): the Image object itself, of course, as well as the location of the upper-left point of the image and its height and width. But we also add a this pointer at the very end. Because handling graphics is so important in Java, there is a special class named the ImageObserver class, whose job it is to oversee loading and handling of images (e.g., if loading the image takes too long, the ImageObserver object can take appropriate action). If you set up an object of that class, you can pass it to the drawImage() method so that your ImageObserver can watch what's happening. Here, we will just pass a this pointer, with no other special action.

Now the user can load and stretch our **figure.jpg** image as desired and as shown in Figure 7.2. Our applet is a success. The code for this applet appears in Listing 7.1.

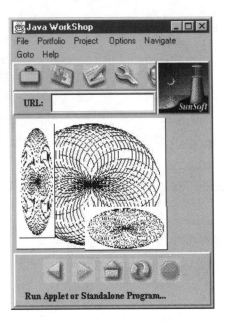

Figure 7.2 Stretching our figure with Stretch.class.

Listing 7.1 Stretch.java

```
import java.awt.*;
import java.lang.Math;
import java.applet.Applet;
```

```java
public class Stretch extends Applet {

    Image stretchImage;
    boolean bMouseDownFlag = false;
    boolean bMouseUpFlag = false;
    Point ptAnchor, ptDrawTo;

    public void init() {
        stretchImage = getImage(getCodeBase(), "figure.jpg");
    }

    public boolean mouseDown(Event e, int x, int y){
        bMouseDownFlag = true;
        bMouseUpFlag = false;
        ptAnchor = new Point(x, y);
        return true;
    }

    public boolean mouseUp(Event e, int x, int y){
        bMouseDownFlag = false;
        bMouseUpFlag = true;

        ptDrawTo = new Point(Math.max(x, ptAnchor.x),
            Math.max(y, ptAnchor.y));
        ptAnchor = new Point(Math.min(x, ptAnchor.x),
            Math.min(y, ptAnchor.y));
        repaint();
        return true;
    }

    public void paint (Graphics g) {
        int drawWidth, drawHeight;

        if(bMouseUpFlag){
            drawWidth = ptDrawTo.x - ptAnchor.x;
            drawHeight = ptDrawTo.y - ptAnchor.y;
            g.drawRect(ptAnchor.x, ptAnchor.y, drawWidth,
                drawHeight);
            g.drawImage(stretchImage, ptAnchor.x, ptAnchor.y,
                drawWidth, drawHeight, this);
        }
    }
}
```

That's a good introduction to image handling in Java. As you can see, it is easy and powerful. Now let's turn to text and font handling.

Fonts: The Writer Applet

In our next example, named Writer, we'll let the user draw text in our applet in various fonts, styles, and sizes. All the user needs to do is click a spot with the mouse, select a font style by clicking a button, and type:

```
-----------------------------------------------------
|                                                   |
|    ------   -------   ---   ----   ------   -----  |
|   |TRoman| |Courier| |Big| |Bold| |Italic| |Plain||
|    ------   -------   ---   ----   ------   -----  |
|                                                   |
|                                                   |
|            Hello World!                           |
|                                                   |
|                                                   |
|                                                   |
|                                                   |
|                                                   |
|                                                   |
|                                                   |
-----------------------------------------------------
```

The options we'll allow include: Times Roman or Courier font, using a large font size (36 point), bold text, italic text, and plain text. You may be surprised to see a text example in a chapter on graphics; however, in an applet, drawing text (outside of text controls) is just as much graphics as drawing lines is. Let's start our applet by declaring our six buttons in Writer:

```java
import java.applet.Applet;
import java.awt.*;
import java.awt.Graphics;

public class Writer extends Applet {
```

```
-->              Button buttonFont1, buttonFont2, buttonBig;
-->              Button buttonBold, buttonItalic, buttonPlain;
                        .
                        .
                        .
```

We also create and add these buttons in an init() function, as usual:

```
          public void init() {

-->              buttonFont1 = new Button("TRoman");
-->              buttonFont2 = new Button("Courier");
-->              buttonBig = new Button("Big");
-->              buttonBold = new Button("Bold");
-->              buttonItalic = new Button("Italic");
-->              buttonPlain = new Button("Plain");

-->              add(buttonFont1);
-->              add(buttonFont2);
-->              add(buttonBig);
-->              add(buttonBold);
-->              add(buttonItalic);
-->              add(buttonPlain);
          }
```

And we can set up a flag to match each button, as we did in the last chapter for the Painter applet:

```
     import java.applet.Applet;
     import java.awt.*;
     import java.awt.Graphics;

     public class Writer extends Applet {

          Button buttonFont1, buttonFont2, buttonBig;
          Button buttonBold, buttonItalic, buttonPlain;
-->       boolean bMouseDownFlag = false;
-->       boolean bMouseUpFlag = false;
-->       boolean bFont1Flag = false;
-->       boolean bFont2Flag = false;
-->       boolean bBigFlag = false;
```

```
-->          boolean bBoldFlag = false;
-->          boolean bItalicFlag = false;
-->          boolean bPlainFlag = false;
                   .
                   .
                   .
```

Notice that now, however, these buttons are no longer exclusive. That is, it's possible to select as many as four options at once: a font like Courier, making it bold, large, and even italicized. For that reason, we take care to set the flags correctly when the user clicks a button, noticing that some options are exclusive. For example, you can't use both Times Roman and Courier at the same time. So when we set one font flag true, we'll set the other flag false:

```
     public boolean action(Event e, Object o){
          if(e.target.equals(buttonFont1)){
-->              bFont1Flag = true;
-->              bFont2Flag = false;
          }            .
                       .
                       .
```

Here is how we set all the buttons in the action() method. Notice that selecting plain text (the last button) resets all the other flags:

```
     public boolean action(Event e, Object o){
          if(e.target.equals(buttonFont1)){
               bFont1Flag = true;
               bFont2Flag = false;
          }
          if(e.target.equals(buttonFont2)){
               bFont2Flag = true;
               bFont1Flag = false;
          }
          if(e.target.equals(buttonBig)){
               bBigFlag = true;
          }
          if(e.target.equals(buttonBold)){
               bBoldFlag = true;
          }
          if(e.target.equals(buttonItalic)){
               bItalicFlag = true;
          }
```

```
                    if(e.target.equals(buttonPlain)){
                            bPlainFlag = true;
                            bFont2Flag = false;
                            bBigFlag = false;
                            bBoldFlag = false;
                            bItalicFlag = false;
                            bFont1Flag = false;
                    }
                    return true;
            }
```

Now let's start handling the mouse. When the user presses the mouse button, we can record the mouse position as the start location of our text string (i.e., when they type text, it will start at this position). We set aside two integers to hold the x and y coordinates of the start position:

```
        public class Writer extends Applet {

                int StartX = 0;
                int StartY = 0;
                      .
                      .
                      .
```

And we load those coordinates when the mouse button goes down:

```
                public boolean mouseDown(Event e, int x, int y){
-->                     StartX = x;
-->                     StartY = y;
                          .
                          .
                          .
```

In addition, we can store the text itself in a Java string called inString:

```
        public class Writer extends Applet {

-->             String inString = "";
                int StartX = 0;
                int StartY = 0;
                      .
                      .
                      .
```

We also should clear inString when the mouse button goes down. Then, when the user selects a new mouse position to type text, they can start a whole new text string:

```
public boolean mouseDown(Event e, int x, int y){
        StartX = x;
        StartY = y;
        inString = "";
        return true;
}
```

Now we can add the keyDown() event handler. Here, we'll read the key the user typed and echo it directly in our applet—no textfields, no textareas. The keyDown() method looks like this:

```
public boolean keyDown(Event e, int k){
            .
            .
            .
```

The integer we've called k holds the code for the key that was pressed, and we can add it to our text string inString like this:

```
          public boolean keyDown(Event e, int k){
-->               inString = inString + (char)k;
                      .
                      .
                      .
```

Now we're ready to read keystrokes directly, just as in the last chapter we learned how to use the mouse directly. After we read the struck key, we call repaint() to paint inString in our applet with code we'll add to the paint() method:

```
          public boolean keyDown(Event e, int k){
                  inString = inString + (char)k;
-->               repaint();
                  return true;
          }
```

Let's write the paint() method now. Here, our task is to display the text in inString at the location (StartX, StartY) in our applet, with the font, font size, and style the user selects. We begin the paint() method by selecting default values for all the font selections (e.g., in case the user didn't select a font or other options):

```
          public void paint (Graphics g) {

-->               String fontName = "TimesRoman"; //default face
-->               int fontType = Font.PLAIN;      //default type
-->               int fontSize = 18;              //default size
                              .
                              .
                              .
```

As you can see, we set the variables we'll use to set the text font and style in our applet. In particular, we set the font to Times Roman and the type to the predefined constant Font.PLAIN (other values include Font.BOLD and Font.ITALIC) and select an 18-point font size. These values will all be installed in a Font object named drawFont:

```
          public void paint (Graphics g) {

                  String fontName - "TimesRoman"; //default face
                  int fontType = Font.PLAIN;      //default type
                  int fontSize = 18;              //default size
-->               Font drawFont;
                              .
                              .
                              .
```

The Java Font class's constructors and methods appear in Table 7.2.

Table 7.2 Font Class's Constructors and Methods

```
java.lang.Object
   |
   +----java.awt.Font
```

Font(String, int, int)	Creates font with specified name, style (Font.BOLD, Font.PLAIN, or Font.ITALIC), and point size
equals(Object)	Compares object to specified object
getFamily()	Returns family name of Font
getFont(String)	Returns a font from system properties list
getFont(String, Font)	Returns specified font from system properties list
getName()	Returns logical name of Font
getSize()	Returns point size of Font
getStyle()	Returns style of Font
hashCode()	Returns a hashcode for Font
isBold()	Returns true if Font is bold
isItalic()	Returns true if Font is italic
isPlain()	Returns true if Font is plain
toString()	Converts object to a string

Now we can check the font options the user specified by clicking the buttons and change the default values we set (if necessary). For example, besides the Times Roman font, we will also offer Courier, which we check for this way:

```
public void paint (Graphics g) {

        String fontName = "TimesRoman"; //default face
        int fontType = Font.PLAIN;      //default type
        int fontSize = 18;              //default size
        Font drawFont;

        if(bFont1Flag){
                fontName = "TimesRoman";
        }
```

```
-->              if(bFont2Flag){
-->                      fontName = "Courier";
              }             .
                            .
                            .
```

Now we check if the user clicked the button labeled **Big**, in which case we can set the font size variable to hold 36 point (instead of 18):

```
public void paint (Graphics g) {

        String fontName = "TimesRoman"; //default face
        int fontType = Font.PLAIN;      //default type
        int fontSize = 18;              //default size
        Font drawFont;

        if(bFont1Flag){
                fontName = "TimesRoman";
        }
        if(bFont2Flag){
                fontName = "Courier";
        }
-->     if(bBigFlag){
-->             fontSize = 36;
-->     }             .
                      .
                      .
```

We also check to see if the user clicked the **Bold** button like this, in which case we set our fontType variable to Font.BOLD:

```
public void paint (Graphics g) {

        String fontName = "TimesRoman"; //default face
        int fontType = Font.PLAIN;      //default type
        int fontSize = 18;              //default size
        Font drawFont;

        if(bFont1Flag){
                fontName = "TimesRoman";
        }             .
                      .
                      .
```

```
                        if(bBigFlag){
                                fontSize = 36;
                        }
      -->               if(bBoldFlag){
      -->                       fontType = Font.BOLD;
      -->               }            .
                                     .
                                     .
                                     .
```

And we can also see if the user wants an italic font like this. Note that we OR the constant Font.ITALIC with our fontStyle variable; we do that because the user may want to type in a font that is both italicized and in bold:

```
        public void paint (Graphics g) {

                String fontName = "TimesRoman"; //default face
                int fontType = Font.PLAIN;      //default type
                int fontSize = 18;              //default size
                Font drawFont;

                if(bFont1Flag){
                        fontName = "TimesRoman";
                }            .
                             .
                             .

                if(bBoldFlag){
                        fontType = Font.BOLD;
                }
      -->       if(bItalicFlag){
      -->               fontType = fontType | Font.ITALIC;
      -->       }
                             .
                             .
                             .
```

Now we create our new font object, passing it the name of the font (a string), the font type (made up of constants like Font.PLAIN and Font.BOLD), and the font size (an integer):

```
        public void paint (Graphics g) {

                String fontName = "TimesRoman"; //default face
                int fontType = Font.PLAIN;      //default type
```

```
          int fontSize = 18;            //default size
          Font drawFont;

          if(bFont1Flag){
                  fontName = "TimesRoman";
          }       .
                  .
                  .
          if(bItalicFlag){
                  fontType = fontType | Font.ITALIC;
          }

-->       drawFont = new Font(fontName, fontType, fontSize);
              .
              .
              .
```

All that's left is to install our font in the graphics object with the setFont()
method and to draw the current text string in our applet with drawLine():

```
public void paint (Graphics g) {

          String fontName = "TimesRoman"; //default face
          int fontType = Font.PLAIN;      //default type
          int fontSize = 18;              //default size
          Font drawFont;

          if(bFont1Flag){
                  fontName = "TimesRoman";
          }       .
                  .
                  .
          if(bItalicFlag){
                  fontType = fontType | Font.ITALIC;
          }

          drawFont = new Font(fontName, fontType, fontSize);
-->       g.setFont(drawFont);
-->       g.drawString(inString, StartX, StartY);
    }
```

Now the user can select font sizes, types, and styles, as we see in Figure 7.3. Our Writer applet is a success. We're able to draw text in our applets directly now. The code for this applet appears Listing 7.2.

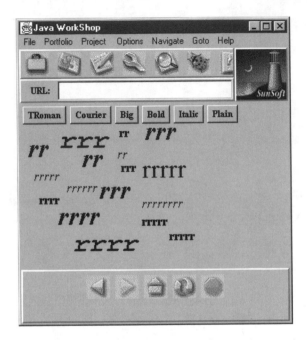

Figure 7.3 Our Writer applet lets the user choose fonts and sizes.

Listing 7.2 Writer.java

```
import java.applet.Applet;
import java.awt.*;
import java.awt.Graphics;

public class Writer extends Applet {

        String inString = "";
        int StartX = 0;
        int StartY = 0;
        Button buttonFont1, buttonFont2, buttonBig;
        Button buttonBold, buttonItalic, buttonPlain;
        boolean bMouseDownFlag = false;
```

```java
boolean bMouseUpFlag = false;
boolean bFont1Flag = false;
boolean bFont2Flag = false;
boolean bBigFlag = false;
boolean bBoldFlag = false;
boolean bItalicFlag = false;
boolean bPlainFlag = false;

public void init() {

        buttonFont1 = new Button("TRoman");
        buttonFont2 = new Button("Courier");
        buttonBig = new Button("Big");
        buttonBold = new Button("Bold");
        buttonItalic = new Button("Italic");
        buttonPlain = new Button("Plain");

        add(buttonFont1);
        add(buttonFont2);
        add(buttonBig);
        add(buttonBold);
        add(buttonItalic);
        add(buttonPlain);
}


public boolean mouseDown(Event e, int x, int y){
        StartX = x;
        StartY = y;
        inString = "";
        return true;
}


public boolean keyDown(Event e, int k){
        inString = inString + (char)k;
        repaint();
        return true;
}


public void paint (Graphics g) {

        String fontName = "TimesRoman"; //default face
        int fontType = Font.PLAIN;      //default type
        int fontSize = 18;              //default size
        Font drawFont;
```

```
        if(bFont1Flag){
                fontName = "TimesRoman";
        }
        if(bFont2Flag){
                fontName = "Courier";
        }
        if(bBigFlag){
                fontSize = 36;
        }
        if(bBoldFlag){
                fontType = Font.BOLD;
        }
        if(bItalicFlag){
                fontType = fontType | Font.ITALIC;
        }

        drawFont = new Font(fontName, fontType, fontSize);
        g.setFont(drawFont);
        g.drawString(inString, StartX, StartY);
}

public boolean action(Event e, Object o){
        if(e.target.equals(buttonFont1)){
                bFont1Flag = true;
                bFont2Flag = false;
        }
        if(e.target.equals(buttonFont2)){
                bFont2Flag = true;
                bFont1Flag = false;
        }
        if(e.target.equals(buttonBig)){
                bBigFlag = true;
        }
        if(e.target.equals(buttonBold)){
                bBoldFlag = true;
        }
        if(e.target.equals(buttonItalic)){
                bItalicFlag = true;
        }
        if(e.target.equals(buttonPlain)){
                bPlainFlag = true;
                bFont2Flag = false;
                bBigFlag = false;
                bBoldFlag = false;
                bItalicFlag = false;
```

```
                            bFont1Flag = false;
                    }
                    return true;
            }

            public void update(Graphics g){
                    paint(g);
            }
    }
```

Now that we've worked somewhat with text, let's get a little more expertise and explore text placement; there's more going on here than you might think.

Justifying Text

When we write with variable-width text, as we do in applets, placement of text is always a little risky. How do we know things will line up? How do we know we won't overlap the edge of the page? We'll look at these questions now as we create an example with three "Hello World!" strings, one of which is left-justified, one centered, and one right-justified:

```
    ------------------------------------
   |Hello World!                        |
   |                                    |
   |                                    |
   |                                    |
   |             Hello World!           |
   |                                    |
   |                                    |
   |                                    |
   |                        Hello World!|
    ------------------------------------
```

We start by declaring a new Font object, justifyFont, in our new applet:

```
import java.applet.Applet;
import java.awt.*;

public class Justify extends java.applet.Applet {
```

```
-->     Font justifyFont;
              .
              .
              .
```

Then we install that font in the Graphics object passed to us in the paint()
method as a 24-point plain Times Roman font:

```
import java.applet.Applet;
import java.awt.*;

public class Justify extends java.applet.Applet {

      Font justifyFont;

      public void paint (Graphics g) {
-->           justifyFont = new Font("TimesRoman", Font.PLAIN, 24);
-->           g.setFont(justifyFont);
              .
              .
              .
```

We want to place this first text string at the top-left corner of our applet:

```
         ----------------------------------------
-->      |Hello World!         .                 |
         |                                       |
         |                                       |
         |                                       |
         |              Hello World!             |
         |                                       |
         |                                       |
         |                                       |
         |                          Hello World!|
         ----------------------------------------
```

You might think that this is location (0, 0) and that we could just pass that location to drawString(). In fact, the location we pass to drawString() is where we

want the bottom left of our text to appear, so our string wouldn't even appear if we passed a value of (0, 0) (the string would be above the applet). Instead, we have to pass a value of 0 for the x coordinate, and, to make sure the text is top justified, the exact height of the text as the y coordinate. Recall that the pixel coordinate system looks like this:

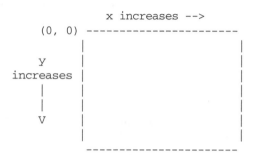

```
                        x increases -->
            (0, 0) ----------------------
                   |                     |
         y         |                     |
     increases     |                     |
         |         |                     |
         |         |                     |
         V         |                     |
                   |                     |
                   ----------------------
```

But how do we find the height of a string of text? We do that with the FontMetrics class, and we add an object of that class to our applet now:

```
public class Justify extends java.applet.Applet {

        Font justifyFont;
  -->   FontMetrics justifyFontMetrics;

        public void paint (Graphics g) {
                justifyFont = new Font("TimesRoman", Font.PLAIN, 24);
                g.setFont(justifyFont);

  -->           justifyFontMetrics = getFontMetrics(justifyFont);
                    .
                    .
                    .
```

The FontMetrics class's constructors and methods appear in Table 7.3.

Table 7.3 FontMetric Class's Constructors and Methods

```
java.lang.Object
      |
      +----java.awt.FontMetrics
```

FontMetrics(Font)	Creates a FontMetrics object with specified font
bytesWidth(byte[], int, int)	Returns width of array of bytes
charWidth(int)	Returns width of specified character in font
charWidth(char)	Returns width of specified character in font
charsWidth(char[], int, int)	Returns width of specified character array
getAscent()	Returns font ascent
getDescent()	Returns font descent
getFont()	Returns font
getHeight()	Returns total height of font
getLeading()	Returns standard line spacing for font
getMaxAdvance()	Returns maximum advance width of any character
getMaxAscent()	Returns maximum ascent of all characters
getMaxDescent()	Returns maximum descent of all characters
getWidths()	Returns widths of first 256 characters
stringWidth(String)	Returns width of specified string
toString()	Returns string representation of FontMetric's values

We can get a string's height and width with the FontMetrics class's getHeight() and stringWidth() methods. For example, we can place our first string at the top-left corner of the applet like this:

```
public class Justify extends java.applet.Applet {

        Font justifyFont;
        FontMetrics justifyFontMetrics;
        String msg = "Hello World!";
        int XPos, YPos;

        public void paint (Graphics g) {
                justifyFont = new Font("TimesRoman", Font.PLAIN, 24);
                g.setFont(justifyFont);

                justifyFontMetrics = getFontMetrics(justifyFont);

-->             XPos = 0;
-->             YPos = justifyFontMetrics.getHeight();
-->             g.drawString(msg, XPos, YPos);
                    .
                    .
                    .
```

Now we can place our second string in the exact center of the page this way, where we use the Java size() method to find the dimensions of our applet [size().width is the width of our applet in pixels, and size().height is the height]:

```
public void paint (Graphics g) {
        justifyFont = new Font("TimesRoman", Font.PLAIN, 24);
        g.setFont(justifyFont);

        justifyFontMetrics = getFontMetrics(justifyFont);

        XPos = 0;
        YPos = justifyFontMetrics.getHeight();
        g.drawString(msg, XPos, YPos);

-->     XPos = (size().width - justifyFontMetrics.stringWidth(msg)) / 2;
-->     YPos = (size().height + justifyFontMetrics.getHeight()) / 2;
-->     g.drawString(msg, XPos, YPos);
            .
            .
            .
```

Finally, we must place the third "Hello World!" string at the lower-right corner of the applet. To do that, we have to start displaying it at a point on the bottom line, leaving just enough horizontal space for the text string. We can find how wide the string is with stringWidth() and place our final string, right-justified, in the applet this way:

```
public void paint (Graphics g) {
        justifyFont = new Font("TimesRoman", Font.PLAIN, 24);
        g.setFont(justifyFont);

        justifyFontMetrics = getFontMetrics(justifyFont);

        XPos = 0;
        YPos = justifyFontMetrics.getHeight();
        g.drawString(msg, XPos, YPos);
              .

              .

              .
-->     XPos = size().width - justifyFontMetrics.stringWidth(msg);
-->     YPos = size().height;
-->     g.drawString(msg, XPos, YPos);
```

The results of these string placement manipulations appear in Figure 7.4. As you can see, our text string is left-justified at the top and right-justified at the bottom. And the text in the center is indeed centered. Our applet is a success. The code for this applet appears in Listing 7.3.

Figure 7.4 Our Justify applet justifies text.

Listing 7.3 Justify.java

```
import java.applet.Applet;
import java.awt.*;

public class Justify extends java.applet.Applet {

    Font justifyFont;
    FontMetrics justifyFontMetrics;
```

```
String msg = "Hello World!";
int XPos, YPos;

public void paint (Graphics g) {
        justifyFont = new Font("TimesRoman", Font.PLAIN, 24);
        g.setFont(justifyFont);

        justifyFontMetrics = getFontMetrics(justifyFont);

        XPos = 0;
        YPos = justifyFontMetrics.getHeight();
        g.drawString(msg, XPos, YPos);

        XPos = (size().width - justifyFontMetrics.stringWidth(msg)) / 2;
        YPos = (size().height + justifyFontMetrics.getHeight()) / 2;
        g.drawString(msg, XPos, YPos);

        XPos = size().width - justifyFontMetrics.stringWidth(msg);
        YPos = size().height;
        g.drawString(msg, XPos, YPos);
    }
}
```

Let's get back to images. In our next example, we'll see how to enable imagemaps.

Imagemaps

If you've surfed the Web, you've almost certainly seen imagemaps, images with active spots that you can click to jump to another URL. For example, we might display some graphics with the text "Java" and "Sun" set off in boxes, forming their own graphical "buttons":

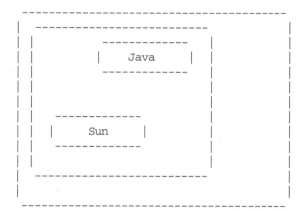

When the user clicks the **Java** button, for example, we can jump to a new URL: **http://java.sun.com**. Let's see this at work. The graphic image we can use for our imagemap, called, for example, **imagemap.gif**, appears in Figure 7.5.

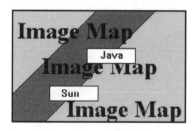

Figure 7.5 Our imagemap's graphics file.

The first step is to display our new imagemap in an applet, and we do that by starting out with an object of class Image named, for example, Imap, this way:

```
import java.applet.Applet;
import java.awt.*;
import java.net.*;
```

```
         public class Imagemap extends Applet {

-->              Image Imap;
                        .
                        .
                        .
```

In the init() function, we load the Image object Imap with the graphics file
Imagemap.gif:

```
         import java.applet.Applet;
         import java.awt.*;
         import java.net.*;

         public class Imagemap extends Applet {

                 Image Imap;

                 public void init(){
-->                      Imap = getImage(getCodeBase(), "Imagemap.gif");
                 }         .
                           .
                           .
```

All that's left is to display the image, and we do so with the drawImage() method
in the paint() method (our image is 240 pixels wide and 155 pixels high):

```
            public void paint (Graphics g) {
                g.drawImage(Imap, 10, 10, 240, 155, this);
            }
```

At this point, our imagemap appears in the applet. But how do we make it
active? We can let the user click the name **Java** or **Sun** and jump to those Web
sites by using mouse events, such as mouseDown():

```
         import java.applet.Applet;
         import java.awt.*;
         import java.net.*;

         public class Imagemap extends Applet {
```

```
                Image Imap;

                public void init(){
                        Imap = getImage(getCodeBase(), "Imagemap.gif");
                }

-->             public boolean mouseDown(Event e, int x, int y){
                    .
                    .
                    .
```

To jump to a new location, we need a Java URL object. We can create one named, for example, newURL, like this:

```
        public class Imagemap extends Applet {

                Image Imap;

                public void init(){
                        Imap = getImage(getCodeBase(), "Imagemap.gif");
                }

                public boolean mouseDown(Event e, int x, int y){
-->                     URL newURL = null;
                            .
                            .
                            .
```

The URL Class's constructors and methods appear in Table 7.4.

Table 7.4 URL Class's Constructors and Methods

```
        java.lang.Object
           |
           +----java.net.URL
```

URL(String, String, int, String)	Creates absolute URL from specified protocol, host, port, and file
URL(String, String, String)	Creates absolute URL from specified protocol, host, and file

URL(String)	Creates URL from unparsed absolute URL
URL(URL, String)	Creates URL from unparsed URL in specified context
equals(Object)	Compares two URL objects
getContent()	Returns contents from opened connection
getFile()	Returns filename
getHost()	Returns host name
getPort()	Returns port number
getProtocol()	Returns protocol name
hashCode()	Creates integer for hash table indexing
openConnection()	Creates a URLConnection object that contains a connection to the URL
openStream()	Opens an input stream
sameFile(URL)	Compares two URLs
set(String, String, int, String, String)	Sets fields of the URL
setURLStreamHandlerFactory (URLStreamHandlerFactory)	Sets URLStreamHandler factory
toExternalForm()	Reverses parsing of URL
toString()	Converts the URL to text-readable form

Now we can check if we are supposed to jump to a new URL by seeing where the user clicked the mouse button. If it was inside a graphical button, we should jump to a new URL. We first check to see if the mouseDown event took place in the graphical button marked **Java**:

```
    public boolean mouseDown(Event e, int x, int y){
            URL newURL = null;
-->         if( x > 104 + 10 && x < 171 + 10 && y > 53 + 10 &&
                 y < 75 + 10){ //Java
              .
              .
              .
```

If so, we create a new URL using our declared newURL object:

```
public boolean mouseDown(Event e, int x, int y){
        URL newURL = null;
        if( x > 104 + 10 && x < 171 + 10 && y > 53 + 10 &&
                    y < 75 + 10){ //Java
-->          try { newURL = new URL("http://java.sun.com"); }
                    .
                    .
                    .
```

Notice the *try* keyword here. This is part of exception handling, and it means that we are attempting an operation that might generate an error. We'll see more about exceptions later in Chapter 10. For now, we just use this code. If the operation generates an error, we can "catch" and handle the error, which is an error of type MalformedURLexception with the catch keyword this way:

```
public boolean mouseDown(Event e, int x, int y){
        URL newURL = null;
        if( x > 104 + 10 && x < 171 + 10 && y > 53 + 10 &&
                    y < 75 + 10){ //Java
                try { newURL = new URL("http://java.sun.com"); }
-->          catch (MalformedURLException e1) {}
                    .
                    .
                    .
```

If there is no error, we jump to the new location this way in Java: getAppletContext().showDocument(newURL),   where getAppletContext() returns the Web browser itself to us:

```
public boolean mouseDown(Event e, int x, int y){
        URL newURL = null;
        if( x > 104 + 10 && x < 171 + 10 && y > 53 + 10 &&
                    y < 75 + 10){ //Java
                try { newURL = new URL("http://java.sun.com"); }
                catch (MalformedURLException e1) {}
-->          getAppletContext().showDocument(newURL);
        }
                    .
                    .
                    .
```

Our Java button in the imagemap is active. We can do the same for the **Sun** button, causing the Web browser to jump to **http://www.sun.com** if it is clicked. We check to see if it is clicked based on the mouse down position:

```
public boolean mouseDown(Event e, int x, int y){
        URL newURL = null;
        if( x > 104 + 10 && x < 171 + 10 && y > 53 + 10 &&
                y < 75 + 10){ //Java
                try { newURL = new URL("http://java.sun.com"); }
                catch (MalformedURLException e1) {}
                getAppletContext().showDocument(newURL);
        }
-->     if( x > 54 + 10 && x < 118 + 10 && y > 105 + 10 &&
                y < 125 + 10){ //Sun
                                .
                                .
                                .
```

If the **Sub** graphical button is clicked, we can jump to the Sun URL much as we did for the Java URL:

```
public boolean mouseDown(Event e, int x, int y){
        URL newURL = null;
        if( x > 104 + 10 && x < 171 + 10 && y > 53 + 10 &&
                y < 75 + 10){ //Java       .
                try { newURL = new URL("http://java.sun.com"); }
                catch (MalformedURLException e1) {}
                getAppletContext().showDocument(newURL);
        }
        if( x > 54 + 10 && x < 118 + 10 && y > 105 + 10 &&
                y < 125 + 10){ //Sun
-->             try { newURL = new URL("http://www.sun.com"); }
-->             catch (MalformedURLException e2) {}
-->             getAppletContext().showDocument(newURL);
        }
        return true;
}
```

When you run the applet, our imagemap appears as in Figure 7.6, and the graphical buttons are active. Our imagemap is a success. The code for this applet appears in Listing 7.4.

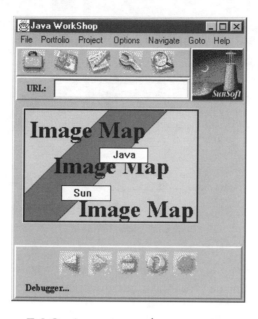

Figure 7.6 Our Imagemap applet supports imagemaps.

Listing 7.4 Imagemap.java

```java
import java.applet.Applet;
import java.awt.*;
import java.net.*;

public class Imagemap extends Applet {

    Image Imap;

    public void init(){
            Imap = getImage(getCodeBase(), "Imagemap.gif");
    }

    public boolean mouseDown(Event e, int x, int y){
            URL newURL = null;
            if( x > 104 + 10 && x < 171 + 10 && y > 53 + 10 &&
                y < 75 + 10){ //Java
                    try { newURL = new URL("http://java.sun.com"); }
                    catch (MalformedURLException e1) {}
                    getAppletContext().showDocument(newURL);
```

```
        }
        if( x > 54 + 10 && x < 118 + 10 && y > 105 + 10 &&
            y < 125 + 10){  //Sun
                try { newURL = new URL("http://www.sun.com"); }
                catch (MalformedURLException e2) {}
                getAppletContext().showDocument(newURL);
        }
        return true;
    }


    public void paint (Graphics g) {
        g.drawImage(Imap, 10, 10, 240, 155, this);
    }


}
```

The last topic we'll explore in this chapter is the Canvas class. This class lets you draw anywhere inside it (unlike other controls).

Canvases

Java Canvases are just like controls in which you can draw (you can't draw inside any other type of control):

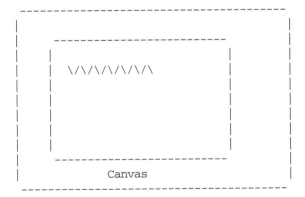

Like panels, you derive your Canvas controls from a base class and then customize the result. Let's see this at work. We can derive a new class named, for example, circleCanvas:

```
class circleCanvas extends java.awt.Canvas {      <--
                  .
                  .
                  .
}
```

Let's just draw a circle inside this Canvas for now:

```
class circleCanvas extends java.awt.Canvas {

  -->    public void paint (Graphics g) {
  -->            g.drawOval(10, 10, 40, 40);
  -->     }
}
```

Then we declare an object of our new circleCanvas class in an applet:

```
import java.applet.Applet;
import java.awt.*;

public class Canvases extends java.applet.Applet {

  -->    circleCanvas firstCanvas;
                  .
                  .
                  .
```

Finally, we add our new Canvas to the applet in the usual way, by creating the object and then using the add() method:

```
import java.applet.Applet;
import java.awt.*;

public class Canvases extends java.applet.Applet {

      circleCanvas firstCanvas;

      public void init(){
  -->          firstCanvas = new circleCanvas();
  -->          add(firstCanvas);
      }
```

```
class circleCanvas extends java.awt.Canvas {

      public void paint (Graphics g) {
             g.drawOval(10, 10, 40, 40);
      }
}
```

Our new canvas displays a circle, as shown in Figure 7.7.

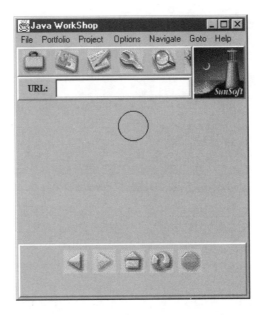

Figure 7.7 Our first Canvas example.

We have seen a great deal of image handling in this chapter, including reading images in, storing them in memory, displaying them in an applet, stretching them as we like, handling and justifying fonts, creating imagemaps, and now working with Canvases. Because Canvas is a Java component, it has a move() method, which means that you can move the Canvas object around the screen like this: `firstCanvas.move()`. The motion is smooth and easy to code; it will be the first example in the next chapter.

CHAPTER EIGHT

GRAPHICS ANIMATION

Welcome to graphics animation! In this chapter, we'll explore one of the most popular of Java topics. After all, what could be more startling than to have your Web pages start moving before an unsuspecting user's eyes? Here, we'll see easy animation techniques, including using the Java Animator class, launching new multitasking threads to support animation, and using clipping, new repainting methods, and double buffering to avoid flicker. We'll also look at interactive animation using XOR drawing and more. Let's get started upgrading our Canvases example Chapter 7 to support animation the easy way.

Using Canvases for Animation

One easy method of animation is to put your graphics in a Canvas control and to use the control's move() method to move the control around, creating the impression that the graphics figure is moving around by itself:

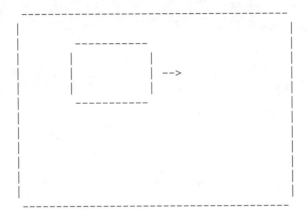

Let's update our Canvases example of the previous chapter by adding a button that the user can press to see the circle in our Canvas move across the applet. We start our applet as usual:

```
class circleCanvas extends java.awt.Canvas {
        .
        .
        .
```

Next, we set up our circleCanvas class, drawing the circle in it:

```
class circleCanvas extends java.awt.Canvas {

        public void paint (Graphics g) {
                g.drawOval(10, 10, 40, 40);
        }
}
```

Now we declare a Canvas named movingCanvas and the button we'll need to start the Canvas moving:

```
import java.applet.Applet;
import java.awt.*;

public class Canvases extends java.applet.Applet {

-->     circleCanvas movingCanvas;
-->     Button button1;
          .
          .
          .
```

Then we create movingCanvas and add it to our applet:

```
import java.applet.Applet;
import java.awt.*;

public class Canvases extends java.applet.Applet {

        circleCanvas movingCanvas;
        int loop_index;
        Button button1;

        public void init(){
-->             movingCanvas = new circleCanvas();
-->             movingCanvas.resize(60, 60);
-->             add(movingCanvas);
              .
              .
              .
```

And we add the button as well:

```
import java.applet.Applet;
import java.awt.*;

public class Canvases extends java.applet.Applet {

        circleCanvas movingCanvas;
```

```
      int loop_index;
      Button button1;

      public void init(){
              movingCanvas = new circleCanvas();
              movingCanvas.resize(60, 60);
              add(movingCanvas);
-->           button1 = new Button("Click Me");
-->           add(button1);
        }            .

                     .

                     .
```

Next, we connect the button to the code that will move the Canvas:

```
      public boolean action (Event e, Object o){
-->           if(e.target.equals(button1)){
                      .

                      .

                      .
```

If the button is pushed, we set up a loop of 200 iterations, which will move our Canvas to the right:

```
      public boolean action (Event e, Object o){
          if(e.target.equals(button1)){
-->           for(loop_index = 0; loop_index < 200; loop_index++){
                  .

                  .

                  .
              }
          }
          return true;
      }
```

To actually move the Canvas, we just use the move() method like this:

```
      public boolean action (Event e, Object o){
          if(e.target.equals(button1)){
              for(loop_index = 0; loop_index < 200; loop_index++){
-->               movingCanvas.move(loop_index, 0);
              }
```

```
        }
        return true;
    }
```

Now when we run the applet as in Figure 8.1 and click the **Click Me** button, the circle (which is inside our movingCanvas object) moves to the right across the applet. The code appears in Listing 8.1. That's one easy way of performing animation, but there are drawbacks. For example, if there were more items in our applet, it would be obvious as the object moved over them that our circle is embedded in a square Canvas object. In addition, our loop monopolizes the computer:

```
for(loop_index = 0; loop_index < 200; loop_index++){
    movingCanvas.move(loop_index, 0);
}
```

This is no way to do animation, since all the time given to our Web page is taken over by this loop while it runs, and if this kind of loop were infinite (i.e., for an animation that just keeps going), it would monopolize all our Web browser's capabilities. But there is a better way.

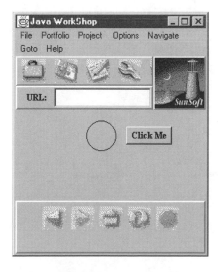

Figure 8.1 Our moving Canvas example allows easy animation.

Listing 8.1 Canvases Version 2

```
import java.applet.Applet;
import java.awt.*;

public class Canvases extends java.applet.Applet {

        circleCanvas movingCanvas;
        int loop_index;
        Button button1;

        public void init(){
                movingCanvas = new circleCanvas();
                movingCanvas.resize(60, 60);
                add(movingCanvas);
                button1 = new Button("Click Me");
                add(button1);
        }
                public boolean action (Event e, Object o){
                        if(e.target.equals(button1)){
                            for(loop_index = 0; loop_index < 200; loop_index++){
                                movingCanvas.move(loop_index, 0);
                            }
                        }
                        return true;
                }
}

class circleCanvas extends java.awt.Canvas {

        public void paint (Graphics g) {
                g.drawOval(10, 10, 40, 40);
        }
}
```

Let's turn now to seeing true animation at work. In Java, true animation is multitasking.

Welcome to Animation: The Wheel Applet

For our first true animation example, we'll place a circle on the screen in our applet:

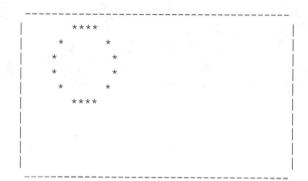

We can make the circle half red, half blue, and make it spin around continuously. To do this, we'll launch the actual working details of our animation in a new *thread*. We'll see in the next chapter that multitasking in Java is based on threads, or independent execution streams, and that each task in the multitasking environment gets its own thread. Each thread is given some time by the computer, and those tasks can operate independently. Seeing how this works in overview now will give us a good start on the next chapter. To allow our applet to support multitasking, we add the line "implements Runnable" this way in our applet:

```
        import java.awt.*;
        import java.applet.Applet;

    public class Wheel extends Applet
-->      implements Runnable{
            .
            .
            .
```

This allows us to start new threads easily, as we'll see in a minute. For now, we use a graphics program (such as Windows Paintbrush) to create four images of a red and blue wheel in the process of running, as shown in Figure 8.2. We'll save these images in the files **Wheel1.gif**, **Wheel2.gif**, **Wheel3.gif**, and **Wheel4.gif**.

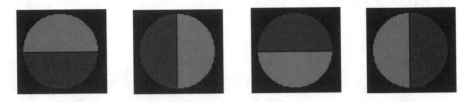

Figure 8.2 Our animation images.

Next, we set up space to store these images in an array named wheelImages[]:

```
import java.awt.*;
import java.applet.Applet;

public class Wheel extends Applet
    implements Runnable{

-->    Image wheelImages[] = new Image[4];
              .
              .
              .
```

And, in the init() function, we load the images into the image array:

```
import java.awt.*;
import java.applet.Applet;

public class Wheel extends Applet
    implements Runnable{

Image wheelImages[] = new Image[4];
```

```
      public void init() {
-->           wheelImages[0] = getImage(getCodeBase(), "Wheel1.gif");
-->           wheelImages[1] = getImage(getCodeBase(), "Wheel2.gif");
-->           wheelImages[2] = getImage(getCodeBase(), "Wheel3.gif");
-->           wheelImages[3] = getImage(getCodeBase(), "Wheel4.gif");
      }       .
              .
              .
```

Next, we can launch our new thread. We'll see how this process really works in the next chapter. Here, we just use the code, which is based on the start() method. This method is called when the applet starts. In it we'll create a new Java Thread object named wheelThread, and start that new thread running this way:

```
      import java.awt.*;
      import java.applet.Applet;

   public class Wheel extends Applet
      implements Runnable{

      Image wheelImages[] = new Image[4];
-->   Thread wheelThread;

      public void init() {
            wheelImages[0] = getImage(getCodeBase(), "Wheel1.gif");
            wheelImages[1] = getImage(getCodeBase(), "Wheel2.gif");
            wheelImages[2] = getImage(getCodeBase(), "Wheel3.gif");
            wheelImages[3] = getImage(getCodeBase(), "Wheel4.gif");
      }


      public void start() {
-->             wheelThread = new Thread(this);
-->             wheelThread.start();
      }         .
                .
                .
```

In addition, when we leave our Web page, we should stop the new thread, which is independent of our applet and would otherwise keep running. We do that in our applet's stop() method, called when the applet stops, this way:

```
          import java.awt.*;
          import java.applet.Applet;

     public class Wheel extends Applet
          implements Runnable{

          Image wheelImages[] = new Image[4];
          Thread wheelThread;

          public void init() {
                  wheelImages[0] = getImage(getCodeBase(), "Wheel1.gif");
                  wheelImages[1] = getImage(getCodeBase(), "Wheel2.gif");
                  wheelImages[2] = getImage(getCodeBase(), "Wheel3.gif");
                  wheelImages[3] = getImage(getCodeBase(), "Wheel4.gif");
          }

          public void start() {
                      wheelThread = new Thread(this);
                      wheelThread.start();
          }

          public void stop() {
  -->                   wheelThread.stop();
          }                         .
                                    .
                                    .
```

Now we are ready to write the code that will be executed in our new thread. We place that code in the applet's run() method. (We'll see why in the next chapter. For now, we'll just use the following code.) Since this code is in our new thread, which can be managed by the computer as an independent process, we have no problem using an infinite loop [using the while() loop] to keep our animation going:

```
     public class Wheel extends Applet
          implements Runnable{

          Image wheelImages[] = new Image[4];
          Image nowImage;
```

```
        int wheelIndex = 0;
        Thread wheelThread;

        public void init() {
                wheelImages[0] = getImage(getCodeBase(), "Wheel1.gif");
                wheelImages[1] = getImage(getCodeBase(), "Wheel2.gif");
                wheelImages[2] = getImage(getCodeBase(), "Wheel3.gif");
                wheelImages[3] = getImage(getCodeBase(), "Wheel4.gif");
        }


-->     public void run() {
-->             while(true){
                        .
                        .
                        .
                }
        }
```

The run() method is where our new thread will do the work of animating the four images we have stored. The first task is to determine what image to display. We can do that with a new integer named, for example, wheelIndex, which will cycle through the numbers 1 to 4 and then start over with 1 again. Using this as the index in the wheelImages[] array, we can load the correct image into a new Image object named nowImage:

```
    public class Wheel extends Applet
        implements Runnable{

        Image wheelImages[] = new Image[4];
-->     Image nowImage;
-->     int wheelIndex = 0;
        Thread wheelThread;

        public void init() {
                wheelImages[0] = getImage(getCodeBase(), "Wheel1.gif");
                wheelImages[1] = getImage(getCodeBase(), "Wheel2.gif");
                wheelImages[2] = getImage(getCodeBase(), "Wheel3.gif");
                wheelImages[3] = getImage(getCodeBase(), "Wheel4.gif");
        }

        public void run() {
                while(true){
```

```
    -->                     nowImage = wheelImages[wheelIndex++];
    -->                     if(wheelIndex > 3)wheelIndex = 0;
                                        .
                                        .
                                        .

                    }
            }
```

All that remains is to display nowImage in our applet. We do that by calling repaint():

```
public class Wheel extends Applet
    implements Runnable{

    Image wheelImages[] = new Image[4];
    Image nowImage;
    int wheelIndex = 0;
    Thread wheelThread;

    public void init() {
            wheelImages[0] = getImage(getCodeBase(), "Wheel1.gif");
            wheelImages[1] = getImage(getCodeBase(), "Wheel2.gif");
            wheelImages[2] = getImage(getCodeBase(), "Wheel3.gif");
            wheelImages[3] = getImage(getCodeBase(), "Wheel4.gif");
    }

    public void run() {
            while(true){
                    nowImage = wheelImages[wheelIndex++];
                    if(wheelIndex > 3)wheelIndex = 0;
    -->             repaint();
                            .
                            .
                            .

                }
            }
    }
```

In addition, we can wait a while before placing the next image on the screen; otherwise, the wheel would simply whip around at top speed. We do that by putting the thread to *sleep* for, say 0.2 second with the Thread object sleep(), which we enclose in a try and catch exception block. This method takes the number of milliseconds (thousandths of a second) to sleep, so we pass it a value of 200, which is 0.2 second:

```
public class Wheel extends Applet
    implements Runnable{

    Image wheelImages[] = new Image[4];
    Image nowImage;
    int wheelIndex = 0;
    Thread wheelThread;

    public void init() {
            wheelImages[0] = getImage(getCodeBase(), "Wheel1.gif");
            wheelImages[1] = getImage(getCodeBase(), "Wheel2.gif");
            wheelImages[2] = getImage(getCodeBase(), "Wheel3.gif");
            wheelImages[3] = getImage(getCodeBase(), "Wheel4.gif");
    }

    public void run() {
            while(true){
                    nowImage = wheelImages[wheelIndex++];
                    if(wheelIndex > 3)wheelIndex = 0;
                    repaint();
-->                 try {Thread.sleep(200);}
-->                 catch(InterruptedException e) { }
            }
    }
}
```

Now all that's left is to put together the paint() method to draw the image in the nowImage object. We can draw that image with drawImage():

```
public void paint (Graphics g) {
        g.drawImage(nowImage, 10, 10, this);
}
```

Now when you start the applet, our animation also starts the wheel spinning, as in Figure 8.3. Our animation example is a success, even if we do have to wait for the next chapter to see how the mutlithreading part works. The code for this applet appears in Listing 8.2.

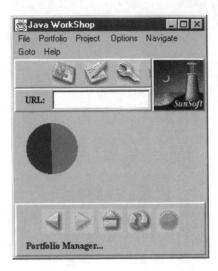

Figure 8.3 Our Wheel applet supports animation.

Listing 8.2 Wheel.java

```java
import java.awt.*;
import java.applet.Applet;

public class Wheel extends Applet
    implements Runnable{

    Image wheelImages[] = new Image[4];
    Image nowImage;
    int wheelIndex = 0;
    Thread wheelThread;

    public void init() {
            wheelImages[0] = getImage(getCodeBase(), "Wheel1.gif");
            wheelImages[1] = getImage(getCodeBase(), "Wheel2.gif");
            wheelImages[2] = getImage(getCodeBase(), "Wheel3.gif");
            wheelImages[3] = getImage(getCodeBase(), "Wheel4.gif");
    }

    public void start() {
                wheelThread = new Thread(this);
                wheelThread.start();
    }
```

```
public void stop() {
            wheelThread.stop();
}

public void run() {
        while(true){
                nowImage = wheelImages[wheelIndex++];
                if(wheelIndex > 3)wheelIndex = 0;
                repaint();
                try {Thread.sleep(200);}
                catch(InterruptedException e) { }
        }
}

public void paint (Graphics g) {
        g.drawImage(nowImage, 10, 10, this);
}

}
```

Our first animation example flickers as the whole page is redrawn each time we redraw our wheel. Let's see what we can do about reducing flicker, which is always an animation problem, as we turn to some advanced animation techniques.

Using Transparent GIFs in Animation

You might notice in Figure 8.3 that the wheel appears round on the Web page background, although they were actually drawn on a black (Color(0, 0, 0)) background, as shown in Figure 8.2. That's because we made the images in *transparent* GIFs. That is, we can select one color to be "transparent" in our **.gif** files, and we chose black, the background color. That makes the background show through instead of being covered, as in Figure 8.3. It's often desirable to do this to allow background graphics to show through your graphics, avoiding the blocky effects of always having to use rectangles for graphics images. There are many ways to produce transparent GIFs. You can use the utility LView Pro 1B mentioned in Chapter 1; just select the

Background Color... menu item in the Options menu, click the color you want to have as the transparent color, and save the file in Gif 89a format.

Using Clipping and Overriding update() to Reduce Flicker

We'll use two methods to reduce animation flicker here: overriding the Java update() method and using clipping. When we call repaint(), what really happens is that the update() method is called so that the entire applet's display is cleared before it is repainted. In animation, this results in flickering. There is, however, a way to avoid having the entire applet repainted each time; we can override the update() method by including our own version:

```
public void update(Graphics g) {

}
```

Here, we just call the paint() method:

```
public void update(Graphics g) {
        paint(g);
}
```

We've reduced flicker tremendously just by not having Java automatically clear the whole page in the update method. That technique doesn't always work for animation. There are cases when you would like the applet cleared before you draw new images, but it often can be used very well.

We can also use another animation trick. Instead of redrawing the whole applet, we can instruct Java to just redraw the immediate region around our spinning wheel. We do that with the clipRect() method. All we have to do to use clipRect() is to pass it the coordinates of a rectangle, and Java will restrict repainting operations to that rectangle. In our update() method, that looks like this:

```
        public void update(Graphics g) {
-->             g.clipRect(10, 10, 100, 100);
                paint(g);
        }
```

Now flicker is gone from our applet. We've stopped the entire applet from being cleared and restricted actual drawing to the immediate space around our animation. Our Wheel applet has been very much improved. The new version appears in Listing 8.3.

Listing 8.3 Wheel.java Version 2

```
        import java.awt.*;
        import java.applet.Applet;

    public class Wheel extends Applet
        implements Runnable{

        Image wheelImages[] - new Image[4];
        Image nowImage;
        int wheelIndex = 0;
        Thread wheelThread;

        public void init() {
                wheelImages[0] = getImage(getCodeBase(), "Wheel1.gif");
                wheelImages[1] = getImage(getCodeBase(), "Wheel2.gif");
                wheelImages[2] = getImage(getCodeBase(), "Wheel3.gif");
                wheelImages[3] = getImage(getCodeBase(), "Wheel4.gif");
        }

        public void start() {
                    wheelThread = new Thread(this);
                    wheelThread.start();
        }

        public void stop() {
                    wheelThread.stop();
        }

        public void run() {
                while(true){
                        nowImage = wheelImages[wheelIndex++];
                        if(wheelIndex > 3)wheelIndex = 0;
```

```
              repaint();
              try {Thread.sleep(200);}
              catch(InterruptedException e) { }
        }
    }

    public void paint (Graphics g) {
          g.drawImage(nowImage, 10, 10, this);
    }

    public void update(Graphics g) {
          g.clipRect(10, 10, 100, 100);
          paint(g);
    }
  }
```

Because animation is such a popular thing in Java, you would think that they would support it with a built-in Animator class, and they do, sort of.

Sun's Animator Class Example

Sun's Animator class is available directly from Sun at **http://java.sun /applets/applets/animator**, and you'll need three class files:

> Animator.class
>
> ImageNotFoundException.class
>
> ParseException.class

After you've downloaded these **.class** files, you can load the Java Animator with an <APPLET> tag in your HTML files. Here is Sun's own documentation on how that works for Animator:

```
<APPLET CODE="Animator.class"
     WIDTH = "aNumber"            -- the width (in pixels) of
                                     the widest frame
     HEIGHT = "aNumber">          -- the height (in pixels) of
                                     the tallest frame
<PARAM NAME="IMAGESOURCE"
```

```
        VALUE="aDirectory">           -- the directory that has the
                                         animation frames (a series
                                         of pictures in GIF or JPEG
                                         format, by default named
                                         T1.gif, T2.gif, ...)
<PARAM NAME="STARTUP"
    VALUE="aFile">                    -- an image to display at
                                         load time
<PARAM NAME="BACKGROUND"
    VALUE="aFile">                    -- an image to paint the
                                         frames against
<PARAM NAME="STARTIMAGE"
    VALUE="aNumber">                  -- number of the starting
                                         frame (1..n)
<PARAM NAME="ENDIMAGE"
    VALUE="aNumber">                  -- number of the end frame
                                         (1..n)
<PARAM NAME="NAMEPATTERN"
    VALUE="dir/prefix%N.suffix">      -- a pattern to use for
                                         generating names
                                         based on STARTIMAGE and
                                         ENDIMAGE (See below.)
<PARAM NAME="PAUSE"
    VALUE="100">                      -- milliseconds to pause
                                         between images
                                         default (can be overridden
                                         by PAUSES)
<PARAM NAME="PAUSES"
    VALUE="300|200||400|200">         -- millisecond delay per
                                         frame. Blank
                                         uses default PAUSE value
<PARAM NAME="REPEAT"
    VALUE="true">                     -- repeat the sequence?
<PARAM NAME="POSITIONS"
    VALUE="100@200||200@100||200@200|100@100|105@105">
                                      -- positions (X@Y) for each
                                         frame.  Blank
                                         means use previous frame's
                                         position
<PARAM NAME="IMAGES"
    VALUE="3|3|2|1|2|3|17">           -- explicit order for frames
                                         - see below
<PARAM NAME="SOUNDSOURCE"
    VALUE="aDirectory">               -- the directory that has the
                                         audio files
<PARAM NAME="SOUNDTRACK"
```

```
        VALUE="aFile">                 -- an audio file to play
                                          throughout
    <PARAM NAME="SOUNDS"
        SOUNDS="aFile.au|||||bFile.au">
                                    -- audio files keyed to
                                       individual frames

    </APPLET>
```

The gist of this for us in our Wheel applet is that we should rename our **Wheel1.gif** to **Wheel4.gif** files to **T1.gif** to **T4.gif**, because the Java Animator expects graphics images to be stored as **T1.gif** to **Tn.gif** (where *n* is the number of the last image). In addition, since this is not a Java Workshop project, we put together a **.html** file to run the Animator like this:

```
<HTML>
<BODY>


<CENTER>
<APPLET CODE = Animator.class WIDTH = 200 HEIGHT = 200>
<PARAM NAME = endimage VALUE = 4>
<PARAM NAME = pause VALUE = 300>
<PARAM NAME = repeat VALUE = true>
</APPLET>
</CENTER>


</HTML>
</BODY>
```

Finally, we make sure that all the files we need are in our directory:

Animator.class

ImageNotFoundException.class

ParseException.class

T1.gif

T2.gif

T3.gif

T4.gif

Animator.html

When you load the **.html** file into a browser, you'll see our spinning wheel once again. Using the Java Animator, you can create animations with many effects, including sound, and that's very powerful. Let's look at another powerful technique—creating animation in response to the user's actions.

Interactive Animation: Updating the Painter Applet

In this next example, we'll examine a little about interactive animation, that is, animating what happens in our Web page to match the user's wishes. In particular, we can update our Painter applet from Chapter 7 so that when the user moves the mouse around, it appears that they are "dragging" the graphics figure they are working on to the size they want it, much like commercial paint programs do. That is, they may start drawing a rectangle:

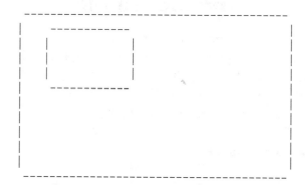

As they drag the mouse, the rectangle they are drawing expands to match:

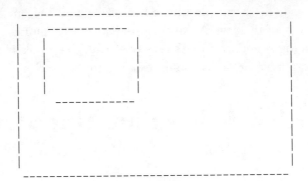

This will teach us more than creating animation with the mouse. One important aspect of animation is making sure that you don't disturb background graphics as you move your animation around in the foreground. We'll see how that works with the setXORMode() method here.

Starting the Xpainter Applet

We need to rewrite our Painter program to allow the user to "stretch" graphics images, because in Chapter 7, we were interested in only two points: the Anchor point and the DrawTo point. Now, however, the process is more complex. When the user first moves the mouse away from the Anchor point, we draw the graphics figure we are supposed to draw, for example, a rectangle:

If the user moves the mouse again to a new DrawTo point:

We have to erase the old rectangle from the Anchor point to the old DrawTo point to give the impression that the rectangle is stretching:

Then we draw a new rectangle from the Anchor point to the new DrawTo point:

```
Anchor point x------------------------
             |                        |
             |                        |
             |                        |
             |                        |
             |                        |
             |                        |
             -----------------------x DrawTo point
```

We'll successively draw new rectangles and erase old ones as the mouse moves. Let's see how this looks. We can handle the mouse first. In the mouseDown method, we begin by setting the mouse flags correctly:

```
        public boolean mouseDown(Event e, int x, int y){
-->             bMouseDownFlag = true;
-->             bMouseUpFlag = false;
                  .
                  .
                  .
```

Next, we set the Anchor point, ptAnchor:

```
        public boolean mouseDown(Event e, int x, int y){
                bMouseDownFlag = true;
                bMouseUpFlag = false;

-->             ptAnchor = new Point(x, y);
                return true;
        }
```

In the mouseUp method(), we do the same thing, setting the mouse flags first:

```
        public boolean mouseUp(Event e, int x, int y){
-->             bMouseDownFlag = false;
-->             bMouseUpFlag = true;
                        .
                        .
                        .
```

In addition, we also set the location at which the mouse went up to be the final extent (from the Anchor point) of our rectangle by setting the DrawTo point to this location:

```
        public boolean mouseUp(Event e, int x, int y){
                bMouseDownFlag = false;
                bMouseUpFlag = true;

-->             ptDrawTo = new Point(x, y);
                        .
                        .
                        .
```

We should not forget, however, that we still need to erase the last rectangle drawn, which we do by storing the old DrawTo point (we will use the old DrawTo point for the rectangle we want to erase) as ptOldDrawTo:

```
        public boolean mouseUp(Event e, int x, int y){
                bMouseDownFlag = false;
                bMouseUpFlag = true;
```

```
-->          ptOldDrawTo = ptDrawTo;
             ptDrawTo = new Point(x, y);
                   .
                   .
                   .
```

After that, we call repaint() so that the old rectangle can be erased and the new one drawn:

```
public boolean mouseUp(Event e, int x, int y){
        bMouseDownFlag = false;
        bMouseUpFlag = true;

        ptOldDrawTo = ptDrawTo;
        ptDrawTo = new Point(x, y);
-->     repaint();
        return true;
  }
```

That's it for mouseUp(). Now let's turn to the mouseDrag() method. We can retain the code we had earlier to record points as the mouse moves for our freehand drawing process (i.e., if the dDrawFlag is true, indicating the user clicked the **Draw** button):

```
     public boolean mouseDrag(Event e, int x, int y){
-->          if(bDrawFlag){
-->                  pts[ptindex] = new Point(x, y);
-->                  ptindex++;
-->          }            .
                          .
                          .
```

Next, we store the old DrawTo point as before (so we can clear the last rectangle drawn) by placing the old DrawTo point in ptOldDrawTo and storing the new DrawTo point:

```
     public boolean mouseDrag(Event e, int x, int y){
          if(bDrawFlag){
                  pts[ptindex] = new Point(x, y);
                  ptindex++;
          }
```

```
-->          ptOldDrawTo = ptDrawTo;
-->          ptDrawTo = new Point(x, y);
                    .
                    .
                    .
```

Finally, we call repaint() to redraw our rectangle:

```
public boolean mouseDrag(Event e, int x, int y){
        if(bDrawFlag){
                pts[ptindex] = new Point(x, y);
                ptindex++;
        }

        ptOldDrawTo = ptDrawTo;
        ptDrawTo = new Point(x, y);
-->     repaint();
        return true;
    }
```

That finishes mouseDrag() and, with it, all the mouse actions. Now let's put together the paint() method, where the real action is. First, we retain code we had before to handle freehand drawing, because that doesn't change:

```
    public void paint (Graphics g) {
-->         int loop_index;

-->         if(bDrawFlag){
-->             for(loop_index = 0; loop_index < ptindex; loop_index++){
-->                 g.drawLine(pts[loop_index].x, pts[loop_index].y,
-->                     pts[loop_index + 1].x, pts[loop_index + 1].y);
-->             }
-->             return;
-->         }   .
                    .
                    .
```

Now that the user has moved the mouse to a new location, we'll erase the old graphics figure we drew in response to the previous mouse move.

Setting the XOR Drawing Mode

At this point, we'll use a special drawing mode that is very useful for animation—the XOR drawing mode. XOR is the exclusive OR instruction, and it works by taking two arguments and matching them up bit by bit. If a zero meets a zero, the result is zero. If a one meets a zero, the result is one, just as with the OR operator. But if a one meets a one, the result is still zero:

```
XOR | 0  1
-----------
  0 | 0  1
  1 | 1  0
```

When you XOR a number with itself, all ones are sure to meet ones and all zeros are sure to meet zeros, so the result is zero. And here's the interesting part: if you XOR a value with some number, you get a certain result. If you XOR the same value with that result, you'll get back the original number again. That's why XOR drawing is useful. We can make sure we don't disturb the background graphics (if there are any) by XORing our figures with what's already there. To erase our graphics, we do precisely the same thing again, XORing our figure with what's on the screen, and we get back the original screen, erasing our graphics entirely.

In other words, we can draw our stretched rectangle in the XOR drawing mode, making it show up in the applet, and then we can simply draw it again to erase it when we need to. This is a very powerful animation technique. Note, however, that when you XOR a figure onto background graphics, the result is not your original graphic figure, but a numerical mix of your values and what was already there. For example, if you XOR a graphic figure onto a white screen, you'll end up getting an inverted image (e.g., red becomes green and so on). However, this is perfect for the purpose we are putting it to use here. An XORed image always shows up against the background (e.g., if the background is black, we'll end up drawing lines in white). The first task in the paint() method is to erase the old graphics figure (which goes from the Anchor point to the Old DrawTo point) before redrawing the new one now that the mouse has moved:

We will do this with the XOR drawing mode. To set the XOR drawing mode, we first set the drawing color to black: (`Color(0, 0, 0)`). Next, we call the Graphics class method setXORMode(), passing it the current background color. This means that when we draw on the current background color, it is switched to the current drawing color. If we draw on pixels that are the current drawing color, they are set to the background color we specified:

```
public void paint (Graphics g) {
        int loop_index;

        if(bDrawFlag){
            for(loop_index = 0; loop_index < ptindex; loop_index++){
                g.drawLine(pts[loop_index].x, pts[loop_index].y,
                    pts[loop_index + 1].x, pts[loop_index + 1].y);
            }
            return;
        }

-->     g.setColor(new Color(0, 0, 0));
-->     g.setXORMode(getBackground());
                    .
                    .
                    .
```

Now that we've set up XOR drawing [you can reset the drawing mode with setPaintMode()], we can erase the old graphics figure just by drawing it again. We do that by simply drawing that same figure between the Anchor and the Old DrawTo point, ptOldDrawTo.

For the Java Graphics methods, we'll need to know which of these points represents the top left of the graphics figure, so we add two new points, TopLeft and BottomRight:

```
        public void paint (Graphics g) {
                int loop_index;
-->             Point TopLeft, BottomRight;

                if(bDrawFlag){
                    for(loop_index = 0; loop_index < ptindex; loop_index++){
                        g.drawLine(pts[loop_index].x, pts[loop_index].y,
                            pts[loop_index + 1].x, pts[loop_index + 1].y);
                    }
                    return;
                }

                g.setColor(new Color(0, 0, 0));
                g.setXORMode(getBackground());
-->             TopLeft = new Point(Math.min(ptAnchor.x, ptOldDrawTo.x),
                    Math.min(ptAnchor.y, ptOldDrawTo.y));
-->             BottomRight = new Point(Math.max(ptAnchor.x, ptOldDrawTo.x),
                    Math.max(ptAnchor.y, ptOldDrawTo.y));
                        .
                        .
                        .
```

This is better than relying on the ptAnchor and ptOldDrawTo points, because now we know which point is at the top left:

```
TopLeft point x-------------------------
               |                       |
               |                       |
               |                       |
               |                       |
               |                       |
               |                       |
               -------------------------x BottomRight point
```

In addition, we need the width and height of the figure we are about to erase by redrawing so that we add two new variables, drawWidth and drawHeight:

```
        public void paint (Graphics g) {
                int loop_index;
-->             int drawWidth, drawHeight;
                Point TopLeft, BottomRight;

                if(bDrawFlag){
```

```
        for(loop_index = 0; loop_index < ptindex; loop_index++){
            g.drawLine(pts[loop_index].x, pts[loop_index].y,
                pts[loop_index + 1].x, pts[loop_index + 1].y);
        }
        return;
    }

    g.setColor(new Color(0, 0, 0));
    g.setXORMode(getBackground());
    TopLeft = new Point(Math.min(ptAnchor.x, ptOldDrawTo.x),
        Math.min(ptAnchor.y, ptOldDrawTo.y));
    BottomRight = new Point(Math.max(ptAnchor.x, ptOldDrawTo.x),
        Math.max(ptAnchor.y, ptOldDrawTo.y));
-->     drawWidth = Math.abs(ptOldDrawTo.x - ptAnchor.x);
-->     drawHeight = Math.abs(ptOldDrawTo.y - ptAnchor.y);
            .
            .
            .
            .
```

Finally, we just draw the required figure (checking the bRectFlag and others to make sure what figure we are to draw), which erases it now that we are using XOR mode:

```
public void paint (Graphics g) {
        int loop_index;
        int drawWidth, drawHeight;
        Point TopLeft, BottomRight;

        if(bDrawFlag){
            for(loop_index = 0; loop_index < ptindex; loop_index++){
                g.drawLine(pts[loop_index].x, pts[loop_index].y,
                    pts[loop_index + 1].x, pts[loop_index + 1].y);
            }
            return;
        }

        g.setColor(new Color(0, 0, 0));
        g.setXORMode(getBackground());
        TopLeft = new Point(Math.min(ptAnchor.x, ptOldDrawTo.x),
            Math.min(ptAnchor.y, ptOldDrawTo.y));
        BottomRight = new Point(Math.max(ptAnchor.x, ptOldDrawTo.x),
            Math.max(ptAnchor.y, ptOldDrawTo.y));
        drawWidth = Math.abs(ptOldDrawTo.x - ptAnchor.x);
        drawHeight = Math.abs(ptOldDrawTo.y - ptAnchor.y);
```

```
-->        if(bLineFlag){
-->                g.drawLine(ptAnchor.x, ptAnchor.y, ptOldDrawTo.x,
-->                    ptOldDrawTo.y);
-->        }
-->        if(bOvalFlag){
-->                g.drawOval(TopLeft.x, TopLeft.y, drawWidth,
-->                    drawHeight);
-->        }
-->        if(bRectFlag){
-->                g.drawRect(TopLeft.x, TopLeft.y, drawWidth,
-->                    drawHeight);
-->        }
-->        if(b3DRectFlag){
-->                g.draw3DRect(TopLeft.x, TopLeft.y, drawWidth,
-->                    drawHeight, true);
-->        }
-->        if(bRoundedFlag){
-->                g.drawRoundRect(TopLeft.x, TopLeft.y, drawWidth,
-->                    drawHeight, 10, 10);
-->        }           .
                       .
                       .
```

Now the old graphics figure is erased:

```
Anchor point x


                                        x Old DrawTo point

                                        x DrawTo point
```

But this raises a problem. This erasing code depends on ptOldDrawTo being filled before we execute it. However, the very first time we draw any rectangle at all, this point, which specifies the extent of the old graphics image we are to erase, will not be set correctly. For that reason, we set ptOldDrawTo to the Anchor point when the mouse goes down first, in mouseDown(), making sure there will be no error for this first rectangle:

```
public boolean mouseDown(Event e, int x, int y){
        bMouseDownFlag = true;
        bMouseUpFlag = false;
```

```
              ptAnchor = new Point(x, y);
    -->       ptOldDrawTo = new Point(x, y);
              return true;
      }
```

Having erased the old graphics figure, it's time to draw the new one (to the new location of the mouse, in ptDrawTo):

We'll draw the figure in black, which means a Color value of `Color(0, 0, 0)`. Since we have already set the XOR drawing mode to `g.setXORMode(getBackground())`, we simply set the current drawing color to the background color, because values XORed with themselves result in 0, which is what we want for a black drawing color:

```
public void paint (Graphics g) {
        int loop_index;
                .
                .
                .
        if(bRectFlag){
                g.drawRect(TopLeft.x, TopLeft.y, drawWidth,
                    drawHeight);
        }
        if(b3DRectFlag){
                g.draw3DRect(TopLeft.x, TopLeft.y, drawWidth,
                    drawHeight, true);
        }
        if(bRoundedFlag){
                g.drawRoundRect(TopLeft.x, TopLeft.y, drawWidth,
                    drawHeight, 10, 10);
        }
```

```
-->            g.setColor(getBackground());
                       .
                       .
                       .
```

The new figure we are to draw extends from the Anchor point, ptAnchor, to the new DrawTo point, ptDrawTo, so we set the TopLeft and BottomRight points to match, as well as find the figure's new height and width:

```
                .
                .
                .
            g.setColor(getBackground());
-->         TopLeft = new Point(Math.min(ptAnchor.x, ptDrawTo.x),
                Math.min(ptAnchor.y, ptDrawTo.y));
-->         BottomRight = new Point(Math.max(ptAnchor.x, ptDrawTo.x),
                Math.max(ptAnchor.y, ptDrawTo.y));
-->         drawWidth = Math.abs(ptDrawTo.x - ptAnchor.x);
-->         drawHeight = Math.abs(ptDrawTo.y - ptAnchor.y);
                .
                .
                .
```

After that, we just draw the new figure as we have done before:

```
            g.setColor(getBackground());
            TopLeft = new Point(Math.min(ptAnchor.x, ptDrawTo.x),
                Math.min(ptAnchor.y, ptDrawTo.y));
            BottomRight = new Point(Math.max(ptAnchor.x, ptDrawTo.x),
                Math.max(ptAnchor.y, ptDrawTo.y));
            drawWidth = Math.abs(ptDrawTo.x - ptAnchor.x);
            drawHeight = Math.abs(ptDrawTo.y - ptAnchor.y);
-->         if(bLineFlag){
-->             g.drawLine(ptAnchor.x, ptAnchor.y, ptDrawTo.x,
-->                 ptDrawTo.y);
-->         }
-->         if(bOvalFlag){
-->             g.drawOval(TopLeft.x, TopLeft.y, drawWidth,
-->                 drawHeight);
-->         }
-->         if(bRectFlag){
-->             g.drawRect(TopLeft.x, TopLeft.y, drawWidth,
-->                 drawHeight);
```

```
-->        }
-->        if(b3DRectFlag){
-->                g.draw3DRect(TopLeft.x, TopLeft.y, drawWidth,
-->                    drawHeight, true);
-->        }
-->        if(bRoundedFlag){
-->                g.drawRoundRect(TopLeft.x, TopLeft.y, drawWidth,
-->                    drawHeight, 10, 10);
-->        }
    }
```

Now the user can stretch graphics figures in our new Painter applet, as shown in Figure 8.4. Our new applet is a success, and the code appears in Listing 8.4.

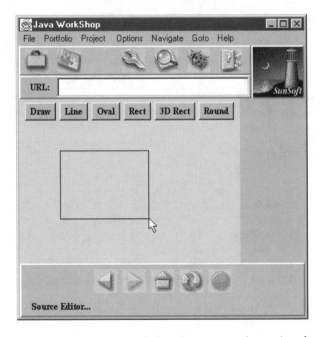

Figure 8.4 Our Xpainter applet lets the user stretch graphics figures.

Listing 8.4 Xpainter.java

```
import java.awt.Graphics;
import java.awt.*;
```

```java
import java.lang.Math;
import java.applet.Applet;

public class Xpainter extends Applet {

    Button buttonDraw, buttonLine, buttonOval, buttonRect, button3DRect;
    Button buttonRounded;

    Point pts[] = new Point[100];
    Point ptAnchor, ptDrawTo, ptOldAnchor, ptOldDrawTo;
    int ptindex = 0;

    boolean bMouseDownFlag = false;
    boolean bMouseUpFlag = false;
    boolean bDrawFlag = false;
    boolean bLineFlag = false;
    boolean bOvalFlag = false;
    boolean bRectFlag = false;
    boolean b3DRectFlag = false;
    boolean bRoundedFlag = false;

    public void init() {

            buttonDraw = new Button("Draw");
            buttonLine = new Button("Line");
            buttonOval = new Button("Oval");
            buttonRect = new Button("Rect");
            button3DRect = new Button("3D Rect");
            buttonRounded = new Button("Round");

            add(buttonDraw);
            add(buttonLine);
            add(buttonOval);
            add(buttonRect);
            add(button3DRect);
            add(buttonRounded);
    }

    public boolean mouseDown(Event e, int x, int y){
            bMouseDownFlag = true;
            bMouseUpFlag = false;

            ptAnchor = new Point(x, y);
            ptOldDrawTo = new Point(x, y);
```

```
                return true;
        }

        public boolean mouseUp(Event e, int x, int y){
                bMouseDownFlag = false;
                bMouseUpFlag = true;

                ptOldDrawTo = ptDrawTo;
                ptDrawTo = new Point(x, y);
                repaint();
                return true;
        }

        public boolean mouseDrag(Event e, int x, int y){
                if(bDrawFlag){
                        pts[ptindex] = new Point(x, y);
                        ptindex++;
                }

                ptOldDrawTo = ptDrawTo;
                ptDrawTo = new Point(x, y);
                repaint();
                return true;
        }

        public void paint (Graphics g) {
                int loop_index;
                int drawWidth, drawHeight;
                Point TopLeft, BottomRight;

                if(bDrawFlag){
                    for(loop_index = 0; loop_index < ptindex; loop_index++){
                        g.drawLine(pts[loop_index].x, pts[loop_index].y,
                            pts[loop_index + 1].x, pts[loop_index + 1].y);
                    }
                    return;
                }

                g.setColor(new Color(0, 0, 0));
                g.setXORMode(getBackground());
                TopLeft = new Point(Math.min(ptAnchor.x, ptOldDrawTo.x),
                    Math.min(ptAnchor.y, ptOldDrawTo.y));
                BottomRight = new Point(Math.max(ptAnchor.x, ptOldDrawTo.x),
                    Math.max(ptAnchor.y, ptOldDrawTo.y));
```

```
drawWidth = Math.abs(ptOldDrawTo.x - ptAnchor.x);
drawHeight = Math.abs(ptOldDrawTo.y - ptAnchor.y);
if(bLineFlag){
        g.drawLine(ptAnchor.x, ptAnchor.y, ptOldDrawTo.x,
            ptOldDrawTo.y);
}
if(bOvalFlag){
        g.drawOval(TopLeft.x, TopLeft.y, drawWidth,
            drawHeight);
}
if(bRectFlag){
        g.drawRect(TopLeft.x, TopLeft.y, drawWidth,
            drawHeight);
}
if(b3DRectFlag){
        g.draw3DRect(TopLeft.x, TopLeft.y, drawWidth,
            drawHeight, true);
}
if(bRoundedFlag){
        g.drawRoundRect(TopLeft.x, TopLeft.y, drawWidth,
            drawHeight, 10, 10);
}


g.setColor(getBackground());
TopLeft = new Point(Math.min(ptAnchor.x, ptDrawTo.x),
     Math.min(ptAnchor.y, ptDrawTo.y));
BottomRight = new Point(Math.max(ptAnchor.x, ptDrawTo.x),
     Math.max(ptAnchor.y, ptDrawTo.y));
drawWidth = Math.abs(ptDrawTo.x - ptAnchor.x);
drawHeight = Math.abs(ptDrawTo.y - ptAnchor.y);
if(bLineFlag){
        g.drawLine(ptAnchor.x, ptAnchor.y, ptDrawTo.x,
            ptDrawTo.y);
}
if(bOvalFlag){
        g.drawOval(TopLeft.x, TopLeft.y, drawWidth,
            drawHeight);
}
if(bRectFlag){
        g.drawRect(TopLeft.x, TopLeft.y, drawWidth,
            drawHeight);
}
if(b3DRectFlag){
        g.draw3DRect(TopLeft.x, TopLeft.y, drawWidth,
            drawHeight, true);
```

```
            }
        if(bRoundedFlag){
                g.drawRoundRect(TopLeft.x, TopLeft.y, drawWidth,
                    drawHeight, 10, 10);
            }


    }

    public boolean action(Event e, Object o){
        if(e.target.equals(buttonDraw)){
                bDrawFlag = !bDrawFlag;
                bLineFlag = false;
                bOvalFlag = false;
                bRectFlag = false;
                b3DRectFlag = false;
                bRoundedFlag = false;
            }
        if(e.target.equals(buttonLine)){
                bLineFlag = !bLineFlag;
                bDrawFlag = false;
                bOvalFlag = false;
                bRectFlag = false;
                b3DRectFlag = false;
                bRoundedFlag = false;
            }
        if(e.target.equals(buttonOval)){
                bOvalFlag = !bOvalFlag;
                bLineFlag = false;
                bDrawFlag = false;
                bRectFlag = false;
                b3DRectFlag = false;
                bRoundedFlag = false;
            }
        if(e.target.equals(buttonRect)){
                bRectFlag = !bRectFlag;
                bLineFlag = false;
                bOvalFlag = false;
                bDrawFlag = false;
                b3DRectFlag = false;
                bRoundedFlag = false;
            }
        if(e.target.equals(button3DRect)){
                b3DRectFlag = !b3DRectFlag;
                bLineFlag = false;
                bOvalFlag = false;
```

```
                bRectFlag = false;
                bDrawFlag = false;
                bRoundedFlag = false;
        }
        if(e.target.equals(buttonRounded)){
                bRoundedFlag = !bRoundedFlag;
                bLineFlag = false;
                bOvalFlag = false;
                bRectFlag = false;
                b3DRectFlag = false;
                bDrawFlag = false;
        }
        return true;
    }
  }
```

Before leaving this topic, we'll look into one last animation method—double buffering.

Double Buffering

If you have complex graphics as part of your animation, you probably don't want to construct them on the screen as the user watches. It would be much better to develop them off-screen and then pop the graphics on-screen as needed for your animation:

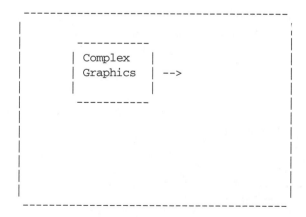

Double-buffering is all about developing complex graphics off-screen and then placing them on-screen as needed. Let's develop this now. Assume we have an image of 20 overlapping rectangles to draw and don't want to draw them right in front of the user. How can we do it?

We start with the usual thread-oriented animation applet:

```
        import java.awt.*;
        import java.applet.Applet;
        import java.util.Random;

public class Dbuf extends Applet
        implements Runnable{              <--
           .
           .
           .
```

Then we create an Image object with the createImage() method:

```
        import java.awt.*;
        import java.applet.Applet;
        import java.util.Random;

public class Dbuf extends Applet
        implements Runnable{

  -->    Image nowImage;

        public void init() {
  -->          nowImage = createImage(100, 100);
                .
                .
                .
```

To draw in our new Image object, we create a new Graphics object with the Image class's getGraphics() method:

```
        import java.awt.*;
        import java.applet.Applet;
        import java.util.Random;
```

```
public class Dbuf extends Applet
        implements Runnable{

        Image nowImage;
        Graphics nowGraphics;

        public void init() {
                nowImage = createImage(100, 100);
                nowGraphics = nowImage.getGraphics();
        }             .
                      .
                      .
```

Now we can draw in the Image object nowImage just as we could in a paint()
method by using a Graphics object.

As before, we write a start() method to start the animation thread:

```
public void start() {
        dbufThread = new Thread(this);
        dbufThread.start();
}
```

We also write a stop() method:

```
public void stop() {
        dbufThread.stop();
}
```

Now we're ready to write the run() method, in which we call repaint() and
pause for 200 milliseconds:

```
    public void run() {
-->         while(true){
-->                 repaint();
-->                 try {Thread.sleep(200);}
-->                 catch(InterruptedException e) { }
-->         }
    }
```

All that is left is to implement double-buffering in the paint() method:

```
public void paint (Graphics g) {
                          .
                          .
                          .
```

We will create our graphics in the (off-screen) Image object. Here, we'll draw 20 overlapping rectangles, so we set up a loop:

```
public void paint (Graphics g) {

        int Xinterval, loop_index;
        for(loop_index = 20; loop_index > 0; loop_index--){
                          .
                          .
                          .
```

We set up a random drawing color in the new Graphics object nowGraphics (corresponding to our off-screen buffer) with the Math.random() method:

```
public void paint (Graphics g) {

        int Xinterval, loop_index;
        for(loop_index = 20; loop_index > 0; loop_index--){
-->            nowGraphics.setColor(new Color((int) (255 *
                    Math.random()), (int) (255 * Math.random()),
                    (int) (255 * Math.random()))));
                          .
                          .
                          .
```

Then we draw rectangles filled with the new color:

```
public void paint (Graphics g) {

        int Xinterval, loop_index;
        for(loop_index = 20; loop_index > 0; loop_index--){
            nowGraphics.setColor(new Color((int) (255 *
                Math.random()), (int) (255 * Math.random()), (int)
                (255 * Math.random()))));
-->            nowGraphics.fillRect(0, 0, 5 * loop_index, 5 * loop_index);
        }
                          .
                          .
                          .
```

Finally, now that our graphics image is ready to go, we draw it on-screen with the applet's Graphics object's drawImage() method:

```
public void paint (Graphics g) {

    int Xinterval, loop_index;
    for(loop_index = 20; loop_index > 0; loop_index--){
        nowGraphics.setColor(new Color((int) (255 *
            Math.random()), (int) (255 * Math.random()), (int)
            (255 * Math.random()))));
        nowGraphics.fillRect(0, 0, 5 * loop_index, 5 * loop_index);
    }
    g.drawImage(nowImage, 10, 10, this);
}
```

We've created our graphics image off-screen and moved it on-screen as required. That's what double-buffering is all about. It's a useful technique in animation, since it allows you to develop complex graphics off-screen and display them as you like. The result appears in Figure 8.5. Our double-buffering animation example is a success. The code for this applet appears in Listing 8.5.

Figure 8.5 Our Dbuf applet uses double-buffering animation.

Listing 8.5 Dbuf.java

```java
import java.awt.*;
import java.applet.Applet;
import java.util.Random;

public class Dbuf extends Applet
        implements Runnable{

        Image nowImage;
        Graphics nowGraphics;
        Thread dbufThread;

        public void init() {
                nowImage = createImage(100, 100);
                nowGraphics = nowImage.getGraphics();
        }

        public void start() {
                        dbufThread = new Thread(this);
                        dbufThread.start();
        }

        public void stop() {
                        dbufThread.stop();
        }

        public void run() {
                while(true){
                        repaint();
                        try {Thread.sleep(200);}
                        catch(InterruptedException e) { }
                }
        }

        public void paint (Graphics g) {

                int Xinterval, loop_index;
                for(loop_index = 20; loop_index > 0; loop_index--){
                    nowGraphics.setColor(new Color((int) (255 *
                        Math.random()), (int) (255 * Math.random()), (int)
                        (255 * Math.random()))); 
                    nowGraphics.fillRect(0, 0, 5 * loop_index, 5 * loop_index);
                }
```

```
        g.drawImage(nowImage, 10, 10, this);
    }
}
```

That's it for graphics animation. In this chapter, we've progressed from simple animation to transparent GIFs, true animation, double buffering, flicker-reducing techniques, using Sun's Animator class, and interactive animation. We've come far. In the next chapter, we'll explore multitasking.

CHAPTER NINE

JAVA MULTITHREADING

In this chapter, we'll explore the multitasking capabilities of Java. Multitasking is the (apparent) ability of the computer to do several things at once. If you have several things that you should be working on at the same time, you should be using multitasking. Unlike other platforms in which multitasking is still somewhat of a curiosity, multitasking in Java is a central topic. A major reason for this is, of course, that the Internet is slow, and you don't necessarily want the user to have to wait for your whole Web page to load before being able to do anything. In addition, certain processes like animation lend themselves naturally to multitasking. For example, if we did not do something like split off a new multitasking thread (we'll define threads are shortly), the animation would take over all the system's resources.

Let's look at the simplest type of multitasking first. Here we'll simply derive a new class from the Java Thread class.

Creating a New Thread

In our first multitasking example, let's put together a basic applet that will create a new *thread*. What exactly is a thread? You might define a thread as an independent execution stream, but that definition isn't really helpful.

The best way to think about threads is in terms of their results. With threads, the result is that we can make many things appear to happen at the same time. That is, although the user is working in one part of our applet, we might be simultaneously loading graphics into another part at the same time or displaying numerical results. We might even be loading a Web page from the Internet. Threads allow us to perform multiple, and seemingly independent, tasks at the same time. Each of these tasks has its own thread, which is what ensures that its instructions are run. In this way, we can think of threads as the central part of a process that actually makes it run—the "thread" of execution that runs through any process's instructions. It's possible to have many threads (in many processes) being executed by your computer at once, and that's what this chapter is about.

Let's set up our first example with two buttons: **Start thread** and **Stop thread**:

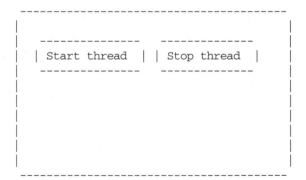

When the user clicks the **Start thread** button, we start our new thread. At this time, we can print out a message to the Java WorkShop's log file, as we'll see. When the user clicks **Stop thread**, we terminate the new thread.

The most basic way to set up a new thread is to derive a new class with the Java Thread class as the base class; here, we can make our new thread print out "Hello World!" so we'll call the new thread class HelloThread:

```
class HelloThread extends Thread {
        .
        .
        .
```

The Java Thread class's constructors and methods appear in Table 9.1.

Table 9.1 Thread Class's Constructors and Methods

```
java.lang.Object
       |
       +----java.lang.Thread
```

Thread()	Constructs a thread
Thread(Runnable)	Constructs Thread, which uses the run() method of the specified target
Thread(ThreadGroup, Runnable)	Constructs a thread in specified Thread group that uses the run() method of specified target
Thread(String)	Constructs a thread with specified name
Thread(ThreadGroup, String)	Constructs a thread in specified thread group with specified name
Thread(Runnable, String)	Constructs a thread with specified name and uses the run() method of specified target
Thread(ThreadGroup, Runnable, String)	Constructs a thread in specified thread group with specified name and uses run() method of the specified target
activeCount()	Returns number of active threads in thread group

checkAccess()	Checks if current Thread is allowed to modify access
countStackFrames()	Returns number of stack frames in Thread
currentThread()	Returns reference to currently executing Thread object
destroy()	Destroys Thread, without cleaning up
dumpStack()	Debugging procedure to print stack trace
enumerate(Thread[])	Places references to every thread in thread group in array
getName()	Gets and returns Thread's name
getPriority()	Returns Thread's priority, one of MAX_PRIORITY, MIN_PRIORITY, or NORM_PRIORITY
getThreadGroup()	Returns Thread's group
interrupt()	Sends interrupt to Thread
interrupted()	Checks if thread has been interrupted
isAlive()	Returns true if Thread is active
isDaemon()	Returns daemon flag of Thread
isInterrupted()	Checks if another thread has been interrupted
join(long)	Joins Thread, waits for it to die for specified time
join(long, int)	Joins Thread, waits for it to die, with more precise time
join()	Joins Thread, waits forever for it to die
resume()	Resumes Thread execution
run()	Body of this Thread
setDaemon(boolean)	Marks Thread as daemon Thread or user Thread
setName(String)	Sets Thread's name

setPriority(int)	Sets Thread's priority to one of MAX_PRIORITY, MIN_PRIORITY, or NORM_PRIORITY
sleep(long)	Makes Thread pause for specified milliseconds
sleep(long, int)	Pauses Thread for specified milliseconds and additional nanoseconds
start()	Starts Thread
stop()	Stops Thread
stop(Throwable)	Stops Thread by throwing an object
suspend()	Suspends Thread's execution
toString()	Returns String representation of Thread (includes thread's name, priority, and thread group)
yield()	Makes Thread object yield time slices to other threads

The body of a Thread object's code is in its run() method, which is called after the thread is initialized:

```
        class HelloThread extends Thread {

-->           public void run(){
                  .
                  .
                  .
              }
        }
```

Note that our thread is severely limited. We based it on the Thread class, not the Applet class, so we can't easily reach the screen or communicate with our applet object. One thing we can do, however, is to print out to the Java WorkShop log, which is a file named **weblog** (e.g., in Windows 95, **weblog** is stored as **c:\windows\.jde\weblog**). We do that with the System.out.println() method, where we print our "Hello World!" message like this:

```
class HelloThread extends Thread {

        public void run(){
-->             System.out.println("Hello World!");
        }
    }
```

That's it for our Thread class. Now we need to make sure that this thread is started and run. We do that in a new multithreaded applet named Multi. To start, we declare our two buttons (**Start thread** and **Stop thread**) and the new thread object of class HelloThread, which we might call Thread1:

```
import java.applet.Applet;
import java.awt.*;

public class Multi extends Applet {

-->     Button button1, button2;
-->     HelloThread Thread1;
            .
            .
            .
```

Next, we set up the two buttons in the init() method:

```
import java.applet.Applet;
import java.awt.*;

public class Multi extends Applet {

        Button button1, button2;
        HelloThread Thread1;

-->     public void init(){
-->             button1 = new Button("Start thread");
-->             add(button1);
-->             button2 = new Button("Stop thread");
```

```
-->                     add(button2);
-->                     Thread1 = new HelloThread();
-->            }
                    .
                    .
                    .
```

All that's left is to start and stop the new thread Thread1 when the user clicks the buttons. We begin with the **Start thread** button, button1. To start the new thread, Thread1, we use that object's start() method:

```
          public boolean action (Event e, Object o){

-->               if(e.target.equals(button1)){
-->                     Thread1.start();
-->               }           .
                             .
                             .
```

We can terminate Thread1 when the user clicks the **Stop thread** button, button2. To terminate the thread, we use its stop() method like this:

```
          public boolean action (Event e, Object o){

                  if(e.target.equals(button1)){
                        Thread1.start();
                  }
-->               if(e.target.equals(button2)){
-->                     Thread1.stop();
-->               }
                  return true;
          }
```

When we run the applet, we see our two buttons, as in Figure 9.1. Using those buttons, we can start and stop the new thread, which adds this string to the **weblog** file:

```
Hello World!
```

Figure 9.1 Our Thread-based multitasking example.

Our first multithreaded example is a success. The code for this applet appears in Listing 9.1.

Listing 9.1 Multi.java

```java
import java.applet.Applet;
import java.awt.*;

public class Multi extends Applet {

        Button button1, button2;
        HelloThread Thread1;

        public void init(){
                button1 = new Button("Start thread");
                add(button1);
                button2 = new Button("Stop thread");
                add(button2);
                Thread1 = new HelloThread();
        }

        public boolean action (Event e, Object o){

                if(e.target.equals(button1)){
                        Thread1.start();
                }
```

```
                    if(e.target.equals(button2)){
                            Thread1.stop();
                    }
                    return true;
            }
    }

    class HelloThread extends Thread {

            public void run(){
                    System.out.println("Hello World!");
            }
    }
```

That's fine as far as it goes, but of course we don't want to restrict our multi-threaded applets to printing to the **weblog** file. How do we connect our new threads directly to our applet objects so they can work with what appears on the screen or handle applet internal data? We'll look into that now.

Using Runnable

We would like to be able to derive a new class from *both* the Thread and Applet classes, but Java doesn't allow multiple inheritance yet. What we can do instead is to use the *Runnable* keyword like this when we declare our new class:

```
        import java.awt.*;
        import java.applet.Applet;

-->     public class aClass extends Applet implements Runnable{
                .
                .
                .
```

This way, our applet will be based on the Applet class and still support threads. We've already seen this at work, in fact, in the last chapter on animation. Let's review our Wheel example, looking especially at the thread-based parts of the program. That applet displayed a wheel in red and blue that spun around:

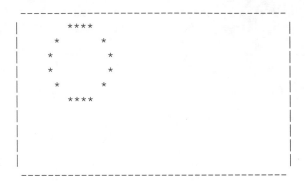

We started the Wheel applet by making our class Runnable:

```
        import java.awt.*;
        import java.applet.Applet;

--> public class Wheel extends Applet implements Runnable{
                    .
                    .
                    .
```

Next, we set up the new thread object, which we named wheelThread, and overrode the start() method, which is called when the applet first starts running:

```
        import java.awt.*;
        import java.applet.Applet;

    public class Wheel extends Applet implements Runnable{

        Image wheelImages[] = new Image[4];
        Image nowImage;
        int wheelIndex = 0;
-->     Thread wheelThread;

        public void init() {
                wheelImages[0] = getImage(getCodeBase(), "Wheel1.gif");
                wheelImages[1] = getImage(getCodeBase(), "Wheel2.gif");
                wheelImages[2] = getImage(getCodeBase(), "Wheel3.gif");
                wheelImages[3] = getImage(getCodeBase(), "Wheel4.gif");
        }
```

```
-->    public void start() {
                              .
-->    }              .
                      .
```

In the start() method, we created our new thread object and started it:

```
       public void start() {
-->                   wheelThread = new Thread(this);
-->                   wheelThread.start();
       }
```

And in the stop() method, we stopped the new thread (unless you stop the thread, it will keep going even when the user has left your Web page):

```
       public void start() {
                      wheelThread = new Thread(this);
                      wheelThread.start();
       }

-->    public void stop() {
-->                   wheelThread.stop();
       }
```

In the run() method, we put the actual code for the animation:

```
       public void run() {
              while(true){
                      nowImage = wheelImages[wheelIndex++];
                      if(wheelIndex > 3)wheelIndex = 0;
                      repaint();
                              .
                              .
                              .


                      }
              }
```

With applets that implement Runnable and want to start new threads, you put the code for the new thread into the run() method.

In addition, we paused for 0.2 second between animation frames by using the Thread sleep() method, which must be contained in a try/catch block (which we'll see more about in the next chapter):

```
public void run() {
        while(true){
                nowImage = wheelImages[wheelIndex++];
                if(wheelIndex > 3)wheelIndex = 0;
                repaint();
-->             try {Thread.sleep(200);}
-->             catch(InterruptedException e) { }
        }
    }
```

Our wheel animation was launched in a new thread, and the wheel spins are as shown in Figure 9.2. The listing of **Wheel.java** appears in Listing 9.2 for reference.

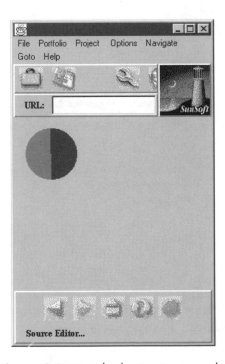

Figure 9.2 Our Wheel animation example.

Implementing the multitasking process in Java is simple. You declare your class so that it implements Runnable, declare your new thread(s), and start and stop it (them) in the start() and stop() applet methods. Finally, you place the thread's main code in the run() method. That's all there is to it.

Listing 9.2 Wheel.java

```java
import java.awt.*;
import java.applet.Applet;

public class Wheel extends Applet implements Runnable{

    Image wheelImages[] = new Image[4];
    Image nowImage;
    int wheelIndex = 0;
    Thread wheelThread;

    public void init() {
            wheelImages[0] = getImage(getCodeBase(), "Wheel1.gif");
            wheelImages[1] = getImage(getCodeBase(), "Wheel2.gif");
            wheelImages[2] = getImage(getCodeBase(), "Wheel3.gif");
            wheelImages[3] = getImage(getCodeBase(), "Wheel4.gif");
    }

    public void start() {
                wheelThread = new Thread(this);
                wheelThread.start();
    }

    public void stop() {
                wheelThread.stop();
    }

    public void run() {
            while(true){
                    nowImage = wheelImages[wheelIndex++];
                    if(wheelIndex > 3)wheelIndex = 0;
                    repaint();
                    try {Thread.sleep(200);}
                    catch(InterruptedException e) { }
            }
    }
```

```
public void paint (Graphics g) {
        g.drawImage(nowImage, 10, 10, this);
}

public void update(Graphics g) {
        g.clipRect(10, 10, 100, 100);
        paint(g);
}
}
```

There is considerably more to learn about multithreading than this basic technique. Let's begin our exploration of multitasking by setting threads' multi-tasking priorities.

Setting Thread Priority

Not all threads are equal; some might be considered more important than others. For example, you might want a thread to execute something in the background (a good example is the print spooler in Windows, which handles the printer in the background), and that thread should not get as much time as the one that is operating with the user in the foreground. In the same way, we can set the thread priority of our own threads with the setPriority() method, which takes the predefined constants Thread.MAX_PRIORITY, Thread.MIN_PRIORITY, or Thread.NORM_PRIORITY (threads are started with normal priority, Thread.NORM_PRIORITY). To see this in action, we can change our wheel animation thread to low priority like this:

```
      public void start() {
                  wheelThread = new Thread(this);
-->               WheelThread.setPriority(Thread.MIN_PRIORITY);
                  wheelThread.start();
      }
```

That's all it takes. At this time, however, not much beyond these priority levels are defined in Java's multitasking scheme, although this will probably change in the future.

Another common activity with threads is to suspend them for a while, letting them resume when there is more time or when necessary resources are available. Let's look into this activity next.

Suspending and Resuming Threads

To see how to make threads pause and then start again, let's add two buttons to our Wheel applet, **Suspend** and **Resume**, the real names for these processes:

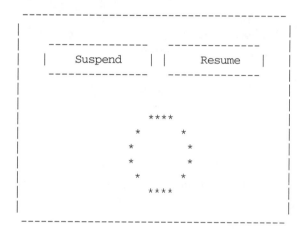

To modify our Wheel applet, we add suspendButton and resumeButton like this:

```
import java.awt.*;
import java.applet.Applet;

public class Suspend extends Applet
    implements Runnable{

    Image wheelImages[] = new Image[4];
    Image nowImage;
    int wheelIndex = 0;
    Thread wheelThread;
--> Button suspendButton, resumeButton;
        .

        .

        .
```

Next, we add those buttons to our layout:

```
        public void init() {
                wheelImages[0] = getImage(getCodeBase(), "Wheel1.gif");
                wheelImages[1] = getImage(getCodeBase(), "Wheel2.gif");
                wheelImages[2] = getImage(getCodeBase(), "Wheel3.gif");
                wheelImages[3] = getImage(getCodeBase(), "Wheel4.gif");
-->             suspendButton = new Button("Suspend");
-->             add(suspendButton);
-->             resumeButton = new Button("Resume");
-->             add(resumeButton);
        }
```

Now we make this buttons active in the action() method. First, we check if the
Suspend button was pushed:

```
        public boolean action (Event e, Object o){
-->             if(e.target.equals(suspendButton)){
                        .
                        .
                        .
```

If so, we just suspend our animation thread, which is named wheelThread,
using its suspend() method:

```
        public boolean action (Event e, Object o){
                if(e.target.equals(suspendButton)){
-->                     wheelThread.suspend();
-->             }           .
                            .
                            .
```

If the **Resume** button is clicked, we can execute the animation thread's resume() method:

```
public boolean action (Event e, Object o){
        if(e.target.equals(suspendButton)){
                wheelThread.suspend();
        }
-->     if(e.target.equals(resumeButton)){
-->             wheelThread.resume();
-->     }
        return true;
}
```

Finally, we set aside some space for our buttons by moving the animated wheel from (10, 10) to (100, 100):

```
public void paint (Graphics g) {
-->     g.drawImage(nowImage, 100, 100, this);
}


public void update(Graphics g) {
-->     g.clipRect(100, 100, 200, 200);
-->     paint(g);
}
```

Now we can suspend the wheel's motion by clicking the **Suspend** button, as shown in Figure 9.3. Clicking **Resume** starts the wheel spinning again. Our new version of the Wheel applet is a success. The code for this new applet appears in Listing 9.3.

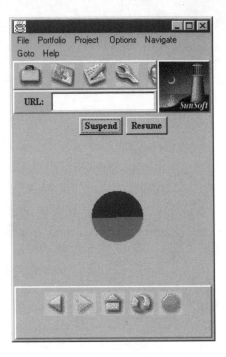

Figure 9.3 We suspend and resume the threaded animation in our Wheel applet.

Listing 9.3 Suspend.java

```java
import java.awt.*;
import java.applet.Applet;

public class Suspend extends Applet implements Runnable{

    Image wheelImages[] = new Image[4];
    Image nowImage;
    int wheelIndex = 0;
    Thread wheelThread;
    Button suspendButton, resumeButton;

    public void init() {
            wheelImages[0] = getImage(getCodeBase(), "Wheel1.gif");
            wheelImages[1] = getImage(getCodeBase(), "Wheel2.gif");
            wheelImages[2] = getImage(getCodeBase(), "Wheel3.gif");
            wheelImages[3] = getImage(getCodeBase(), "Wheel4.gif");
```

```java
        suspendButton = new Button("Suspend");
        add(suspendButton);
        resumeButton = new Button("Resume");
        add(resumeButton);
}

public boolean action (Event e, Object o){
        if(e.target.equals(suspendButton)){
                wheelThread.suspend();
        }
        if(e.target.equals(resumeButton)){
                wheelThread.resume();
        }
        return true;
}

public void start() {
                wheelThread = new Thread(this);
                wheelThread.start();
}

public void stop() {
                wheelThread.stop();
}

public void run() {
        while(true){
                nowImage = wheelImages[wheelIndex++];
                if(wheelIndex > 3)wheelIndex = 0;
                repaint();
                try {Thread.sleep(200);}
                catch(InterruptedException e) { }
        }
}

public void paint (Graphics g) {
        g.drawImage(nowImage, 100, 100, this);
}

public void update(Graphics g) {
        g.clipRect(100, 100, 200, 200);
        paint(g);
}
}
```

Animation is one way of using threads in our applets. Loading graphic images into our applets but not waiting for them before allowing the user to continue is another way that is almost as useful.

Loading Graphics in the Background

A good use of threads is loading time-consuming graphics into your applet in the background, allowing other things to happen while you do. For this example, we can modify our Imagemap applet, which just displays an image map that the user can click, into a new applet, Multimap. In Multimap, we load the imagemap into the applet in a new thread, allowing the user to do other things while the graphics are downloaded:

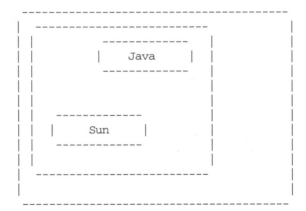

Let's look into this applet now. We modify our Imagemap applet by making Multimap a Runnable class:

```
        import java.applet.Applet;
        import java.awt.*;
        import java.net.*;

  -->   public class Multimap extends Applet implements Runnable {
                 .
                 .
                 .
```

We declare our new thread, Thread1, and an Image object named IMap to hold the Imagemap itself:

```
import java.applet.Applet;
import java.awt.*;
import java.net.*;

public class Multimap extends Applet implements Runnable {

-->          Thread Thread1;
-->          Image Imap;
                .
                .
                .
```

The real work of this applet is done in the mouseDown() function. We leave that as before, simply jumping to a new URL when the graphics buttons are pushed:

```
public boolean mouseDown(Event e, int x, int y){
        URL newURL = null;
        if( x > 104 + 10 && x < 171 + 10 && y > 53 + 10 && y <
            75 + 10){ //Java
                try { newURL = new URL("http://java.sun.com"); }
                catch (MalformedURLException e1) {}
                getAppletContext().showDocument(newURL);
        }
        if( x > 54 + 10 && x < 118 + 10 && y > 105 + 10 && y <
            125 + 10){ //Sun
                try { newURL = new URL("http://www.sun.com"); }
                catch (MalformedURLException e2) {}
                getAppletContext().showDocument(newURL);
        }
        return true;
}
```

We can start loading the graphics in the background when the applet starts by creating a new Thread object and placing it into Thread1. We create and start Thread1 in Multimap's start() method:

```
                    public void start() {
                            Thread1 = new Thread(this, "Thread1");
                            Thread1.start();
                    }
```

Similarly, we stop Thread1 when the applet stops:

```
                    public void stop() {
                            Thread1.stop();
                    }
```

Now, in the run() method, we can load the image into the Imap Image object. This process occurs in our Thread1 thread, so the user can do other things in our applet as it loads:

```
                    public void run(){
   -->                       Imap = getImage(getCodeBase(), "Imagemap.gif");
                              .
                              .
                              .
```

Note that we don't want the paint() method to try to display the image in Imap until we have loaded our imagemap into Imap, so let's set up a flag that indicates when the imagemap is fully loaded and ready to be displayed. We might call that flag ImageLoaded and set it to false initially:

```
            import java.applet.Applet;
            import java.awt.*;
            import java.net.*;

            public class Multimap extends Applet implements Runnable {

                    Thread Thread1;
                    Image Imap;
   -->              boolean ImageLoaded = false;
                        .
                        .
                        .
```

After the image is loaded in run(), we can set the ImageLoaded flag to true:

```
          public void run(){
                  Imap = getImage(getCodeBase(), "Imagemap.gif");
  -->             ImageLoaded = true;
                        .
                        .
                        .
```

And we can stop the current thread because it is no longer needed:

```
          public void run(){
                  Imap = getImage(getCodeBase(), "Imagemap.gif");
                  ImageLoaded = true;
  -->             Thread1.stop();
          }
```

The last thing to do is to make sure that the paint() method doesn't try to display the imagemap until it is loaded:

```
          public void paint (Graphics g) {
  -->         if(ImageLoaded){
                  g.drawImage(Imap, 10, 10, 240, 155, this);
  -->         }
          }
```

The result appears in Figure 9.4, where the imagemap was loaded in the background. Our Multimap applet is a success. The code for this applet appears in Listing 9.4.

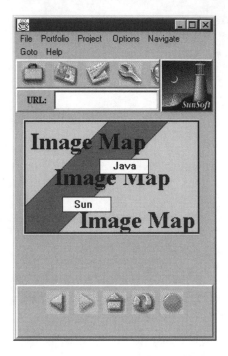

Figure 9.4 Our imagemap is loaded in by a background thread.

Listing 9.4 Multimap.java

```
import java.applet.Applet;
import java.awt.*;
import java.net.*;

public class Multimap extends Applet implements Runnable {

        Thread Thread1;
        Image Imap;
        boolean ImageLoaded = false;

        public void init(){

        }

        public void start() {
                Thread1 = new Thread(this, "Thread1");
```

```
        Thread1.start();
}

public void stop() {
        Thread1.stop();
}

public void run(){
        Imap = getImage(getCodeBase(), "Imagemap.gif");
        ImageLoaded = true;
        Thread1.stop();
}

public boolean mouseDown(Event e, int x, int y){
        URL newURL = null;
        if( x > 104 + 10 && x < 171 + 10 && y > 53 + 10 && y <
            75 + 10){ //Java
                try { newURL = new URL("http://java.sun.com"); }
                catch (MalformedURLException e1) {}
                getAppletContext().showDocument(newURL);
        }
        if( x > 54 + 10 && x < 118 + 10 && y > 105 + 10 && y <
            125 + 10){ //Sun
                try { newURL = new URL("http://www.sun.com"); }
                catch (MalformedURLException e2) {}
                getAppletContext().showDocument(newURL);
        }
        return true;
}

public void paint (Graphics g) {
    if(ImageLoaded){
        g.drawImage(Imap, 10, 10, 240, 155, this);
    }
}

}
```

We've see a lot about handling graphics with threads, but of course we can also handle textfields, having the data in a textfield updated automatically by a thread even while the user is doing something else. Let's look into that now in an example that will also introduce us to handling multiple threads.

Using Multiple Threads

Let's say that we have two new threads, each of which prints out square root values in a textfield, giving us two textfields like this:

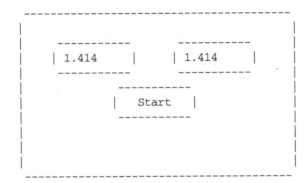

When the user clicks the **Start** button, we can start two threads, T1 and T2. T1 can print out square roots in textfield1, and T2 can print out square roots in textfield2.

Let's begin this applet, which we'll call **Sqrts.java**, by importing **java.lang.Math**, because that class has the square root routine we'll need to get square roots. Next, we declare our two threads, our text-matching textfields, and the **Start** button:

```
        import java.awt.*;
        import java.applet.Applet;
 -->    import java.lang.Math;

    public class Sqrts extends Applet implements Runnable{

 -->       Thread Thread1, Thread2;
 -->       TextField text1, text2;
 -->       Button button1;
               .
               .
               .
```

In the init() method, we can set up our textfields and the **Start** button:

```
public void init() {
        text1 = new TextField(20);
        text2 = new TextField(20);
        add(text1);
        add(text2);
        button1 = new Button("Start");
        add(button1);
}
```

Next, we connect our **Start** button, button1, to the action() method:

```
        public boolean action (Event e, Object o){

-->             if(e.target.equals(button1)){
                        .
                        .
                        .
```

When the user presses the **Start** button, we can start the first thread, giving it the name T1:

```
        public boolean action (Event e, Object o){

                if(e.target.equals(button1)){
-->                     Thread1 = new Thread(this, "T1");
-->                     Thread1.start();
                           .
                           .
                           .
```

We also start the second thread, giving it the name T2:

```
        public boolean action (Event e, Object o){

                if(e.target.equals(button1)){
                        Thread1 = new Thread(this, "T1");
                        Thread1.start();
-->                     Thread2 = new Thread(this, "T2");
-->                     Thread2.start();
                }
                return true;
        }
```

Now our threads, T1 and T2, are started. The real action—placing square roots in the textfields—takes place in the applet's run() method:

```
public void run() {
        .
        .
        .
```

T1 and T2 will both call this run() method. How do we tell them apart? How can we make sure that they put their output in the correct textfield? The answer is that we can actually check which thread is running by checking its name, using the thread getName() method.

Let's write the run() method now. We can have the applet print the square roots of the numbers from 1 to 500 by placing a loop in the run() method:

```
      public void run() {
-->           int loop_index;
-->           for(loop_index = 1; loop_index < 500; loop_index++){
                   .
                   .
                   .
```

Inside that loop, the first thing we do is to check to see if thread T1 is running this code:

```
      public void run() {
              int loop_index;
              for(loop_index = 1; loop_index < 500; loop_index++){
-->               if(((Thread.currentThread()).getName()).equals("T1")){
                       .
                       .
                       .
```

Note that we found the current thread's name like this: (Thread.currentThread()).getName(). If that thread's name is T1, we want to place the current square root (just the square root of the loop index) into textfield text1. We do that like this, where we can easily reach text1 because it is a member of the current applet object we are running in:

```
       public void run() {
               String out_string;
               int loop_index;
               out_string = new String();
               for(loop_index = 1; loop_index < 500; loop_index++){
                   if(((Thread.currentThread()).getName()).equals("T1")){
-->                    text1.setText(out_string.
-->                        valueOf(Math.sqrt((double)loop_index)));
                   }          .
                              .
                              .
```

Here we've used the Math class's sqrt() method to get a square root. Next, we do the same for thread T2, except we make sure that its output goes into textfield text2:

```
       public void run() {
               String out_string;
               int loop_index;
               out_string = new String();
               for(loop_index = 1; loop_index < 500; loop_index++){
                   if(((Thread.currentThread()).getName()).equals("T1")){
                       text1.setText(out_string.
                           valueOf(Math.sqrt((double)loop_index)));
                   }
-->                if(((Thread.currentThread()).getName()).equals("T2")){
-->                    text2.setText(out_string.
-->                        valueOf(Math.sqrt((double)loop_index)));
-->                }
               }
       }
```

Now our multithreaded applet supports two threads, each of which places square roots into a different textfield, as shown in Figure 9.5. The Sqrts applet is a success. The code for this applet appears in Listing 9.5.

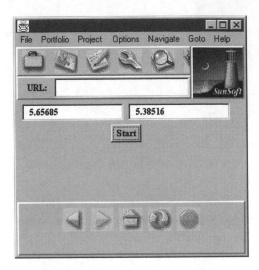

Figure 9.5 We place square roots into textfields with two different threads.

Listing 9.5 Sqrts.java

```java
import java.awt.*;
import java.applet.Applet;
import java.lang.Math;

public class Sqrts extends Applet implements Runnable{

    Thread Thread1, Thread2;
    TextField text1, text2;
    Button button1;

    public void init() {
        text1 = new TextField(20);
        text2 = new TextField(20);
        add(text1);
        add(text2);
        button1 = new Button("Start");
        add(button1);
    }

    public boolean action (Event e, Object o){
```

```
        if(e.target.equals(button1)){
                Thread1 = new Thread(this, "T1");
                Thread1.start();
                Thread2 = new Thread(this, "T2");
                Thread2.start();
        }
        return true;
}

public void stop() {
        Thread1.stop();
        Thread2.stop();
}

public void run() {
        String out_string;
        int loop_index;
        out_string = new String();
        for(loop_index = 1; loop_index < 500; loop_index++){
            if(((Thread.currentThread()).getName()).equals("T1")){
                text1.setText(out_string.
                   valueOf(Math.sqrt((double)loop_index)));
            }
            if(((Thread.currentThread()).getName()).equals("T2")){
                text2.setText(out_string.
                   valueOf(Math.sqrt((double)loop_index)));
            }
        }
    }
}
```

Now that we've started to work with multiple threads, let's see how Java supports methods of coordinating such threads.

Coordinating Multiple Threads

In this next example, we'll see a few new things: we'll see how to coordinate threads using the yield() method, and we'll also see that it doesn't have to be the Applet object in which we use the implements Runnable keywords. Until now, we've done some work controlling the flow of our threads with suspend() and resume(), as well as making a thread sleep for 200 milliseconds before placing another animation frame on the screen. But we haven't allowed Java to coordinate multiple threads for us. In our applet, we can have two new threads, which we start with a **Start threads** button and stop with a **Stop threads** button:

```
-----------------------------------------
|                                       |
|   ---------------   -------------      |
|   | Start threads | | Stop threads |   |
|   ---------------   -------------      |
|                                       |
|                                       |
|                                       |
|                                       |
|                                       |
-----------------------------------------
```

One thread will print out "Hello" and the other thread will print out "World" to the **weblog** file. In addition, we'll let Java schedule our two threads so that they take turns, and the result will be "Hello World" over and over again in the **weblog** file.

As we write this applet, let's experiment by adding a new class that is Runnable instead of making our applet class runnable. The advantage is that we will create two objects of this class, so they don't have to share the same run() method as in our Sqrts applet. We can call our new class HelloRunnable:

```
-->    class HelloRunnable implements Runnable{
          .
          .
          .
```

This is what the new threads we will start will run, so we include a run() method:

```
       class HelloRunnable implements Runnable{

-->           public void run(){
                 .
                 .
                 .
```

To have one thread print out "Hello" and the other print "World," we can give each thread those strings as their names, which means that we simply need to print the thread's name to the **weblog** file here inside a loop that loops, for example, 500 times:

```
class HelloRunnable implements Runnable{

    public void run(){

-->             int loop_index;
-->             for(loop_index = 1; loop_index < 500; loop_index++){
-->                 System.out.println((Thread.currentThread()).
-->                     getName());
                        .
                        .
                        .

                }
        }
}
```

Here is where the coordination of our threads comes in. We want the threads to alternate writing to the **weblog** file so that the result will be "Hello World" over and over again. How do we do that? We do it with the Thread class's yield() method like this:

```
class HelloRunnable implements Runnable{

    public void run(){

            int loop_index;
            for(loop_index = 1; loop_index < 500; loop_index++){
                System.out.println((Thread.currentThread()).
                    getName());
-->                 Thread.yield();
            }
        }
}
```

This means that the current thread yields control to the Java system so that another thread can run. But that thread, of course, also completes its task and then yields control. (Both threads are executing identical copies of the preceding code.), We come back to the first thread for one more iteration of the loop and one more text output to the **weblog** file.

When the user clicks the **Start threads** button as shown in Figure 9.6, the result of this applet is indeed "Hello World" over and over again in the **weblog** file as the two threads take turns writing to that file. Our new applet is a success. The code for this applet appears in Listing 9.6.

Figure 9.6 This applet starts and coordinates two threads that write to a log file.

Listing 9.6 Multi2.java

```java
import java.applet.Applet;
import java.awt.*;

public class Multi2 extends Applet {

        Button button1, button2;
        HelloRunnable helloRun;
        Thread Thread1, Thread2;

        public void init(){
                button1 = new Button("Start threads");
                add(button1);
```

```
                button2 = new Button("Stop threads");
                add(button2);
                helloRun = new HelloRunnable();
                Thread1 = new Thread(helloRun, "Hello");
                Thread2 = new Thread(helloRun, " World");
        }

        public boolean action (Event e, Object o){

                if(e.target.equals(button1)){
                        Thread1.start();
                        Thread2.start();
                }
                if(e.target.equals(button2)){
                        Thread1.stop();
                        Thread2.stop();
                }
                return true;
        }
}

class HelloRunnable implements Runnable{

        public void run(){

                int loop_index;
                for(loop_index = 1; loop_index < 500; loop_index++){
                    System.out.println((Thread.currentThread()).
                        getName());
                    Thread.yield();
                }
        }
}
```

So far, we've looked at coordinating threads. However, it can also happen that you have less control over threads than we have used here, where we made our threads yield when we wanted another thread to run. If we have less control over how other threads run, or when they run, then it becomes more important to protect the resources that we use in our thread. We need to make sure other threads (which we don't control) can't get to and change those resources at the very time we are working with them. Let's look into this now.

Synchronizing Resource Use

Now we'll turn from controlling other thread's actions to controlling what they have access to. In particular, we'll tell the Java system that, when we are working on a specific piece of data, we don't want anyone else to be able to alter it under us (something that other threads specialize in).

For example, we might have a data object named dataInt, which holds an integer. This dataInt object might be an object of class Data, where the Data class looks like this:

```
class Data{
        public int internal_data;
        public void Data(){
                internal_data = 0;
        }
}
```

Here, we just store an internal integer in the Data class and set it to 0 in the class's constructor. We might have an applet named Synchro that sets up our object named dataInt (of our new class Data) like this:

```
    import java.awt.*;
    import java.applet.Applet;

  public class Synchro extends Applet{

-->    Data dataInt;

    public void init() {
-->        dataInt = new Data();
    }           .
                .
                .
```

In addition, let's assume that our Synchro applet is multithreaded with two threads, Thread1 and Thread2, which start running when the applet does:

```
    import java.awt.*;
    import java.applet.Applet;
```

```
        public class Synchro extends Applet implements Runnable{

-->         Thread Thread1, Thread2;
            Data dataInt;

            public void init() {
                    dataInt = new Data();
            }

            public void start() {
-->                 Thread1 = new Thread(this);
-->                 Thread1.start();
-->                 Thread2 = new Thread(this);
-->                 Thread2.start();
            }                     .
                                  .
                                  .
```

In the Synchro applet's run() method, the two threads might increment the dataInt object's internal integer and print the new value out to the **weblog** file. In fact, we can set up a loop where that happens 500 times:

```
        public void run() {
-->             int loop_index;
-->                 for(loop_index = 1; loop_index < 500; loop_index++){
                        .
                        .
                        .
                    }
            }
```

Here is how we increment the dataInt object's internal data and print out the new value to the **weblog** file:

```
        public void run() {
                String out_string;
                int loop_index;
                out_string = new String();
                    for(loop_index = 1; loop_index < 500; loop_index++){
-->                     dataInt.internal_data++;
-->                     System.out.println("data value = " +
```

```
-->                          out_string.valueOf(dataInt.internal_data));
            }
    }
```

When Threads Conflict

A problem arises here. Even the simple statement `dataInt.internal_data++` is made up of several internal steps—reading dataInt's internal_data member, incrementing it, and replacing it in memory. The other thread can easily slip in and disrupt things as we work on them.

For example, if dataInt's internal_data member held the value 100 when we read it, we would increment that to 101 and place it back into internal_data. Next, we would proceed on to the next step, printing the value in internal_data out to the **weblog** file. However, suppose the other thread beat us to this and incremented the value in internal_data to 102. In that case, we'd be left fetching this new value, 102, and printing that to the **weblog** file instead of the number we should be printing, 101. In this way, our two

threads are interfering with each other. We have to guard the data in the dataInt object some way, and we'll look into that next. The current, unguarded version of **Synchro.java** appears in Listing 9.7.

Listing 9.7 Synchro.java

```java
import java.awt.*;
import java.applet.Applet;

public class Synchro extends Applet implements Runnable{

    Thread Thread1, Thread2;
    Data dataInt;

    public void init() {
            dataInt = new Data();
    }

    public void start() {
                    Thread1 = new Thread(this);
                    Thread1.start();
```

```
                    Thread2 = new Thread(this);
                    Thread2.start();
        }

        public void stop() {
                    Thread1.stop();
                    Thread2.stop();
        }

        public void run() {
              String out_string;
              int loop_index;
              out_string = new String();
                  for(loop_index = 1; loop_index < 500; loop_index++){
                      dataInt.internal_data++;
                      System.out.println("data value = " +
                          out_string.valueOf(dataInt.internal_data));
                  }
        }
    }

        class Data{
              public int internal_data;
              public void Data(){
                      internal_data = 0;
              }
        }
```

Our first way of restricting other thread's access to the sensitive data in dataInt.internal_data will be to use synchronized functions.

Synchronizing Functions

We can *synchronize* functions so that only one thread can be inside a particular function at once. To do that, we just use the *synchronized* keyword when declaring the function. In our example, we could place all the sensitive actions dealing with the data in dataInt.internal_data into a new function named, for example, print_out(), which we declare a synchronized function like this:

```
        public synchronized void print_out(){
                          .
                          .
                          .
```

Here we simply increment dataInt.internal_data first:

```
        public synchronized void print_out(){
-->             dataInt.internal_data++;
                    .
                    .
                    .
```

Next, we print the value in that data member using `System.out.println()`:

```
        public synchronized void print_out(){
-->             String out_string;
-->             out_string = new String();
                dataInt.internal_data++;
-->             System.out.println("data value = " +
                    out_string.valueOf(dataInt.internal_data));
        }
```

Because only one thread can be in the print_out() function at a time, we're safe. The last step is to change the run() method so that it calls print_out() instead of handling the data itself:

```
        public void run() {
                int loop_index;
                for(loop_index = 1; loop_index < 500; loop_index++){
-->                     print_out();
                }
        }
```

Our new applet is a success, and the code for it appears in Listing 9.8. We have resolved the thread conflict problem here.

Listing 9.8 Funcsync.java

```java
import java.awt.*;
import java.applet.Applet;

public class Funcsync extends Applet
    implements Runnable{

    Thread Thread1, Thread2;
    Data dataInt;

    public void init() {
            dataInt = new Data();
    }

    public void start() {
                    Thread1 = new Thread(this);
                    Thread1.start();
                    Thread2 = new Thread(this);
                    Thread2.start();
    }

    public void stop() {
                    Thread1.stop();
                    Thread2.stop();
    }

    public void run() {
            int loop_index;
            for(loop_index = 1; loop_index < 500; loop_index++){
                    print_out();
            }
    }

    public synchronized void print_out(){
            String out_string;
            out_string = new String();
            dataInt.internal_data++;
            System.out.println("data value = " +
                out_string.valueOf(dataInt.internal_data));
    }
}
```

```
class Data{
        public int internal_data;
        public void Data(){
                internal_data = 0;
        }
}
```

However, there can still be another problem. Even though we've protected the data from the actions of Thread1 and Thread2, there may be other threads. In other words, we have changed Thread1 and Thread2 to work politely, but if there are still other threads around that we can't control in this way, we should think about protecting our data instead. And that's what we'll do next.

Synchronizing Data

Let's focus on guarding the data in dataInt.internal_data instead. We do that with a synchronized() block. To use such a block, we just have to indicate what data item we want locked; after that, the data we have locked will be inaccessible to any other threads but ours while we execute the code we put in the synchronized block. For example, here is how the run() method appeared originally in our applet:

```
public void run() {
        String out_string;
        int loop_index;
        out_string = new String();
        for(loop_index = 1; loop_index < 500; loop_index++){
            dataInt.internal_data++;
            System.out.println("data value = " +
                out_string.valueOf(dataInt.internal_data));
        }
}
```

The sensitive lines are those that work with dataInt.internal_data, and we can put them in a synchronized block to lock other threads out. We indicate that we want to lock the dataInt object for our exclusive use while in this block by placing "dataInt" in parentheses after the synchronized keyword:

```
       public void run() {
               String out_string;
               int loop_index;
               out_string = new String();
-->            synchronized(dataInt){
                   for(loop_index = 1; loop_index < 500; loop_index++){
                       dataInt.internal_data++;
                       System.out.println("data value = " +
                          out_string.valueOf(dataInt.internal_data));
                   }
-->            }
       }
```

Now the dataInt object will be used by us only when we are in the synchronized block. This has solved the new problem for us. The new listing of our applet appears in Listing 9.9.

Listing 9.9 Synchro.java, Version 2

```
       import java.awt.*;
       import java.applet.Applet;

public class Synchro extends Applet
    implements Runnable{

    Thread Thread1, Thread2;
    Data dataInt;

    public void init() {
            dataInt = new Data();
    }

    public void start() {
                    Thread1 = new Thread(this);
                    Thread1.start();
                    Thread2 = new Thread(this);
                    Thread2.start();
    }

    public void stop() {
                    Thread1.stop();
                    Thread2.stop();
    }
```

```
      public void run() {
              String out_string;
              int loop_index;
              out_string = new String();
              synchronized(dataInt){
                  for(loop_index = 1; loop_index < 500; loop_index++){
                      dataInt.internal_data++;
                      System.out.println("data value = " +
                          out_string.valueOf(dataInt.internal_data));
                  }
              }
      }
  }


      class Data{
              public int internal_data;
              public void Data(){
                      internal_data = 0;
              }
      }
```

We can also solve the problem in a more general way by having dataInt's class *lock itself* when we perform some operation on its internal data. Let's look into that now.

Synchronizing Classes

Our next step is to lock dataInt's class—the class we have named Data—when anyone starts working with its internal data. We do that by controlling access to the internal_data member of Data by making it private with the private keyword (note that the other examples so far, which modified this class's internal data directly, should not really have done so; it is better form to control access to internal data through callable methods):

```
      class Data{
  -->         private int internal_data;
              public void Data(){
                      internal_data = 0;
              }               .
                              .
                              .
```

Let's introduce another security risk. Here we might make internal_data a *static* data member:

```
        class Data{
-->             private static int internal_data;
                public void Data(){
                        internal_data = 0;
                }       .
                        .
                        .
```

In other words, although there may be many objects of class Data throughout your applet, they all share the same value of internal_data. That means that if you have five Data objects and you change the value of internal_data in one of them, it changes in them all.

This is obviously something we have to consider; we don't want the data in internal_data to change as we work with it. To let other objects increment internal_data, we set up a new method in the Data class named, for example, incData():

```
        class Data{
                private static int internal_data;
                public void Data(){
                        internal_data = 0;
                }
>               public int incData(){
                        .
                        .
                        .
                }
        }
```

Here, we just increment internal_data and return the new value to the caller:

```
        class Data{
                private static int internal_data;
                public void Data(){
                        internal_data = 0;
                }
                public int incData(){
-->                     internal_data++;
```

```
-->                     return internal_data;
                              .
                              .
                              .

              }
      }
```

However, this is very unsafe. What if some other thread is working on internal_data at the same time we are? Another thread could even be calling our incData() function at the same time that we are in it. To fix this, we use a synchronized block in which we lock the *whole class* at the same time (we get the Java identifier for the current class with the getClass() method):

```
class Data{
        private static int internal_data;
        public void Data(){
                internal_data = 0;
        }
        public int incData(){
-->             synchronized(getClass()){
                     internal_data++;
                     return internal_data;
-->             }
        }
}
```

This fixes the problem of other threads working with internal_data at the same time, even if they try to modify internal_data from another Data object. The last step is to modify code in our applet to use incData() instead of modifying internal_data directly:

```
public void run() {
        String out_string;
        int loop_index;
        out_string = new String();
        for(loop_index = 1; loop_index < 500; loop_index++){
            System.out.println("data value = " +
-->             out_string.valueOf(dataInt.incData()));
        }
}
```

We've made our applet much more thread-safe. The new version appears in Listing 9.10. Our applet is a success.

Listing 9.10 Classync.java

```java
import java.awt.*;
import java.applet.Applet;

public class Classync extends Applet
    implements Runnable{

    Thread Thread1, Thread2;
    Data dataInt;

    public void init() {
            dataInt = new Data();
    }

    public void start() {
                    Thread1 = new Thread(this);
                    Thread1.start();
                    Thread2 = new Thread(this);
                    Thread2.start();
    }

    public void stop() {
                    Thread1.stop();
                    Thread2.stop();
    }

    public void run() {
            String out_string;
            int loop_index;
            out_string = new String();
            for(loop_index = 1; loop_index < 500; loop_index++){
                System.out.println("data value = " +
                    out_string.valueOf(dataInt.incData()));
            }
    }
}

class Data{
        private static int internal_data;
```

```
            public void Data(){
                    internal_data = 0;
            }
            public int incData(){
                    synchronized(getClass()){
                        internal_data++;
                        return internal_data;
                    }
            }
    }
```

In this chapter, we've seen many new multitasking techniques, including using new threads, creating Runnables, synchronizing threads, using multiple threads, and letting threads yield to other threads. In the next chapter, we'll turn to another important topic—Java exception handling and debugging.

CHAPTER TEN

HANDLING JAVA EXCEPTIONS

In this chapter, we are going to examine Java exceptions, an important part of Java programming. Just what is exception handling? *Exception handling* is a technique that lets you handle unusual circumstances in your applets without making the applet crash. For example, you might be trying to allocate more memory, but what if there isn't any more? An exception occurs, and you can add provisions to you code to handle and recover from such cases without the applet freezing up or crashing. Handling exceptions in this way allows you to take alternate actions, such as get along without the new memory or alert the user to stop a few other programs. Here we'll see what exceptions are, how to handle them, and how to extend them. Let's start with an overview of exceptions.

What Is Exception Handling?

The out-of-memory case does not really cause an exception. It really causes an error, but in Java, error and exception handling are often thought of interchangeably. Both error classes and exception classes are derived from the same Java class: the *Throwable* class (we'll deal with what it means to *throw* an exception shortly). The Java exceptions appear in Table 10.1, and the Java errors appear in Table 10.2.

Table 10.1 The Java Exceptions

ArithmeticException

ArrayIndexOutOfBoundsException

ArrayStoreException

AWTException

ClassCastException

ClassNotFoundException

CloneNotSupportedException

EmptyStackException

EOFException

FileNotFoundException

IllegalAccessException

IllegalArgumentException

IllegalMonitorStateException

IllegalThreadStateException

IndexOutOfBoundsException

InstantiationException

InterruptedException

InterruptedIOException

IOException

MalformedURLException

NegativeArraySizeException

NoSuchElementException

NoSuchMethodException

NullPointerException

NumberFormatException

ProtocolException

RuntimeException

SecurityException

SocketException

StringIndexOutOfBoundsException

uncaughtException

UnknownHostException

UnknownServiceException

UTFDataFormatException

Table 10.2 The Java Errors

AbstractMethodError

AWTError

ClassCircularityError

ClassFormatError

IllegalAccessError

IncompatibleClassChangeError

InstantiationError

InternalError

LinkageError

NoClassDefFoundError

NoSuchFieldError

NoSuchMethodError

OutOfMemoryError

StackOverflowError

UnknownError

UnsatisfiedLinkError

VirtualMachineError

How do exceptions work? And what does throwing an exception mean? As you may recall, we've already used exception handling. We'll review those cases now. The first is our imagemap applet in which we place an image with graphical buttons in our applet and let the user click a button to jump to a new URL:

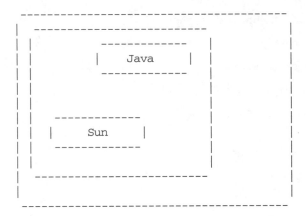

Reviewing the Imagemap Applet

The code for the Imagemap applet appears in Listing 10.1 for reference. We used exception handling in the mouseDown() method when we created our new URL object, like this:

```
        public boolean mouseDown(Event e, int x, int y){
                URL newURL = null;
                if( x > 104 + 10 && x < 171 + 10 && y > 53 + 10 &&
                    y < 75 + 10){ //Java
-->                     try { newURL = new URL("http://java.sun.com"); }
-->                     catch (MalformedURLException e1) {}
                        getAppletContext().showDocument(newURL);
```

```
                    }
                    if( x > 54 + 10 && x < 118 + 10 && y > 105 + 10 &&
                        y < 125 + 10){ //Sun
-->                         try { newURL = new URL("http://www.sun.com"); }
-->                         catch (MalformedURLException e2) {}
                            getAppletContext().showDocument(newURL);
                    }
                    return true;
            }
```

This shows the typical use of exception handling. We enclose sensitive (i.e., error-prone) code inside a *try block* this way:

```
        try{
          [sensitive operation]
        }        .
                 .
                 .
```

If there is no problem and no exception was thrown, the thread leaves the try block and continues on with the post-exception-handling code:

```
        try{
          [sensitive operation]
        }        .
                 .
                 .

        [post-exception-handling code]
```

On the other hand, if an exception was thrown, we can *catch* it. In other words, the exception recovery code in a catch block will be run:

```
        try{
          [sensitive operation]
        }
-->     catch (exception_type e){
-->       [exception recovery code]
-->     }
        [post-exception-handling code]
```

Note that the exception recovery code is run only if one particular type of exception occurs, the type the catch block is set up to catch. Back in our mouseDown() method, the exception we catch is the MalformedURLException exception:

```
public boolean mouseDown(Event e, int x, int y){
        URL newURL = null;
        if( x > 104 + 10 && x < 171 + 10 && y > 53 + 10 &&
            y < 75 + 10){ //Java
                try { newURL = new URL("http://java.sun.com"); }
                catch (MalformedURLException e1) {}
                getAppletContext().showDocument(newURL);
        }
```

(With `-->` arrow pointing to the `catch` line.)

Now let's take another look at exception handling as we have already used it in our Wheel animation applet.

Listing 10.1 Imagemap.java

```
import java.applet.Applet;
import java.awt.*;
import java.net.*;

public class Imagemap extends Applet {

    Image Imap;

    public void init(){
            Imap = getImage(getCodeBase(), "Imagemap.gif");
    }

    public boolean mouseDown(Event e, int x, int y){
            URL newURL = null;
            if( x > 104 + 10 && x < 171 + 10 && y > 53 + 10 &&
                y < 75 + 10){ //Java
                    try { newURL = new URL("http://java.sun.com"); }
                    catch (MalformedURLException e1) {}
                    getAppletContext().showDocument(newURL);
            }
            if( x > 54 + 10 && x < 118 + 10 && y > 105 + 10 &&
                y < 125 + 10){ //Sun
                    try { newURL = new URL("http://www.sun.com"); }
                    catch (MalformedURLException e2) {}
                    getAppletContext().showDocument(newURL);
```

```
            }
            return true;
    }

    public void paint (Graphics g) {
        g.drawImage(Imap, 10, 10, 240, 155, this);
    }


}
```

Let's review the Wheel applet now.

Reviewing the Wheel Applet

Our Wheel applet presented a red and blue wheel that spun when launched in its own thread:

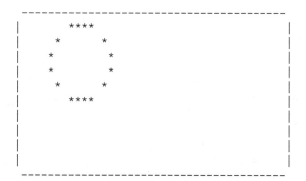

We also used try and catch blocks in our Wheel applet. The code for this applet appears in Listing 10.2. Here's how we used exception handling in the Wheel applet:

```
    public void run() {
        while(true){
            nowImage = wheelImages[wheelIndex++];
            if(wheelIndex > 3)wheelIndex = 0;
            repaint();
-->         try {Thread.sleep(200);}
-->         catch(InterruptedException e) { }
        }
    }
```

In this case, we catch the InterruptedException exception, which occurs when another thread interrupts ours. This is a good one to catch if you use threads in an applet, catching this exception will let you know that your thread has been interrupted. That is useful in case we really need to limit the thread's sleep time to 200 milliseconds. If the thread was interrupted and therefore suspended by another thread, more time may have passed than we think.

Listing 10.2 Wheel.java

```java
import java.awt.*;
import java.applet.Applet;

public class Wheel extends Applet
    implements Runnable{

    Image wheelImages[] = new Image[4];
    Image nowImage;
    int wheelIndex = 0;
    Thread wheelThread;

    public void init() {
            wheelImages[0] = getImage(getCodeBase(), "Wheel1.gif");
            wheelImages[1] = getImage(getCodeBase(), "Wheel2.gif");
            wheelImages[2] = getImage(getCodeBase(), "Wheel3.gif");
            wheelImages[3] = getImage(getCodeBase(), "Wheel4.gif");
    }

    public void start() {
                wheelThread = new Thread(this);
                wheelThread.start();
    }

    public void stop() {
                wheelThread.stop();
    }

    public void run() {
            while(true){
                    nowImage = wheelImages[wheelIndex++];
                    if(wheelIndex > 3)wheelIndex = 0;
                    repaint();
                    try {Thread.sleep(200);}
```

```
                catch(InterruptedException e) { }
        }
    }

    public void paint (Graphics g) {
        g.drawImage(nowImage, 10, 10, this);
    }

    public void update(Graphics g) {
        g.clipRect(10, 10, 100, 100);
        paint(g);
    }
}
```

Now that we've reviewed exception handling as we've already used it, let's look at putting it to use in some of the other applets we've created.

Using Exception Handling

Let's look at using exceptions in the Painter applet we wrote. In that applet, we let the user select a drawing tool and then draw freehand and draw lines, ovals, and so on:

```
-------------------------------------------------
|                                               |
|                                               |
|     ----    ----    ----    ----   -------   ----- |
|    |Draw|  |Line|  |Oval|  |Rect| |3D Rect| |Round| |
|     ----    ----    ----    ----   -------   ----- |
|                                               |
|                                               |
|                                               |
|                                               |
|                                               |
|                                               |
|                                               |
|                                               |
|                                               |
-------------------------------------------------
```

Now let's look at the mouseDrag() method, which is where we recorded mouse locations in the Point array pts[] as the mouse moved:

```
        public boolean mouseDrag(Event e, int x, int y){
                if(bDrawFlag){
   -->                      pts[ptindex] = new Point(x, y);
                          ptindex++;
                }
                ptOldDrawTo = ptDrawTo;
                ptDrawTo = new Point(x, y);
                repaint();
                return true;
        }
```

There is a problem here. The pts[] array is set up to take only 100 points:

```
    public class Xpainter extends Applet {

        Button buttonDraw, buttonLine, buttonOval, buttonRect, button3DRect;
        Button buttonRounded;

 -->    Point pts[] = new Point[100];
                  .
                  .
                  .
```

After 100 points are recorded, the array will overflow. We can catch that with the ArrayIndexOutOfBoundsException exception. First, we enclose the sensitive part of the code in a try block:

```
        public boolean mouseDrag(Event e, int x, int y){
                if(bDrawFlag){
   -->                  try{
   -->                      pts[ptindex] = new Point(x, y);
   -->                      ptindex++;
   -->                  }        .
                                  .
                                  .

                }
```

```
                    ptOldDrawTo = ptDrawTo;
                    ptDrawTo = new Point(x, y);
                    repaint();
                    return true;
        }
```

The exception we expect here is the Java exception ArrayIndexOutOfBoundsException. Like all exceptions, this exception is based on the Throwable class, which appears in Table 10.3. The Exception class, which appears in Table 10.4, is derived from the Throwable class. Further down the line, the ArrayIndexOutOfBoundsException class, which appears in Table 10.5, is derived from the Exception class.

Table 10.3 The Throwable Class's Constructors and Methods

```
        java.lang.Object
            |
        +----java.lang.Throwable
```

Throwable()	Constructs a Throwable with no detail message
Throwable(String)	Constructs a Throwable with specified detail message
fillInStackTrace()	Fills in stack trace
getMessage()	Returns detail message of Throwable
printStackTrace()	Prints Throwable and Throwable's stack trace
printStackTrace(PrintStream)	Prints Throwable and Throwable's stack trace to PrintStream
toString()	Returns a short description of the Throwable

Table 10.4 The Exception Class's Constructors and Methods

```
Class java.lang.Exception

java.lang.Object
   |
   +----java.lang.Throwable
            |
            +----java.lang.Exception
```

| Exception() | Constructs Exception with no specified detail message |
| Exception(String) | Constructs Exception with specified detail message |

Table 10.5 ArrayIndexOutOfBoundsException's Constructors and Methods

```
java.lang.Object
   |
   +--java.lang.Throwable
        |
        +--java.lang.Exception
            |
            +--java.lang.RuntimeException
                |
                +--java.lang.IndexOutOfBoundsException
                    |
                    +----java.lang.ArrayIndexOutOfBoundsException
```

ArrayIndexOutOfBoundsException()	Constructs newArrayIndexOutOfBoundsException with no detail message
ArrayIndexOutOfBoundsException(int)	Constructs new ArrayIndexOutOfBoundsException initialized to specific index
ArrayIndexOutOfBoundsException(String)	Constructs ArrayIndexOutOfBoundsException with specified detail message

We catch this exception like this:

```
      public boolean mouseDrag(Event e, int x, int y){
             if(bDrawFlag){
                    try{
                           pts[ptindex] = new Point(x, y);
                           ptindex++;
                    }
 -->                catch(ArrayIndexOutOfBoundsException ex)
                    {        .

                                 .

                                 .


             ptOldDrawTo = ptDrawTo;
             ptDrawTo = new Point(x, y);
             repaint();
             return true;
      }
```

If this exception did indeed occur, we might set the array index back to 0 and print out to the weblog file indicating that an exception of this kind occurred:

```
      public boolean mouseDrag(Event e, int x, int y){
             if(bDrawFlag){
                    try{
                           pts[ptindex] - new Point(x, y);
                           ptindex++;
                    }
                    catch(ArrayIndexOutOfBoundsException ex)
                    {
 -->                       ptindex = 0;
 -->                       System.out.println("Point array overflowed.");
                    }
             }

             ptOldDrawTo = ptDrawTo;
             ptDrawTo = new Point(x, y);
             repaint();
             return true;
      }
```

In this way, we have handled the array overflow exception. That's all there is to it. Our new version of the Painter applet is a success. The code for this applet appears in Listing 10.3. As you can see in Table 10.3, objects of the Throwable class have a getMessage() method, which tells more about the exception that occurred. If we want to, we can print out messages like this in our new Painter applet using getMessage():

```
public boolean mouseDrag(Event e, int x, int y){
        if(bDrawFlag){
                try{
                    pts[ptindex] = new Point(x, y);
                    ptindex++;
                }
                catch(ArrayIndexOutOfBoundsException ex)
                {
                    ptindex = 0;
  -->               System.out.println(ex.getMessage());
                }
        }
```

Listing 10.3 Xpainter.java

```
import java.awt.Graphics;
import java.awt.*;
import java.lang.Math;
import java.applet.Applet;

public class Xpainter extends Applet {

Button buttonDraw, buttonLine, buttonOval, buttonRect, button3DRect;
Button buttonRounded;

Point pts[] = new Point[100];
Point ptAnchor, ptDrawTo, ptOldAnchor, ptOldDrawTo;
int ptindex = 0;

boolean bMouseDownFlag = false;
boolean bMouseUpFlag = false;
boolean bDrawFlag = false;
boolean bLineFlag = false;
boolean bOvalFlag = false;
boolean bRectFlag = false;
```

```java
boolean b3DRectFlag = false;
boolean bRoundedFlag = false;

public void init() {

        buttonDraw = new Button("Draw");
        buttonLine = new Button("Line");
        buttonOval = new Button("Oval");
        buttonRect = new Button("Rect");
        button3DRect = new Button("3D Rect");
        buttonRounded = new Button("Round");

        add(buttonDraw);
        add(buttonLine);
        add(buttonOval);
        add(buttonRect);
        add(button3DRect);
        add(buttonRounded);
}

public boolean mouseDown(Event e, int x, int y){
        bMouseDownFlag = true;
        bMouseUpFlag = false;

        ptAnchor = new Point(x, y);
        ptOldDrawTo = new Point(x, y);
        return true;
}

public boolean mouseUp(Event e, int x, int y){
        bMouseDownFlag = false;
        bMouseUpFlag = true;

        ptOldDrawTo = ptDrawTo;
        ptDrawTo = new Point(x, y);
        repaint();
        return true;
}

public boolean mouseDrag(Event e, int x, int y){
        if(bDrawFlag){
                try{
                        pts[ptindex] = new Point(x, y);
                        ptindex++;
                }
```

```
                catch(ArrayIndexOutOfBoundsException ex)
                {
                    ptindex = 0;
                    System.out.println("Point array overflowed.");
                }
            }

        ptOldDrawTo = ptDrawTo;
        ptDrawTo = new Point(x, y);
        repaint();
        return true;
    }

public void paint (Graphics g) {
        int loop_index;
        int drawWidth, drawHeight;
        Point TopLeft, BottomRight;

        if(bDrawFlag){
            for(loop_index = 0; loop_index < ptindex; loop_index++){
                g.drawLine(pts[loop_index].x, pts[loop_index].y,
                    pts[loop_index + 1].x, pts[loop_index + 1].y);
            }
            return;
        }

        g.setColor(new Color(0, 0, 0));
        g.setXORMode(getBackground());
        TopLeft = new Point(Math.min(ptAnchor.x, ptOldDrawTo.x),
            Math.min(ptAnchor.y, ptOldDrawTo.y));
        BottomRight = new Point(Math.max(ptAnchor.x, ptOldDrawTo.x),
            Math.max(ptAnchor.y, ptOldDrawTo.y));
        drawWidth = Math.abs(ptOldDrawTo.x - ptAnchor.x);
        drawHeight = Math.abs(ptOldDrawTo.y - ptAnchor.y);
        if(bLineFlag){
                g.drawLine(ptAnchor.x, ptAnchor.y, ptOldDrawTo.x,
                    ptOldDrawTo.y);
        }
        if(bOvalFlag){
                g.drawOval(TopLeft.x, TopLeft.y, drawWidth,
                    drawHeight);
        }
        if(bRectFlag){
                g.drawRect(TopLeft.x, TopLeft.y, drawWidth,
                    drawHeight);
        }
```

```
        if(b3DRectFlag){
                g.draw3DRect(TopLeft.x, TopLeft.y, drawWidth,
                    drawHeight, true);
        }
        if(bRoundedFlag){
                g.drawRoundRect(TopLeft.x, TopLeft.y, drawWidth,
                    drawHeight, 10, 10);
        }


        g.setColor(getBackground());
        TopLeft = new Point(Math.min(ptAnchor.x, ptDrawTo.x),
            Math.min(ptAnchor.y, ptDrawTo.y));
        BottomRight = new Point(Math.max(ptAnchor.x, ptDrawTo.x),
            Math.max(ptAnchor.y, ptDrawTo.y));
        drawWidth = Math.abs(ptDrawTo.x - ptAnchor.x);
        drawHeight = Math.abs(ptDrawTo.y - ptAnchor.y);
        if(bLineFlag){
                g.drawLine(ptAnchor.x, ptAnchor.y, ptDrawTo.x,
                    ptDrawTo.y);
        }
        if(bOvalFlag){
                g.drawOval(TopLeft.x, TopLeft.y, drawWidth,
                    drawHeight);
        }
        if(bRectFlag){
                g.drawRect(TopLeft.x, TopLeft.y, drawWidth,
                    drawHeight);
        }
        if(b3DRectFlag){
                g.draw3DRect(TopLeft.x, TopLeft.y, drawWidth,
                    drawHeight, true);
        }
        if(bRoundedFlag){
                g.drawRoundRect(TopLeft.x, TopLeft.y, drawWidth,
                    drawHeight, 10, 10);
        }


}


public boolean action(Event e, Object o){
        if(e.target.equals(buttonDraw)){
                bDrawFlag = !bDrawFlag;
                bLineFlag = false;
                bOvalFlag = false;
                bRectFlag = false;
```

```
                    b3DRectFlag = false;
                    bRoundedFlag = false;
        }
        if(e.target.equals(buttonLine)){
                    bLineFlag = !bLineFlag;
                    bDrawFlag = false;
                    bOvalFlag = false;
                    bRectFlag = false;
                    b3DRectFlag = false;
                    bRoundedFlag = false;
        }
        if(e.target.equals(buttonOval)){
                    bOvalFlag = !bOvalFlag;
                    bLineFlag = false;
                    bDrawFlag = false;
                    bRectFlag = false;
                    b3DRectFlag = false;
                    bRoundedFlag = false;
        }
        if(e.target.equals(buttonRect)){
                    bRectFlag = !bRectFlag;
                    bLineFlag = false;
                    bOvalFlag = false;
                    bDrawFlag = false;
                    b3DRectFlag = false;
                    bRoundedFlag = false;
        }
        if(e.target.equals(button3DRect)){
                    b3DRectFlag = !b3DRectFlag;
                    bLineFlag = false;
                    bOvalFlag = false;
                    bRectFlag = false;
                    bDrawFlag = false;
                    bRoundedFlag = false;
        }
        if(e.target.equals(buttonRounded)){
                    bRoundedFlag = !bRoundedFlag;
                    bLineFlag = false;
                    bOvalFlag = false;
                    bRectFlag = false;
                    b3DRectFlag = false;
                    bDrawFlag = false;
        }
        return true;
    }
}
```

That is how we have put the ArrayIndexOutOfBoundsException exception to work. We can also define our own exceptions. Let's look into that now.

Defining Our Own Exceptions

As we've seen, Java provides a number of exceptions for us, but we can also derive our own. To take a look at that, we will re-explore our Writer applet. You might recall that this applet looked like this:

```
------------------------------------------------
|                                              |
|   ------   -------   ---   ----   ------   -----   |
|   |TRoman|  |Courier|  |Big|  |Bold|  |Italic|  |Plain|  |
|   ------   -------   ---   ----   ------   -----   |
|                                              |
|                                              |
|         Hello World!                         |
|                                              |
|                                              |
|                                              |
|                                              |
|                                              |
|                                              |
|                                              |
------------------------------------------------
```

We let the user select a type face, font size, and type; then they can click the mouse anywhere and type. What they type will appear in the applet's window.

Let's say that we want to prevent the user from using the $ key. Clearly, no predefined Java exception is going to help us here. We'll have to define our own. We can call our own exception Is$ and derive this new exception class from the Exception class:

```
class Is$ extends Exception{
}
```

Next, we have to catch the **$** as it is typed. We read keys the user types in the keyDown() method, which currently looks like this in the Writer applet:

```
public boolean keyDown(Event e, int k){

        String new_string;
        new_string = new String();
        new_string += (char)k;
        inString = inString + (char)k;
        repaint();
        return true;

}
```

Here, the sensitive code is the code in which we first read struck keys, in case the user types a **$**. We enclose this code in a try block:

```
        public boolean keyDown(Event e, int k){

-->             try{
-->                     String new_string;
-->                     new_string = new String();
-->                     new_string += (char)k;
-->                     }              .
                                       .
                                       .
                inString = inString + (char)k;
                repaint();
                return true;

        }
```

We check if the user typed a **$**:

```
        public boolean keyDown(Event e, int k){

                try{
                        String new_string;
                        new_string = new String();
                        new_string += (char)k;
-->                     if(new_string.equals("$")){
                                        .
                        }               .
                }                       .
                inString = inString + (char)k;
                repaint();
                return true;

        }
```

If so, then we want to create an Is$ exception. We do that by throwing it with the throw keyword like this:

```
        public boolean keyDown(Event e, int k){

            try{
                    String new_string;
                    new_string = new String();
                    new_string += (char)k;
                    if(new_string.equals("$")){
-->                             throw new Is$();
                    }                     .
            }                             .
                                          .
            inString = inString + (char)k;
            repaint();
            return true;

        }
```

Next, we catch the Is$ exception with a catch block like this:

```
        public boolean keyDown(Event e, int k){

            try{
                    String new_string;
                    new_string = new String();
                    new_string += (char)k;
                    if(new_string.equals("$")){
                            throw new Is$();
                    }
            }
-->         catch(Is$ ex){
                                      .
                                      .
                                      .
            }
            inString = inString + (char)k;
            repaint();
            return true;

        }
```

If an Is$ exception was thrown, we might change the message that appears in the applet to "Do not use the $ sign" like this:

```
public boolean keyDown(Event e, int k){

    try{
            String new_string;
            new_string = new String();
            new_string += (char)k;
            if(new_string.equals("$")){
                    throw new Is$();
            }
    }
    catch(Is$ ex){
-->             inString = "Do not use the $ sign.";
    }
    inString = inString + (char)k;
    repaint();
    return true;
}
```

Now, when the user types **$**, the message "Do not use the $ sign" appears, as shown in Figure 10.1. Now we've handled the custom Is$ exception. Our Xwriter applet is a success, and the code for this applet appears in Listing 10.4.

Figure 10.1 Our custom exception at work.

Listing 10.4 Xwriter.java

```java
import java.applet.Applet;
import java.awt.*;
import java.awt.Graphics;

public class Xwriter extends Applet {

        String inString = "";
        int StartX = 0;
        int StartY = 0;
        Button buttonFont1, buttonFont2, buttonBig;
        Button buttonBold, buttonItalic, buttonPlain;
        boolean bMouseDownFlag = false;
        boolean bMouseUpFlag = false;
        boolean bFont1Flag = false;
        boolean bFont2Flag = false;
        boolean bBigFlag = false;
        boolean bBoldFlag = false;
        boolean bItalicFlag = false;
        boolean bPlainFlag = false;

        public void init() {

                buttonFont1 = new Button("TRoman");
                buttonFont2 = new Button("Courier");
                buttonBig = new Button("Big");
                buttonBold = new Button("Bold");
                buttonItalic = new Button("Italic");
                buttonPlain = new Button("Plain");

                add(buttonFont1);
                add(buttonFont2);
                add(buttonBig);
                add(buttonBold);
                add(buttonItalic);
                add(buttonPlain);
        }

        public boolean mouseDown(Event e, int x, int y){
                StartX = x;
                StartY = y;
                inString = "";
                return true;
        }
```

```java
public boolean keyDown(Event e, int k){

        try{
                String new_string;
                new_string = new String();
                new_string += (char)k;
                if(new_string.equals("$")){
                        throw new Is$();
                }
        }
        catch(Is$ ex){
                inString = "Do not use the $ sign.";
        }
        inString = inString + (char)k;
        repaint();
        return true;

}

public void paint (Graphics g) {

        String fontName = "TimesRoman"; //default face
        int fontType = Font.PLAIN;      //default type
        int fontSize = 18;              //default size
        Font drawFont;

        if(bFont1Flag){
                fontName = "TimesRoman";
        }
        if(bFont2Flag){
                fontName = "Courier";
        }
        if(bBigFlag){
                fontSize = 36;
        }
        if(bBoldFlag){
                fontType = Font.BOLD;
        }
        if(bItalicFlag){
                fontType = fontType | Font.ITALIC;
        }

        drawFont = new Font(fontName, fontType, fontSize);
        g.setFont(drawFont);
```

```
                    g.drawString(inString, StartX, StartY);
        }

        public boolean action(Event e, Object o){
                if(e.target.equals(buttonFont1)){
                        bFont1Flag = true;
                        bFont2Flag = false;
                }
                if(e.target.equals(buttonFont2)){
                        bFont2Flag = true;
                        bFont1Flag = false;
                }
                if(e.target.equals(buttonBig)){
                        bBigFlag = true;
                }
                if(e.target.equals(buttonBold)){
                        bBoldFlag = true;
                }
                if(e.target.equals(buttonItalic)){
                        bItalicFlag = true;
                }
                if(e.target.equals(buttonPlain)){
                        bPlainFlag = true;
                        bFont2Flag = false;
                        bBigFlag = false;
                        bBoldFlag = false;
                        bItalicFlag = false;
                        bFont1Flag = false;
                }
                return true;
        }

        public void update(Graphics g){
                paint(g);
        }
}

class Is$ extends Exception{
}
```

This is fine if there is only one exception like Is$, but what if there are multiple exceptions possible? Let's look into that now.

Handling Multiple Exceptions

When you write Java code, there is often the potential for more than just one type of exception. It turns out that in Java we can handle multiple exceptions almost as easily as we can handle single ones.

As you might recall, our dialog box example allows the user to pop up a dialog box on the screen by selecting the **Open Dialog...** menu item in the File menu:

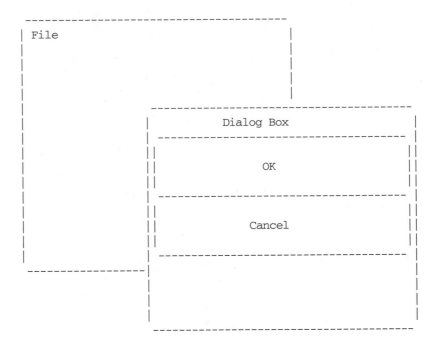

Let's say that we are particularly concerned about the process of creating the new dialog box and want to check for three errors that might occur when we create the dialog box object: stack overflows, out-of-memory errors, and class definition errors (i.e., Java could not find the definition of our dialog box class). The original code looks like this, where we create our dialog box object at the end of the menuFrame() constructor:

```
        menuFrame(String title){
                super(title);
                DisplayText = new TextField("Hello World!");
                setLayout(new GridLayout(1, 1));
                add(DisplayText);
                Menubar1 = new MenuBar();
                Menu1 = new Menu("File");
                Menu1.add(new MenuItem("Hello"));
                Menu1.add(new MenuItem("World!"));
                Menu1.add(new MenuItem("-"));
                Menu1.add(new CheckboxMenuItem("Check this"));
                Menu1.add(new MenuItem("-"));
                SubMenu = new Menu("Sub menus");
                SubMenu.add(new MenuItem("Red"));
                SubMenu.add(new MenuItem("Green"));
                SubMenu.add(new MenuItem("Blue"));
                Menu1.add(new MenuItem("Open Dialog..."));
                Menu1.add(new MenuItem("-"));
                Menu1.add(SubMenu);
                Menubar1.add(Menu1);
                setMenuBar(Menubar1);
-->             dialogBox = new OKDialog(this, "Dialog Box", true);
        }
```

It's easy to check for one error, such as the class definition error, with a standard try and catch block:

```
        menuFrame(String title){
                super(title);
                DisplayText = new TextField("Hello World!");
                setLayout(new GridLayout(1, 1));
                add(DisplayText);
                Menubar1 = new MenuBar();
                Menu1 = new Menu("File");
                Menu1.add(new MenuItem("Hello"));
                Menu1.add(new MenuItem("World!"));
                Menu1.add(new MenuItem("-"));
                Menu1.add(new CheckboxMenuItem("Check this"));
                Menu1.add(new MenuItem("-"));
                SubMenu = new Menu("Sub menus");
                SubMenu.add(new MenuItem("Red"));
                SubMenu.add(new MenuItem("Green"));
                SubMenu.add(new MenuItem("Blue"));
                Menu1.add(new MenuItem("Open Dialog..."));
```

```
                        Menu1.add(new MenuItem("-"));
                        Menu1.add(SubMenu);
                        Menubar1.add(Menu1);
                        setMenuBar(Menubar1);
        -->             try{
                            dialogBox = new OKDialog(this, "Dialog Box", true);
        -->             }
        -->             catch(NoClassDefFoundError class_err){
        -->                 System.out.println("Class def error.");
        -->             }
                                    .
                                    .
                                    .

            }
```

But how do we handle the possibility of three different kinds of errors? It turns
out we just do that with additional catch blocks like this:

```
menuFrame(String title){
        super(title);
        DisplayText = new TextField("Hello World!");
        setLayout(new GridLayout(1, 1));
        add(DisplayText);
        Menubar1 = new MenuBar();
        Menu1 = new Menu("File");
        Menu1.add(new MenuItem("Hello"));
        Menu1.add(new MenuItem("World!"));
        Menu1.add(new MenuItem("-"));
        Menu1.add(new CheckboxMenuItem("Check this"));
        Menu1.add(new MenuItem("-"));
        SubMenu = new Menu("Sub menus");
        SubMenu.add(new MenuItem("Red"));
        SubMenu.add(new MenuItem("Green"));
        SubMenu.add(new MenuItem("Blue"));
        Menu1.add(new MenuItem("Open Dialog..."));
        Menu1.add(new MenuItem("-"));
        Menu1.add(SubMenu);
        Menubar1.add(Menu1);
        setMenuBar(Menubar1);
        try{
            dialogBox = new OKDialog(this, "Dialog Box", true);
        }
```

```
                          catch(NoClassDefFoundError class_err){
                              System.out.println("Class def error.");
                          }
-->                       catch(OutOfMemoryError mem_err){
-->                           System.out.println("Out of memory.");
-->                       }
-->                       catch(StackOverflowError stack_err){
-->                           System.out.println("Stack overflow.");
-->                       }
                  }
```

Now our code checks for three kinds of errors. Our revision is a success. What happens if an error or exception occurs that we don't handle? It goes to Java, which does handle the problem, even if that means terminating the applet with an error message. In fact, there is a whole new topic here. What happens if a function without exception handling causes an exception? Can the exception still be caught? Let's look into that now.

Nested Exception Handlers

Let's say that we want to call a sensitive function in our code and we have a try and catch block set up:

```
        ------------------------------
-->     | try{                        |
        |    sensitive_function();     |
        | }                           |
        |                             |
-->     | catch(sensitive_exception ex){|
        |    System.out.println("Error");|
        | }                           |
        ------------------------------
```

Now we call the sensitive function. Note that this new function does not have exception handling. Even so, an exception occurs inside this new sensitive function like this:

```
        ----------------------------------
        | try{                           |
-------- sensitive_function();           |
|       | }                              |
|       |                                |
|       | catch(sensitive_exception ex){|
|       |    System.out.println("Error");|
|       | }                              |
|       ----------------------------------
|
|       ----------------------------------
------->|void sensitive_function(){       |
        |    [sensitive code]             |
        |                                 |
        |    throw sensitive_exception;   |        <--
        |                                 |
        |}                                |
        ----------------------------------
```

What happens in this case? The sensitive function has no catch block, so the
exception is passed back to the original calling code to be handled there:

```
         ----------------------------------
         | try{                           |
--------- sensitive_function();           |
|        | }                              |
|        |                                |
|   -->| catch(sensitive_exception ex){|
|   |    |    System.out.println("Error");|
|   |    | }                              |
|   |    ----------------------------------
|   |
|   |    ----------------------------------
--|-->|void sensitive_function(){       |
    |    |    [sensitive code]             |
    |    |                                 |
    -------throw sensitive_exception;      |
         |                                 |
         |}                                |
         ----------------------------------
```

In general, exceptions are passed back up call by call in search of a catch block.
(If none is found, Java handles the problem.) Let's take a look at this in code.

You might recall that in our synchronized function example in the last chapter, we called a function named print_out():

```
                  public void run() {
                          int loop_index;
                          for(loop_index = 1; loop_index < 500; loop_index++){
------------------- print_out();
|                         }
|       }
|
--> public synchronized void print_out() throws too_big_exception{
                          String out_string;
                          out_string = new String();
                          dataInt.internal_data++;
                          System.out.println("data value = " +
                              out_string.valueOf(dataInt.internal_data));
                  }
```

In that (synchronized) function, we printed out the value of our internal data:

```
                  public void run() {
                          int loop_index;
                          for(loop_index = 1; loop_index < 500; loop_index++){
                                  print_out();
                          }
                  }

                  public synchronized void print_out() throws too_big_exception{
                          String out_string;
                          out_string = new String();
                          dataInt.internal_data++;
      -->             System.out.println("data value = " +
                              out_string.valueOf(dataInt.internal_data));
                  }
```

Now let's return to the code that calls print_out(), and let's say that we are concerned about exceptions in the print_out() function. To handle that, we enclose the call to that function in a try block:

```
                  public void run() {
                          int loop_index;
                          for(loop_index = 1; loop_index < 500; loop_index++){
```

```
  -->                        try{
                                print_out();
  -->                        }            .
                                          .
                                          .

                    }
           }

           public synchronized void print_out() throws too_big_exception{
                 String out_string;
                 out_string = new String();
                 dataInt.internal_data++;
                 System.out.println("data value = " +
                     out_string.valueOf(dataInt.internal_data));
           }
```

To test this out, we will create our own exception—the too_big_exception—
which we can throw in the print_out() function if, for example, the internal
data value exceeds 100. We will catch this exception in the main code's catch
block after the call to print_out():

```
           public void run() {
                   int loop_index;
                   for(loop_index = 1; loop_index < 500; loop_index++){
                          try{
                              print_out();
                          }
  -->                       catch(too_big_exception tbe){
  -->                           System.out.println("Data too big.");
  -->                       }
                   }
           }

           public synchronized void print_out() throws too_big_exception{
                 String out_string;
                 out_string = new String();
                 dataInt.internal_data++;
                 System.out.println("data value = " +
                     out_string.valueOf(dataInt.internal_data));
           }
```

We set up our new exception, the too_big_exception exception class, this way:

```
class too_big_exception extends Exception{

        public void too_big_exception(){}
    }
```

In the print_out() function, we will not use try and catch blocks because print_out() will not handle the exception, but we *will* throw the exception when the internal data value becomes too big:

```
public void run() {
        int loop_index;
        for(loop_index = 1; loop_index < 500; loop_index++){
            try{
                print_out();
            }
            catch(too_big_exception tbe){
                System.out.println("Data too big.");
            }
        }
    }

public synchronized void print_out() throws too_big_exception{
        String out_string;
        out_string = new String();
        dataInt.internal_data++;
        System.out.println("data value = " +
            out_string.valueOf(dataInt.internal_data));
-->     if (dataInt.internal_data > 100) throw new too_big_exception();
    }
```

Since print_out() generates, but does not handle, the exception, the exception is passed back to the caller where we handle it in our catch block:

```
                public void run() {
                        int loop_index;
                        for(loop_index = 1; loop_index < 500; loop_index++){
                                try{
                                        print_out();
                                }
----------------->      catch(too_big_exception tbe){
|                               System.out.println("Data too big.");
|                               }
|                       }
|               }
|
|       public synchronized void print_out() throws too_big_exception{
|               String out_string;
|               out_string = new String();
|               dataInt.internal_data++;
|               System.out.println("data value = " +
|                       out_string.valueOf(dataInt.internal_data));
---------- if (dataInt.internal_data > 100) throw new too_big_exception();
        }
```

Now we have seen how exceptions can be passed back from function to function until they are handled.

In fact, if we wanted to set things up this way, print_out() could have its own try and catch blocks. If we decide not to handle the too_big_exception, we can simply throw it again, letting the calling code catch it:

```
                public void run() {
                        int loop_index;
                        for(loop_index = 1; loop_index < 500; loop_index++){
                                try{
                                        print_out();
                                }
----------------->      catch(too_big_exception tbe){
|                               System.out.println("Data too big.");
|                               }
|                       }
|               }
|
|       public synchronized void print_out() throws too_big_exception{
|               String out_string;
|               out_string = new String();
|               dataInt.internal_data++;
```

```
    |           System.out.println("data value = " +
    |               out_string.valueOf(dataInt.internal_data));
    |           try{
    |             if (dataInt.internal_data > 100) throw new too_big_exception();
    |           }
    |           catch(too_big_exception ex){
    |               [execute some code]
----------- throw ex;
    |           }
        }
}
```

The new version of our synchronized function, now with exception handling, appears in Listing 10.5.

Listing 10.5 Xfunsync.java

```java
import java.awt.*;
import java.applet.Applet;

public class Xfunsync extends Applet
    implements Runnable{

    Thread Thread1, Thread2;
    Data dataInt;

    public void init() {
            dataInt = new Data();
    }

    public void start() {
                    Thread1 = new Thread(this);
                    Thread1.start();
                    Thread2 = new Thread(this);
                    Thread2.start();
    }

    public void stop() {
                    Thread1.stop();
                    Thread2.stop();
    }

    public void run() {
```

```
        int loop_index;
        for(loop_index = 1; loop_index < 500; loop_index++){
             try{
                 print_out();
             }
             catch(too_big_exception tbe){
                 System.out.println("Data too big.");
             }
        }
    }

    public synchronized void print_out() throws too_big_exception{
        String out_string;
        out_string = new String();
        dataInt.internal_data++;
        System.out.println("data value = " +
             out_string.valueOf(dataInt.internal_data));
        if (dataInt.internal_data > 100) throw new too_big_exception();
    }
}

    class too_big_exception extends Exception{

        public void too_big_exception(){}
    }

    class Data{
        public int internal_data;
        public void Data(){
             internal_data = 0;
        }
    }
```

We've come far in our examination of exception handling, but there is still one more topic to come—using the *finally* keyword.

Using finally

So far, we have seen both try and catch blocks, but there is one more type of exception handling blocks—finally blocks. We put code in a finally block that we want executed even if errors or exceptions have occurred. In fact, such blocks are usually used to clean up after an error (even a serious error) has happened and you have to free a resource or perform some other essential task.

Let's take a look at that now. Recall our threaded imagemap example in which we loaded the imagemap in with a background thread:

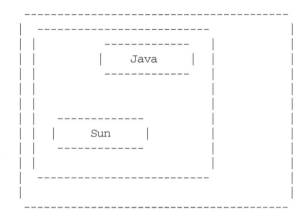

The code for the thread that loaded the graphics looks like this:

```
public void run(){
            Imap = getImage(getCodeBase(), "Imagemap.gif");
            ImageLoaded - true;
            Thread1.stop();
    }
```

Note that if an exception or serious error occurs, we can exit this function without stopping the background thread, Thread1. However, we can use a finally block to make sure that the thread is in fact terminated, even if an error occurs. First, we place the code that might cause an exception or error in a try block:

```
        public void run(){
-->             try{
                    Imap = getImage(getCodeBase(), "Imagemap.gif");
                    ImageLoaded = true;
-->             }               .
                                .
                                .
        }
```

And we place the important thread-termination code into a finally block to make sure it's executed:

```
                public void run(){
                        try{
                            Imap = getImage(getCodeBase(), "Imagemap.gif");
                            ImageLoaded = true;
                        }
 -->                    finally{
 -->                        Thread1.stop();
 -->                    }
                }
```

Now our thread is terminated even if a serious error occurs, since we have placed the correct code in our finally block. Our new applet is a success. The new exception-handling version of the synchronized function example appears in Listing 10.6.

Listing 10.6 Xmultmap.java

```
        import java.applet.Applet;
        import java.awt.*;
        import java.net.*;

        public class Xmultmap extends Applet implements Runnable {

                Thread Thread1;
                Image Imap;
                boolean ImageLoaded = false;

                public void init(){

                }

                public void start() {
                        Thread1 = new Thread(this, "Thread1");
                        Thread1.start();
                }

                public void run(){
                        try{
                            Imap = getImage(getCodeBase(), "Imagemap.gif");
```

```
            ImageLoaded = true;
        }
        finally{
            Thread1.stop();
        }
    }


public boolean mouseDown(Event e, int x, int y){
        URL newURL = null;
        if( x > 104 + 10 && x < 171 + 10 && y > 53 + 10 && y <
                75 + 10){ //Java
            try { newURL = new URL("http://java.sun.com"); }
            catch (MalformedURLException e1) {}
            getAppletContext().showDocument(newURL);
        }
        if( x > 54 + 10 && x < 118 + 10 && y > 105 + 10 && y <
                125 + 10){ //Sun
            try { newURL = new URL("http://www.sun.com"); }
            catch (MalformedURLException e2) {}
            getAppletContext().showDocument(newURL);
        }
        return true;
    }


public void paint (Graphics g) {
    if(ImageLoaded){
        g.drawImage(Imap, 10, 10, 240, 155, this);
    }
}


}
```

That's it for our finally example, and that is also our final example. We've completed our tour of Java and the Java WorkShop. We've come far in this book—from the basics to more advanced techniques; from textfields and buttons to synchronized threads and exceptions; from multitasking to graphics animation and image-handling; from Select controls to Canvas controls. There is a great deal of power in Java programming, and now all that remains is to put it to use. Happy programming!

INDEX

D

J

U